Arizona

Lawrence W. Cheek
Photography by Michael Freeman

COMPASS AMERICAN GUIDES

Arizona

Copyright © 1991, 1993 Fodor's Travel Publications, Inc.
Maps copyright © 1991, 1993 Fodor's Travel Publications, Inc.
First edition 1991
Second edition 1993

LIBRARY OF CONGRESS CATALOGING-IN-PUBLICATION DATA
Cheek, Lawrence W. 1948
Arizona / Lawrence W. Cheek : photography by Michael Freeman. —2nd ed.
Includes bibliographical references and index.
   p.   cm.   — (Discover America)
ISBN 1-878867-32-6 (pbk): $16.95; ISBN 1-878867-46-6 (cloth): $24.95
1. Arizona—Guidebooks   I. Title.
F809.3.C44 1993
917.9104'53—dc20   92-46357   CIP

Editors: Barry Parr, Deke Castleman
Series Editor: Kit Duane
Designers: David Hurst, Christopher Burt
Photography Editor: Christopher Burt

Map Design: Bob Race and
   Eureka Cartography, Berkeley, CA
Produced by Twin Age Ltd., Hong Kong
Printed in Hong Kong

First published in 1991 by Compass American Guides, Inc.
6051 Margarido Drive, Oakland, CA 94618, USA

PHOTO AND ILLUSTRATION CREDITS

   Unless otherwise stated below, all photography is by **Michael Freeman**. The pictures on pages 3, 10-11, 14-15, 49, 119, 172, 173, 180, 185, 194, 215, 223, 228, 243, 251, 261, 264-265, 268, 273, 276, 280-281 are by **Kerrick James**; on pages 91, 109, and 123 by **Paul Chesley**; on page 124 by **R.K. Weis**; on page 154 by **Lawrence W. Cheek**; on page 56 by **Peter Bloomer**; and on page 157 by **Terrence Moore**; page 292 by **Patricia A. Cheek**. Thank you *Image Artist* for the photo by John Drew on page 153. The photos on pages 93, 100, 101, 114, 117, 129, 152, 156, 166, 182, 183, 231 are used with permission of the Arizona Historical Society Library; on page 79 by permission of Helga Tevies and the Arizona State Museum, University of Arizona; page 133 by permission of Bisbee Mining & Historical Museum.
   Compass American Guides would like to thank Anne Hikido, Mark Voss, and Brian Bardwell for their assistance. Thank you Bob Race for the illustration on page 252, and Harry S. Robins for the illustrations on pages 22 and 23. Many thanks to David Laird for his careful reading of the manuscript.

To Patty, who has made my life in the desert complete

CONTENTS

Maps

Literary Extracts

Topical Essays

FACTS ABOUT ARIZONA

Grand Canyon State

CAPITAL: Phoenix

ENTERED UNION: Feb.14,1912

FIRST EUROPEAN SETTLEMENT: 1629

STATE FLOWER: Flower of saguaro cactus

STATE BIRD: Cactus wren

STATE TREE: Paloverde

POPULATION: (1990) 3,619,064

White *(includes some Hispanic)*	80.8%
Hispanic	18.8%
Black	3.0%
Native American	5.6%
Asian	1.5%

FIVE LARGEST CITIES:

Metro Phoenix	2,122,101
Tucson	443,400
Yuma	54,923
Flagstaff	45,857
Sierra Vista	32,983

GEOGRAPHY

Size:	114,000 sq. mi. (6th largest)
Highest point:	12,633 ft. (3828 m) Humphreys Peak
Lowest point:	70 ft. (21 m) Colorado River, Mexican border
Highest temp:	127° F (53° C) July 7,1905 at Parker
Lowest temp:	-40° F (-40° C) Jan. 7,1971 at Hawley Lake
Wettest place:	28.26 in. ann. at Crown King in Yavapai County
Driest place:	2.98 in. ann. at Agua Caliente in Maricopa County

ECONOMY

Major industries:	Manufacturing, tourism, mining, agriculture
Chief crop:	Cotton, sorghum, barley, corn, wheat, sugarbeets, citrus fruits
Minerals:	Copper, molybdenum, gold, silver
Per capita income:	$15,881

FAMOUS ARIZONANS

Cochise, Geronimo, Zane Grey, Carl Hayden, Sandra Day O'Connor,
Percival Lowell, Barry Goldwater, Linda Ronstadt, Bruce Babbitt, Erma Bombeck

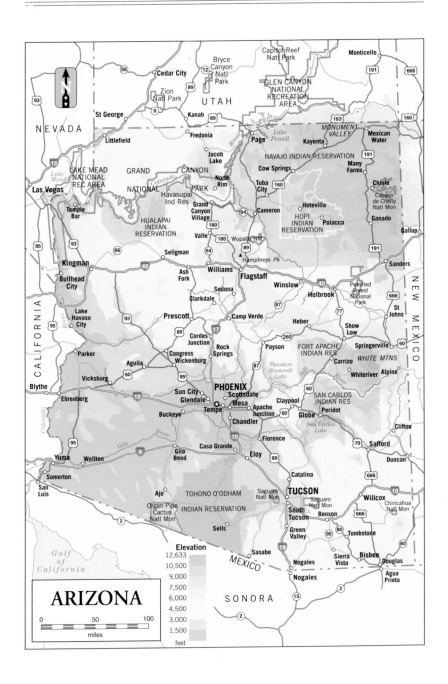

INTRODUCTION

I FIRST STARED AT ARIZONA IN 1973 THROUGH A WINDOW of an airplane, a commercial jet cruising somewhere in the lower stratosphere. I was flying from Des Moines to Tucson for a job interview, and what I still remember with startling clarity, as I pressed my nose to the glass and looked at the Sonoran Desert seven miles below, was a feeling of hollow, gnawing alienation.

I thought: I won't take the job. I cannot live in this place.

The barren earth appeared the color of sun-bleached cardboard. It was raked and torn and furrowed by corrosive wind and bogus rivers that would flow, with luck, 10 days in a year. The mountains seemed equally desolate and hostile; from this altitude I had no inkling of their heroic natural architecture or the kaleidoscopic changes of the plant and animal environments on their slopes every few hundred feet. The entire Arizona landscape appeared to hold no life, no interest, no promise.

Two days later I did indeed turn down the job. I flew back to moist, green Iowa, where my wife, Patty, helped me sort through my feelings. She had been to Arizona once before, as a child, and the place had fascinated her. Was I simply afraid of exploring an exotic environment? If so, wasn't that an odd tic in a journalist's emotional makeup? Finally we agreed we would try it. We would move to Arizona, spend a couple of years pumping up our résumés, and then move on— preferably to California, where in those days even a reporter's salary might land us a house only a few freeway exits from the ocean.

This happened 17 years ago as I write this, and we have not been pried from Arizona. Nor will we be. My feelings mirror those of my friend and fellow author Charles Bowden, who opened his 1986 book *Blue Desert* with this sentence: "I have lived in the Sonoran Desert since I was a boy and unless I get unlucky, I will die here."

My reversal of heart did not come quickly or painlessly. For the first several years I oscillated between a reporter's fascination with the place and a tentative resident's annoyance with it. I didn't like the bugs, the ferocious cutlery that poses as plant life in the desert, or the exhausting summer heat. I missed the sensation of four distinct seasons, and remembered in demented wistfulness the soft, cold feel of snow on my neck. I was peeved at the strange forces that seemed to be pulling on Arizona's political compass. I remember my astonishment one day in 1974 when I first saw a billboard demanding "Get US out of the UN!" on the Interstate between Tucson and the Mexican border. (It's still there, fading but unrelenting.) I detested Phoenix, and over time developed a modest reputation as the Tucson journalist who wrote more vitriolic essays about that other city than anyone in modern history. This mini-specialty peaked with a call from the *Arizona Republic*, Phoenix's morning paper, wanting to interview me about the tradition of hostility between the two cities. I still hadn't come to terms with Arizona, but on certain topics I was at least an authority.

It was my own 14-year tenure at the *Tucson Citizen*, Tucson's afternoon daily, that slowly and inevitably nurtured my affection for the state. There were some pivotal moments.

One came in 1975, the year after a young Phoenix lawyer from an old Arizona pioneer family was elected state attorney general. Before this, the attorney general had always been a passive, stonelike figure on the state's political landscape, quietly issuing opinions on whether this or that state agency had the legal authority to do that or this. The new guy, to the shock of nearly everyone, affixed his constitutional bayonet and began prosecuting price-fixers and land-fraud merchants. He also opened his office one day a month to any Arizonan who wanted to come in and talk about legal problems, consumer problems, sometimes even personal problems. I sat at his right side for one of these long days, taking notes for a story, as he dealt with a torrent of misery. Late in the afternoon, between visitors, he turned to me with hurt in his eyes and said, "These peoples' stories are straight out of Dickens."

For the first time I liked an Arizona politician. He was Bruce Babbitt, who later became governor and then ran for president.

There was another, more personal moment. I was beginning to indulge seriously in bicycling—this after a couple of years of mostly staying indoors, bitching about the sunshine. Finally on Sunday mornings I began a ritual of pedaling out to Saguaro National Monument, a 20-mile (32-km) round trip from my house, and riding the hilly eight-mile (13-km) loop road through the pristine cactus forest in the foothills of the Rincon Mountains. On a spring day in 1983 I was wobbling up a long and pain-inducing hill when a Buick wearing Minnesota plates swished past. Four uncomprehending faces stared at me through sealed windows; their expressions resembled anthropologists observing some primitive aborigine

praying to a pine cone. I realized at that moment that by insulating themselves from the desert— from its physical demands and its miraculous beauty alike— they were failing to understand even the first thing about it. As well as missing the point, probably, of life itself.

More than most other states, Arizona tests its people. Its jagged landscapes and diverse cultures dare us to comprehend them. Its climatic extremes challenge our stamina, will and common sense. The everyday trials of living in a place that has grown more rapidly than sensibly cause many people either to leave or withdraw into their private worlds, taking no part in the public life of the place. We have a volatile population: for every three souls who arrive, two leave. Yet, it is from this instability that opportunity is given birth. In Arizona, whether you lean to art, politics, land fraud, or journalism, you can invent yourself.

This book is partly about that act of inventing, which forms so much of Arizona's history and contemporary culture. It also is a guide to the state's attractions and eccentricities—there are enough things to experience described in here, from hidden canyons to museums of archaeology, to keep any visitor occupied for years. It does not read very much like a conventional guidebook. It is highly opinionated and occasionally cranky, and when it turns to some of the misuse and abuse my sorry species has visited on this magnificent land it bounces peevishly between anger and sorrow. It does manage to say some fairly nice things about Phoenix. (Either I have matured or that city has.) It says even more about the joy of taking part in the extravagant life of the deserts, the canyons, the mountains, and the forests that make up this amazing land. In the end, this book is about falling in love.

(previous pages) December snowstorm, south rim of the Grand Canyon. (Kerrick James)

D E S E R T S

A SONORAN DESERT STORY:

A CROWD OF VACATIONING ISRAELIS PILES OUT OF A BUS at the Arizona-Sonora Desert Museum, the world-famous desert zoo/arboretum a dozen miles west of Tucson. They buy their tickets, then gather under the ramada that overlooks the museum grounds. Their eyes sweep across a forest of saguaro cacti interspersed with woody sprays of ocotillo wearing their flame-shaped orange flowers of spring. The spindly, green-barked paloverde trees are veiled in yellow blossoms, the velvet mesquite and ironwood trees are in luxuriant leaf, and even the homely prickly pear cacti are erupting with peach- and yellow-colored flowers, some the size of coffee cups.

Asks one of the Israelis, not joking: "So where's the desert?"

Another story:

It is July 1980, the benign Sonoran Desert spring a distant memory. Twenty-seven refugees fleeing the civil war in El Salvador gather at Sonoita, a Mexican border town 120 miles southwest of Phoenix. They each pay $1,200 to some Mexican *coyotes*, or "travel guides," to slip them into the United States. They buy 20 gallons (76 liters) of water at a Sonoita restaurant, and an hour after dark they plod north into the cool, starry night.

By 10 the next morning most of the water is gone. The group begins to split up, some fanning out to look for water. The *coyotes* slip away. The Salvadorans' situation rapidly deteriorates into desperation. They drink their cosmetics, try to nibble cacti for moisture, and finally even gulp their own urine. The next day it is 109 (43 C) in the shade and 150 (66 C) on the ground, and before a search party finds them, 13 of the refugees are dead. Two are found face down on their open Bibles—the last solace available in the indescribably harsh, unforgiving Sonoran Desert of midsummer.

In following years, many more Mexican and Central American refugees die the same way—27 in a decade. Finally the U.S. Border Patrol and the Mexican government begin posting signs every summer in the Mexican villages along the border. The words are not minced:

(following pages) To enjoy this view of Monument Valley, visitors must hire a Navajo guide and jeep and make the trip to Hunts Mesa. (Kerrick James)

DESIERTO PELIGROSO	DANGEROUS DESERT
La falta de agua y las altas temperaturas	The lack of water and the high
in el desierto pueden causar la	temperatures in the desert can cause
MUERTE	DEATH
Por tu propia seguridad	For your own safety
NO INTENTES CRUZARLO	DON'T TRY TO CROSS IT

The desert gives life abundantly, the desert revokes it disinterestedly. "Here death is like breathing. Here death simply is," wrote Charles Bowden in *Blue Desert*, a provocative collection of essays. The late Edward Abbey, who was Bowden's inspiration, frequently mused about death in the desert—though never the death *of* the desert. In the closing pages of *Desert Solitaire*, his finest book, he wrote:

> *W*hether we live or die is a matter of absolutely no concern whatsoever to the desert. Let men in their madness blast every city on earth into black rubble and envelop the entire planet in a cloud of lethal gas—the canyons and hills, the springs and rocks will still be here, the sunlight will filter through, water will form and warmth shall be upon the land and after sufficient time, no matter how long, somewhere, living things will emerge and join and stand once again, this time perhaps to take a different and better course.

In the desert, death is exposed, not concealed in the shadows and underbrush of a forest. An hour's walk along any trail in the desert will yield reminders of the fragility of life and the inevitability of its end: a coyote's skull, tufts of coarse, gray-brown fur still clinging to its lower jaw; a century-old saguaro fried by lightning (or perhaps strangled by air pollution) still standing, its naked, woody ribs splaying like a fountain spray and bleaching in the relentless sun. A cottontail darts across the trail and freezes in the shadow of a creosote bush, assuming it's thus invisible to predators—which, of course, it isn't; a coyote's eyes lock easily onto that fluffy white ball of a tail. The bunny adapts by breeding prolifically during its short, timorous life. Bad news for the individual, adequate protection for the species. The desert offers no regrets.

The irony is that this same *desierto peligroso* is also a place that welcomes life. It is extravagantly fecund. Because the desert's plants and animals (and at least its pre-Columbian peoples) are so keenly adapted, they impose themselves on the land with insane determination. A few thimblefuls of sediment wash into a fissure between two boulders, and inevitably a barrel cactus (or something) will sprout, seemingly growing out of rock at whatever crazy angle it needs to stake a claim for some sunlight. The cholla, bloodthirstiest of all cacti, will fight off a human armed with pliers and forceps, yet the cactus wren blithely and safely nests in it. The most common misconception about the deserts of the Southwest is that they are desolate, barren, lifeless places. In fact, they teem with life—weird, colorful, perfectly adapted, interdependent, fiercely obstinate life.

Few *Homo sapiens* fall in love with, or understand, this desert life at first encounter. It appears exotic but threatening. Arizona is home to 11 species of rattlesnake, 30 species each of scorpion and tarantula, the black widow and brown recluse spider, the giant (up to eight inches long) desert centipede and the Gila monster—this last species being one of only two venomous lizards on the planet.

People coming to Arizona from moist, green places frequently ask the natives: "How can you live here with all these rattlesnakes, scorpions and Gila monsters?" The Arizonan, oddly, responds by *exaggerating* the menace of this terrible triad.

Even among Arizonans, who ought to know better, the Gila monster is credited with an amazing list of frightful features: The monster is poisonous because it has no rectum, so a lifetime's waste is stored in its body. When it bites, it will hold on until it hears thunder. And even its breath is poisonous.

According to an 1890 account in the *Tucson Citizen*, "A woodcutter lay down to sleep . . . they found him stone dead, and near his body a Gila Monster . . . as the body of the man bore no marks of a bite or other wounds, we must suppose that his death was caused by the mere exhalation of the lizard."

All this is fanciful nonsense, as is the belief that these shy, waddling, 12- to 16-inch (30- to 41-cm) lizards (hardly "monstrous") will spring out of hiding to attack an unwary human. In fact, virtually all *Heloderma suspectum* bites occur because someone is trying to harass or toy with the lizard.

"This is exactly what one will do if you approach it in the wild," explained Howard Lawler, curator of small animals at the Arizona-Sonora Desert Museum. "First, it will pick up its pace and lumber away with as much dignity as it can manage. If there's any kind of a dark recess nearby, it will crawl inside. If it's cornered it will finally turn around and face the threat and inhale and exhale forcefully. This is its defensive posture. At this point, anything that touches its body or comes within reach of its jaws is going to get bitten."

Even then—contrary to another cherished belief—the bite is not fatal. The Gila monster's venom is chemically primitive, primarily defensive, and sub-lethal. Nature, as usual, is making perfect sense here. If a coyote were bitten by a Gila monster and died from it, the lizard would still have to fret about the next coyote. But if the predator is bitten and (narrowly) survives, it learns that the Gila monster is not part of *its* food chain. Over time, this "knowledge" becomes encoded in the species' genetic memory, and coyotes and Gila monsters give each other a wide berth, to their mutual advantage.

So even though newspaper reports continue to cite human death tolls from Gila monsters (a 1988 article claimed "three in the last decade"), they simply are not true. The best research has unearthed only one possible fatality in Arizona history: that of a "Col. Yearger" in 1878 who, according to reports, also had been on a continuous drunk for a month.

Why all the myths? Because the desert is a strange, and in many ways harsh, environment—and by exaggerating its strangeness and harshness, the people who live in it can convince themselves that they are braver for having conquered it. This mythology is harmless enough to us humans, but not to the rattlesnakes, scorpions and Gila monsters—which people routinely kill even in the wild for no better reason than that they are venomous animals.

Probably Arizona's lizards, snakes, arachnids and insects get more press than they deserve, proportionately speaking. The state's deserts, especially the Sonoran, support a spectacular variety of wildlife. A complete catalog here is impossible, but consider a few.

"Parody pigs with oversize heads and undersize hams" was Abbey's classic description of the collared peccary, or javelina. He wasn't exaggerating their strangeness. If some political party were to adopt a pig as its symbol, a political cartoonist, wanting to portray it as scrappy and aggressive, would draw something like a javelina: small (about two feet high/.75 m at the shoulder), with short, muscular legs, a big head tapering into a long, probelike snout, and dagger-like canine teeth. The desert's most social mammal, javelina invariably forage in groups, usually five to 15 individuals strong.

Seldom does any writer type the word "javelina" without the modifier "bad-tempered." It has become a desert cliché. Hogwash, the javelina would reply, if it could. Every desert animal has evolved some defensive strategy; the collared peccary's is to bristle, snort and stand its ground—en masse. No predator in its right mind would risk charging into such a platoon in search of a tasty youngster. Within the group, javelinas are extremely cordial to each other, the females even nursing each other's offspring—a rare phenomenon in nature. Their sociability makes javelina-watching one of the desert's great pleasures (when undertaken, as with the Gila monster, from a discreet distance).

Coyotes, even though discouraged from dining on javelina and Gila monsters, arguably are the desert's most intelligent and adaptable creatures. They will eat virtually anything else that can't eat them. Because of this, they are the one desert mammal that actually has benefited from the cities now sprawling through their habitat.

"Urban coyotes," as wildlife-management officials term them, are ubiquitous—and urbane. Tom Spalding, a regional supervisor for the Arizona Game & Fish Department, has told of watching a coyote standing at the curb of a busy six-lane thoroughfare in Tucson, carefully monitoring the traffic in both directions, and finally loping across in safety. More often, the animals use their natural freeway system—the normally dry arroyos that cut through the desert cities—to get around and hunt for food. Garbage and household pets are most favored. A coyote can easily kill a domestic cat or a dog its own size (about 30 pounds/14 kg). If a bigger dog chases a coyote, the dog often will find an unpleasant surprise waiting where its prey leads it: more coyotes.

Humans who encounter an abandoned litter of urban coyotes and "adopt" the cute, fuzzy pups also get an unpleasant surprise. At the age of about five months, they begin biting everything in sight, including the hands that feed them. They cannot be domesticated, and it's contrary to state law to try. Coyotes are best enjoyed from a distance. Open the windows on a warm spring night, and eventually, sometimes just before dawn, their uncannily melodic howling and yipping will float miles on the still desert air into the house. It sounds like a celebration, as well it may be. Nothing in the desert seems to live better than a coyote.

Most species have more to regret from the encroachment of *Homo sapiens*. No one would expect the hermit-like spadefoot toad to be among them, but because of advances in recreational technology, it may be.

Scaphiopus couchii spends nearly all its life alone in a sealed burrow three feet underground. No one is quite sure what it does down there except wait for the ground to shake from thunder. When the summer storms come, the spadefoot is thus reminded to burrow to the surface to feed and mate in the shallow ponds that collect on the desert floor after heavy rains. The tadpoles then begin a frantic race to adulthood before the ponds evaporate.

Arizona State University biologist John Alcock, author of two gracefully written books on Sonoran Desert life, described an experiment in which tape recordings of loud motorcycles were played above spadefoots buried in a terrarium. The toads mistook the din for thunder, and burrowed to the surface—a waste of energy that could prove fatal in their marginal existence in the desert. Thus, fumed Alcock, off-roaders enjoying their "trivial human inventions" may endanger one of the least-seen and most elegantly adapted of all the desert's animals.

The desert's plants are no less strange, no less strategically endowed to cope with their environment, and in some sad cases, no less threatened by the humans around them.

Of the four distinct deserts that extend into Arizona, the Sonoran (again) features the most extravagant community of plants. This is a function of climate. The Sonoran is fairly wet, for a desert, with annual rainfall averaging 7.5 inches (19 cm) in Phoenix, 11.09 inches (28 cm) in Tucson, and 8.82 inches (22.4 cm) at Organ Pipe National Monument. (The latter, to keep these measures in perspective, is where the 13 Salvadorans died of dehydration.) Fragile plants also are not in much danger of a hard freeze, at least not below elevations of 3,000 feet (914 m). Tucson, at 2,630 feet (802 m), records an average of 17 freezing lows per year, but it very rarely falls below 25 degrees (-4 C), and never for more than a few hours. If it did, its signature plant, the giant saguaro, would not exist.

The saguaro inhabits a more-or-less horseshoe-shaped chunk of southern Arizona that includes Tucson, Phoenix and the 4,335-square-mile (11,228 sq. km) Tohono O'odham Reservation. They then march south into the Mexican states of Sonora and Baja California. But even though their range is tightly restricted by climate, they have come to serve as a symbol of all Arizona and even the entire frontier West. So essential is their emblematic value that in *Broken Arrow,* the classic 1951 James Stewart western, the film crew scattered plaster-of-Paris saguaro among the red rocks of Sedona. A saguaro would no sooner grow in cool Sedona than in San Francisco.

An average human lifetime, about 75 years, expires before it occurs to a saguaro to perform the act that makes it so impressive to humans, which is to grow its first arm or two. Thus outfitted, the still-adolescent cactus takes on an anthropomorphic character. Some individuals seem to raise their arms in surrender, others in supplication, a few in bewilderment. One monster in the foothills of the Santa Catalina Mountains currently sports 21 arms curling in a swirl around its trunk, like a mutant green Nureyev in a pirouette frozen for eternity. The sentient human, wandering about a forest of these 30-foot (9-meter) creatures, feels like an explorer in the midst of a race of strangely still and silent alien beings. This eerie sensation is multiplied tenfold in the moonlight.

This most prominent living object in the Sonoran Desert is a good citizen, serving the biological community in several remarkable ways. Gila woodpeckers chisel apartments in mature saguaro trunks and nest in them, staying both cool and safe from climbing predators. After the woodpecker moves on, any of several other species will move in—screech and elf owls, purple martins, Wied's crested flycatchers. The saguaro's flower, which grows only at its top on the ends of its arms, provides bats with an energy-rich nectar; the bats reciprocate by pollinating other saguaro. Spanish and Mexican settlers, Tohono O'odham and Pima Indians, and probably their prehistoric ancestors as well harvested the fruit to make jelly and wine, and employed ribs from dead saguaros as roofing material.

This saguaro has sprouted a complex crest.

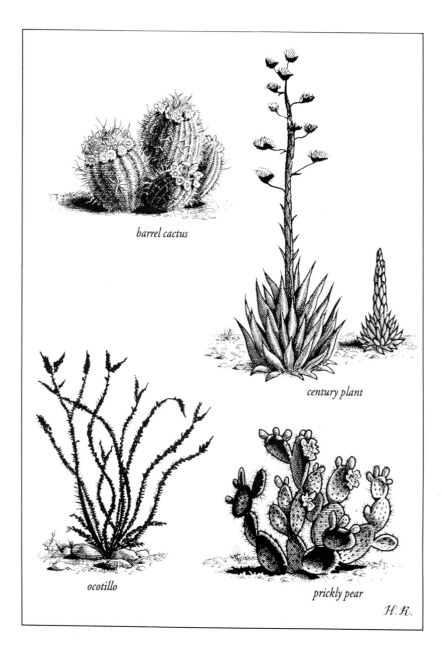

barrel cactus

century plant

ocotillo

prickly pear

H. R.

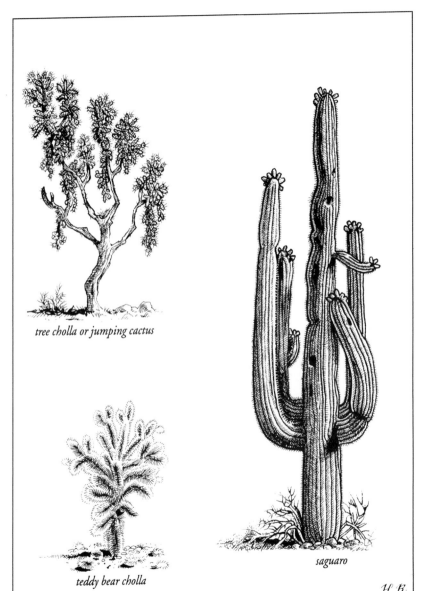

tree cholla or jumping cactus

teddy bear cholla

saguaro

H.R.

FEROCIOUS FLORA

Tree, bush, plant and grass—great and small alike—each has its sting for the intruder. You can hardly stoop to pick a desert flower or pull a bunch of small grass without being aware of a prickle on your hand. Nature seems to have provided a whole arsenal of defensive weapons for these poor starved plants of the desert. Not any of the lovely growths of the earth, like the lilies and the daffodils, are so well defended. And she has given them not only armor but a spirit of tenacity and stubbornness wherewith to carry on the struggle. Cut out the purslain and the iron weed from the garden walk, and it springs up again and again, contending for life. Put heat, drouth, and animal attack against the desert shrubs and they fight back like the higher forms of organic life. How typical they are of everything in and about the desert. There is but one word to describe it and that word—fierce—I shall have worn threadbare before I have finished these chapters.

—John C. Van Dyke, *The Desert* 1901

The brilliant scarlet hedgehog blossom is a springtime ornament for the Sonoran Desert.

Saguaro are prized both by cactus bandits and legitimate landscape architects, but century-old individuals like this seldom survive transplanting.

Yet people also abuse the saguaro. As early as 1854, a pioneer explorer, J.R. Bartlett, found arrows sticking into saguaros in the Yuman Indian lands of far west Arizona. In the early 1980s, a Phoenix man fired a shotgun into a saguaro until it toppled, killing him. Sometimes even *good* intentions doom the plants. Mature saguaros, which landscape architects love to use in their designs, usually die when transplanted. The Arizona-Sonora Desert Museum has seen a 95 percent mortality rate among transplanted saguaros 12 or more feet high, and has quit moving them. Landscapers haven't, because they don't connect the transplant with the cactus's demise. A mature saguaro, perfect symbol of both the desert's perseverance and fragility, takes three to five years to die.

Heat and light also shape the character of Arizona's deserts. Most people naturally think of them as excessive, as a dismaying drawback to year-round residence in at least half of Arizona. A few—Abbey was prime among them—welcome the heat because it discourages at least some people from moving here.

Summer comes early to the low desert and holds it in relentless lock for five long months. On average, Phoenix endures 91 days of 100 (38 C)+ readings per year. Buckeye, Gila Bend and Casa Grande all have been brutalized by 100-degree (38 C) marks in March. The first 100 usually strikes Phoenix by mid-April; Tucson by early May. (In the latter city, the first 100 of the year is hailed as the day "the ice breaks on the Santa Cruz." This is doubly dry humor; the Santa Cruz is a dry riverbed.) By June, the desert is under siege. June 26, 1990, was especially memorable, a torrid day that toppled more weather records than any other date in modern history. A sampler:

CITY	ELEVATION (in feet)	TEMP: HIGH (F)	TEMP: LOW (F)
Bisbee	5,490	106°	68°
Sedona	4,240 .	110°	76°
Safford	2,920	112°	68°
Tucson	2,630	117°	80°
Phoenix	1,092	122°	91°
Yuma	141	122°	85°

Note the predawn "low" of 91 (33 C) for Phoenix. This was a ghastly demonstration of what meteorologists have begun to call the "heat island" effect: the metropolis's immense size is making its summer climate worse. Heat absorbed by asphalt and concrete and roof tiles during the day is radiated at night and trapped by atmospheric inversions. Lows in the 90s (33 C) are no longer unusual in Phoenix.

Chambers of Commerce struggle to put the best possible spin on these numbers. "But it's a *dry* heat!" is their mantra. True, but it's also a relentless heat. A T-shirt popular around Phoenix depicts a couple of bleached skeletons lounging in patio chairs, taking the sun. One remarks, cheerfully, to the other: "But it's a *dry* heat."

According to the U.S. Geological Survey, Arizona has more "hell" place names than any other state—a total of 55. (Utah places second with 46.) Hell Hole Valley, Hellgate Mountain, Hell's Neck Ridge, no fewer than four Hell Canyons—it is a creative list, but no one who has endured a few desert summers would call it fanciful.

Outside on a 115-degree (46 C) midsummer day it is difficult to be conscious of any sensation but the heat. It is like a pressure that pushes on every square inch of the body. Even in shade, the face reddens, the torso moistens, the will to do anything productive—except lurch toward the nearest air-conditioned building—vanishes. Tempers seem shorter; police answer more domestic-disturbance calls in the summer. It isn't unlike Alaskan cabin fever; the seasons are simply reversed.

With the heat comes a quality of light unique in North America. Observed Reyner Banham in *Scenes in America Deserta*, "The full sun of the desert—the Mojave in particular—gives a spectral, hurtful light that is a close brother to heat, and strikes equally hard." John C. Van Dyke, a much earlier essayist, felt that with the pain came an incomparable reward: "In any land what is there more glorious than sunlight! Even here in the desert, where it falls fierce and hot as a rain of meteors, it is the one supreme beauty to which all things pay allegiance." Either interpretation is most true in June, when none of Arizona's deserts can hope for rain, or clouds, or even enough humidity to soften the light. The sky is not quite blue; it appears bleached, almost white. Mountain ranges on the horizon lose both dimension and color; they appear as flat, washed-out cardboard cutouts propped against the sky. Even buildings become painful to look at.

But in other months the desert's light is miraculous. In July, August and early September come the summer storms, romantically if inaccurately termed "monsoons" in Phoenix and Tucson. Even in the mornings, the humidity is higher, diffusing the sun's glaring fury (while rendering evaporative coolers worthless). In the afternoons, platoons of gray, overweight cumulus clouds rumble in from the south. Inside an hour, the sky turns to charcoal and dumps torrents on the desiccated land. Then after maybe 15 minutes, the storm begins to break up and slivers of late-afternoon sunlight scythe through the clouds, selectively highlighting a few acres of mountain, desert or city with golden fire.

In the winter—what passes for winter in the desert—the light is softer still but no less dramatic. Early morning sun will backlight a forest of saguaros in such a way that the light squeezes through their spines, glinting and diffusing on its way, so that each cactus seems to wear a glowing yellow halo. Afternoon light is penetrating and incisive, and if the air is particularly still and dry one can see astounding details in the landscape at preposterous distances. I have stood on a peak near Hannagan Meadow at the eastern edge of the state and traced ridgelines in the Santa Catalina Mountains near my home in Tucson, a straight-line distance of 130 miles (208 km)—with naked eye.

It is the evening light that is the most spectacular, even startling. Arizona's winter sunsets are clichéd *ad nauseam* in curio and commerce—sweat shirts, bus benches, even automatic teller machines are decked out in painted sunsets—but the real thing, the nightly ballet of light in the western sky, is so unpredictable and varied that nobody grows jaded. We do lose perspective. Former Gov. Bruce Babbitt has told a story about watching a group of tourists one evening as a world-class sunset unfolded. Someone snapped a Polaroid, and all turned their backs on the real sunset to watch the photo of it develop. The anecdote may illustrate a peculiar truth about Arizona's light and landscapes: sometimes the reality is so overwhelming that image is easier to comprehend.

■ THE FOUR ARIZONA DESERTS

On frequent occasion a novelist or reporter from someplace east of the Continental Divide will refer in print to "the Arizona desert." Editors ought to fire back: which one? Four deserts, distinctly different in climate, biology and scenery, extend into Arizona. Combined, they make up something between half to two-thirds (scientists quibble about the definition of a "desert") of the state's 113,508 square miles (293,986 sq. km).

The Colorado Plateau, which sprawls north and east of the city of Flagstaff, includes portions of the high Great Basin Desert. (Its Arizona appendage is sometimes called the Painted Desert.) It is strange, haunting country, its geology as bizarre as the Sonoran Desert's more abundant biology. The land is scored by

The Painted Desert almost defines desolation; yet it exudes a starkly awesome beauty.

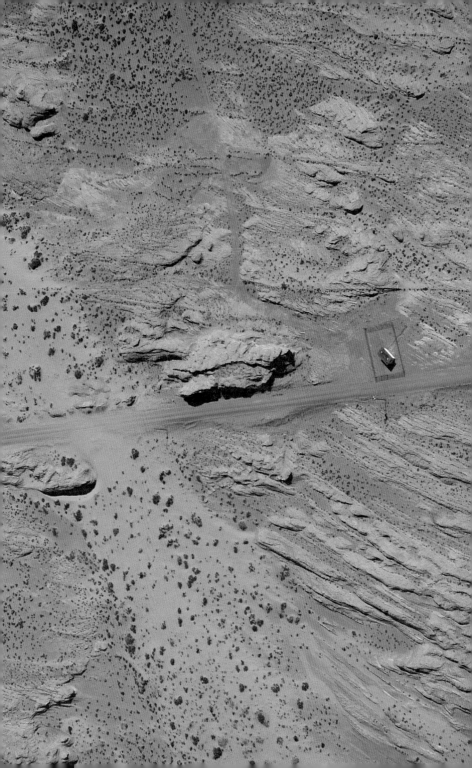

jagged canyons and punctuated by heroic sandstone skylines of cliffs, mesas, buttes and spires up to a thousand feet high. The visitor experiences a palpable, sometimes uncomfortable sensation of insignificance out here; the scale of everything seems too gigantic to comprehend.

Most people assume that water, over a few hundred million years, carved spectacles such as Canyon de Chelly, while wind-whipped sand abraded the buttes of Monument Valley. The truth is a little more disquieting, particularly if one is standing on the rim of a canyon or at the base of a butte. Rivers started the erosion process, and runoff abetted it, but natural weaknesses in the rock formations also allowed pieces to crumble and fall away. Monument Valley, which used to be a solid plateau of sandstone roughly as high as the tops of the "monuments" today, literally is crumbling away in huge splinters and sheets. The reassuring news is that geologic time, like the monuments themselves, is so vast as to be almost irrelevant to the puny humans standing around, gaping in awe.

The Mojave, at Arizona's northwestern edge, is the driest desert. Only 4.52 inches (11.5 cm) of rain falls in an average year at Lake Havasu (a man-made lake, of course). This skimpy precipitation does not nourish much plant life, but what manages to thrive is fiercely tenacious. The ubiquitous creosote bush, a spindly, scruffy shrub, is believed to live as long as 11,000 years, making it the oldest living thing on earth. The Joshua tree, which may see 500 years, is as distinctive a signature plant to the Mojave as the saguaro to the Sonoran. A member of the yucca genus, it grows as high as 30 feet (nine m), sending out a grotesque tangle of arms that terminate in fists spiked with green daggers.

More than the others, the Mojave is a desert of dunes. The land's architecture, sculpted daily by the wind, can appear as soft and fluid as the Great Basin Desert is hard and craggy. Reyner Banham saw "a horizon made of reclining figures by Henry Moore." Its softness, of course, is cruel deceit: no other North American desert is as hot, as inhospitable, as unforgiving.

The Chihuahuan is Arizona's overlooked desert. Many travelers head east out of Tucson on Interstate 10, not even noticing the gradual change that marks the transition from Sonoran into Chihuahuan Desert, which will remain their host across the lower edge of New Mexico and on into the high, barren badlands of West Texas. Most of the Chihuahuan Desert lies in the Mexican state of Chihuahua; only its northwestern sliver edges into Arizona.

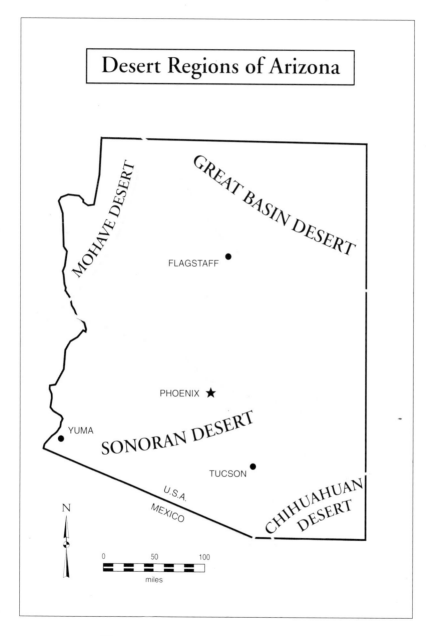

Desert Regions of Arizona

MOHAVE DESERT

GREAT BASIN DESERT

FLAGSTAFF

PHOENIX ★

YUMA

SONORAN DESERT

TUCSON

U.S.A.
MEXICO

CHIHUAHUAN DESERT

N

0   50   100
miles

(following pages) Wind, and occasionally water, have sculpted the land forms
of the Painted Desert.

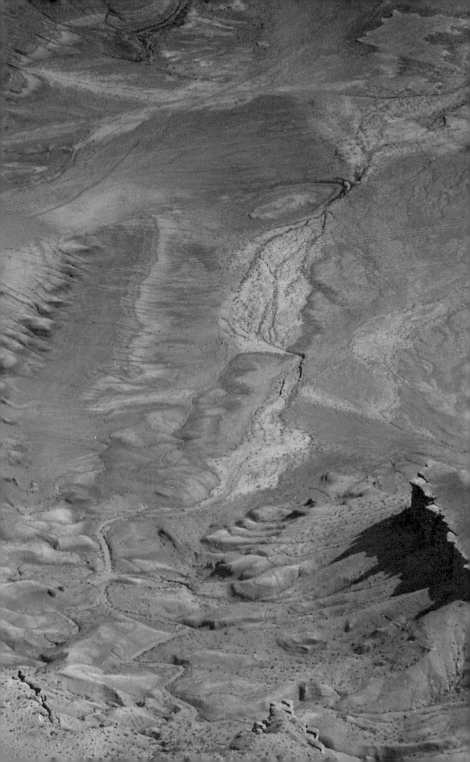

About 50 miles (80 km) east of Tucson, the Interstate traveler has climbed some 1,500 feet (457 m), probably without realizing it. The saguaro have given way to yucca, the shrub cover to rolling hills of straw-colored grass. This edge of the Chihuahuan Desert receives only eight to 10 inches (20 to 25 cm) of rain a year, which is less than Tucson gets, but because it is higher, it is also cooler, and that makes the rain more efficient. Hence the grass.

Two remarkable features mark the edge of the Chihuahuan Desert: Texas Canyon, a mountain range literally made of boulders, and the Willcox Playa. The playa looks like a vast lake shimmering in the distance, but it is a permanent mirage, a cruel optical joke surrealistically imposed on a 50-square-mile (130-sq.-km) basin that *used* to be a lake. Now it is one of the strangest places in Arizona, a parched, table-flat wasteland where absolutely nothing grows from one horizon to another, as far as the eye can see. Ed Severson, a writer for *The Arizona Daily Star*, described it like this: "To walk on the playa is to travel through another dimension. At times, its vast emptiness seems like a gateway to the Twilight Zone." Yet even this most desolate region of the desert supports life. Eggs of three species of miniature shrimp lie dormant below the lake bed for as long as 30 years, and then after an extravagant summer rain, when water puddles into a soupy mud on the playa, the crustaceans hatch. If the water holds out they may last two weeks, which is just long enough to mate, deposit more eggs and then die—having miraculously assured, a shrimp's eon later, the eventual appearance of their offspring.

The Sonoran is the desert of superlatives. It is more colorful, more varied, more lovely, more crowded, more dangerous and more threatened than any of the others. More species of birds, some 300, make their homes in the Sonoran Desert than in any other arid region on the continent. More rain falls in the Sonoran Desert than any other in North America; there literally are forests—called bosques—of mesquite in this desert. It is a noisy desert, and not just because of the intrusions of humans and our mechanized contraptions. Cactus wrens screech at each other in an appalling tenor rasp, cicadas lay down an omnidirectional drone, coyotes yelp, crickets tick, the ubiquitous Western whiptail lizards swish from bush to bush, rattlers helpfully advise stray humans to buzz off. Except in the midday summer sun, when most of these creatures are sensibly taking a snooze, it is hard to feel alone in the Sonoran Desert.

And it is becoming harder all the time. In large part because of its beauty and lushness, more Arizonans live in the Sonoran Desert than in any other geographic region of the state: about 3.1 million of our total of 3.6 million people. This crush of bodies, with the pressures they impose on the desert's modest resources, is the state's most ominous problem. In 1987, then-Gov. Evan Mecham blithely predicted an eventual "giant megalopolis" stretching from Tucson through Phoenix to Wickenburg. Tucson and Wickenburg, near the Sonoran Desert's northwest end, are 167 miles apart.

For now.

THE HORRIBLE "ESCORPION"

Strangest of all was the uncouth, horrible "escorpion," or "Gila monster," which here found its favorite habitat and attained its greatest dimensions. We used to have them not less than three feet long, black, venomous, and deadly, if half the stories told were true. The Mexicans time and time again asserted that the escorpion would kill chickens, and that it would eject a poisonous venom upon them, but, in my own experience, I have to say that the old hen which we tied in front of one for a whole day was not molested, and that no harm of any sort came to her beyond being scared out of a year's growth. Scientists were wont to ridicule the idea of the Gila monster being venomous, upon what ground I do not now remember, beyond the fact that it was a lizard, and all lizards were harmless. But I believe it is now well established that the monster is not to be handled with impunity.

—John G. Bourke, *On the Border with Crook*, 1892

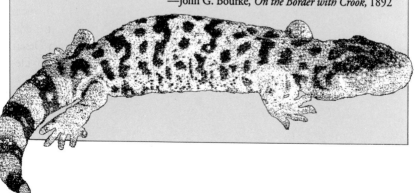

(following pages) The jumping cholla so luxuriates with needles that Sonoran Desert dwellers like to claim it "jumps" to attack unwary passers-by. It doesn't.

■ VISITING THE DESERT

The Sonoran Desert is celebrated, studied and preserved in several parks and museums in central and southern Arizona. In summer, early-morning visits are recommended.

The **Arizona-Sonora Desert Museum** in Tucson regularly appears on lists of the world's ten best zoos. Its world is the animals, plants and natural history of the Sonoran Desert, but its exhibits also encompass this desert's forested mountains, rivers and seacoast on the Gulf of California. The full range of Sonoran Desert animals is on display here, from the one-tenth-ounce (three-gram) calliope hummingbird to the black bear. Docents work the grounds, continually giving demonstrations on topics such as the differences between the jaws of herbivores and carnivores. Allow three hours for a complete visit.

The desert's saguaro forests can be explored at close range at **Saguaro National Monument**, which is split into two units: one is 15 miles (24 km) west of Tucson; the more popular one is on the city's eastern edge in the foothills of the Rincon Mountains. The east unit offers a paved eight-mile (13-km) loop road popular with runners and cyclists, and off the road, wildlife such as javelina and even deer are abundant.

The organ pipe cactus occurs naturally in only one place in the world: **Organ Pipe National Monument**, a 516-square-mile (1,336 sq. km) preserve on the Mexican border. The cactus is a spectacle sprouting a cluster of huge vertical arms (up to 12 feet/3.6 m high) that resemble—vaguely, at least—the pipes of an organ. Quitobaquito Spring, a historic natural watering hole, attracts more than 260 species of birds.

Boyce Thompson Arboretum near the town of Superior superficially resembles the Arizona-Sonora Desert Museum, but there is an important difference: grown on its 1,000 acres are cacti from all around the world. Sixteen inches (41 cm) of rain annually turn this into one of the most extravagantly lush areas of the Sonoran Desert.

In Phoenix, the lovely **Desert Botanical Garden** also features 10,000 desert plants from the Sonoran and other deserts. Its exhibits explain historic uses of plants in the Sonoran Desert, and a demonstration garden struggles (without apparent success) to convince Phoenicians that water-saving desert landscaping is an idea whose time is here.

In the northern high deserts:

Monument Valley, a Navajo tribal park, straddles the Arizona-Utah border near the town of Kayenta. Visitors generally take the 17-mile (27 km) unpaved loop drive through the park, but some of the valley's most fascinating and eerie sandstone totems lie well away from the road. The Navajo strictly forbid hiking, rock climbing and off-road driving. Guided tours with more intimate photo opportunities may be booked at the visitor center. However, **Valley of the Gods**, a similar cluster of enormous spires and buttes only 30 miles (48 km) to the north, can be visited without restrictions. Consult a Utah map for directions.

Petrified Forest National Park and the adjacent **Painted Desert** near Holbrook offer a spectacular 28-mile (45-km) drive through a garden of mineralized logs and Sinagua petroglyphs. Backcountry hiking is permitted here, but anyone leaving the road should pack a plentiful supply of water, even in winter.

DESERT ETIQUETTE

A few tips on desert etiquette:

1. Carry a cooking stove, if you must cook. Do not burn desert wood, which is rare and beautiful and required ages for its creation (an ironwood tree lives for over 1,000 years and juniper almost as long).

2. If you must, out of need, build a fire, then for God's sake allow it to burn itself out before you leave—do not bury it, as Boy Scouts and Campfire Girls do, under a heap of mud or sand. Scatter the ashes; replace any rocks you may have used in constructing a fireplace; do all you can to obliterate the evidence that you camped here. (The Search & Rescue Team may be looking for you.)

3. Do not bury garbage—the wildlife will only dig it up again. Burn what will burn and pack out the rest. The same goes for toilet paper: Don't bury it, burn it.

4. Do not bathe in desert pools, natural tanks, tinajas, potholes. Drink what water you need, take what you need, and leave the rest for the next hiker and, more importantly, for the bees, birds, and animals—bighorn sheep, coyotes, lions, foxes, badgers, deer, wild pigs, wild horses—whose lives depend on that water.

5. Always remove and destroy survey stakes, flagging, advertising signboards, mining claim markers, animal traps, poisoned bait, seismic exploration geophones, and other such artifacts of industrialism. The men who put those things there are up to no good and it is our duty to confound them. Keep America beautiful. Grow a Beard. Take a Bath. Burn a Billboard.

—Edward Abbey, *The Journey Home: Some Words in Defense of the American West,* 1977

Agatized sections of tree trunks are scattered around Petrified Forest National Park. The ruined Agate House (top) was built with this rocklike wood. The wood's structure is revealed in a closeup.

GEOFFREY PLATTS—DESERT ADVOCATE

On a cool January weekend in 1990, 119,000 people showed up at Scottsdale's Tournament Players Club golf course for the Phoenix Open. One of them was Geoffrey Platts, spoilsport and conscience. He stood on the road shoulder near the entrance as golf fans drove in, a picket holding the same sign he had used to welcome the opening of a nearby Jack Nicklaus-designed golf course three years earlier:

GOLF IS KILLING THIS DESERT

Maledicta rained from the passing cars. One fan shouted, "Get a job, you flake." For Platts, that was merely delicious irony. He believes he has a job, one of critical importance, one that he invented. The title on his business card reads:

DESERT ADVOCATE

Platts lives alone in a one-room cabin somewhere in the desert foothills north of Scottsdale. He has no electricity, no phone, no mailbox, no car. He is not a flake. He is an extraordinarily articulate, well-read Englishman who came to the Sonoran Desert in 1962, slowly fell in love with the land, and eventually heard it crying for a defender. To that end, he has spent the last 15 years testifying at legislative hearings, needling public officials, writing polemics for any newspaper that will publish them, serving on the board of The Nature Conservancy, and picketing. It's a full-time, no-pay job; he makes grocery money by giving literary readings at parties in Scottsdale.

"When I started this 15 years ago, people thought, 'what a strange man,'" Platts says. "That's all right; John Muir was thought strange too. The odd thing now is that it's become fashionable to like the desert, and I find myself in the peculiar position of fighting guys who come on like they're the best thing ever to happen to this desert.

"What's happening is that the large developers, under the guise of environmental consciousness, are spending a lot of money to dig up trees and rearrange them and groom the land until it looks totally artificial and sterile—a concept I call 'Disney Desert.' When one of these developers looks at the untouched desert, he sees something that is too scruffy, too wild. It has dense plant growth, and that supports animals . . . creatures . . . creepy-crawly things that might eat . . . bite . . . kill!

"The picketing emerged from a sense of outrage over the golf courses. They're a bloody ecological disaster. When I first picketed Desert Mountain (the Nicklaus course), I didn't know whether I would end up that night in jail, because I wasn't quite sure of the right-of-way—but I was prepared to go to jail, if necessary. I even had in my back pocket a copy of Thoreau's *Civil Disobedience* to read in the cell. As it turned out, I wasn't arrested, and possibly I caused a few people to think.

"I chose to be a solitary picket because one person, interestingly, is more eloquent than five or ten scraggly people. It captures the interest of the media because it isn't diffused. It's the romance of the lone wolf. The protesters should number either one or a hundred; there's nothing more pathetic than a scraggly picket line of five or ten people."

The golf goes on, the scraping and remaking of the desert continues unabated. Does Platts feel futile?

"It's said that in preservation campaigns, there are no victories, only holding actions. My experience has been that there are victories, but they're minimal. All I can do is quote Schweitzer and say that 'Any work done from the heart is done in faith.' You can only hope that by continuing an advocacy, by forever bitching and needling and attacking, that you raise the ambiance of the people's thinking.

"I'll give you a very small example. In the middle of summer, I happened upon a crew pruning and hacking at the trees on the medians in Carefree, Disneyfying them to death, at the very time that a desert tree most needs its foliage to protect itself. I went to see the town manager, a reasonable man, and explained this to him. He said, 'I didn't know this; I'm from another part of the country.' And for the next six months the trees were allowed to grow unmolested. Small, but meaningful to me."

Platts's philosophy derives directly from that of naturalist Aldo Leopold, who wrote: "We abuse land because we regard it as a commodity belonging to us. When we see land as a community to which we belong, we may begin to use it with love and respect."

People who are working to strengthen Arizona's economy—a large part of which is tourism, and a major fraction of that is golf—view critics like Platts as naive annoyances. You can't develop a world-class resort, they will say, without manicuring the desert and providing golf.

Underneath north Scottsdale and the town of Carefree is an aquifer about eight miles long and two miles wide (13 by 3 km); it supplies all the water for the town and the six golf courses in the area. Since the three courses of Desert Mountain opened in 1987, an inverted cone of dry sand has appeared where the greatest concentration of water wells lie. Over the apex of the expanding cone, the water table has dropped 67 feet (20 m) in three years, and a number of wells have gone dry. How long, Geoffrey Platts asks, can this continue?

M O U N T A I N S

It is the summer of 1927, a decade before even rudimentary evaporative air conditioning will begin to become common in Tucson. Editors of *The Arizona Daily Star* and the rival *Tucson Daily Citizen* simmer in their downtown offices, heckling each other and churning out dueling editorials. The issue: how to move Tucson to the cool top of 9,157-foot (2,783 m) Mt. Lemmon for the five long months of summer.

The forward-looking *Star* predicts that by the 1940s, highways and automobiles will be obsolete. It proposes creating a municipal "air line" and shaving the mountaintop for an airstrip.

An air line would bring the cooling breezes and tall pines to within 30 minutes of Congress Street. Summer vacationers could breakfast on top of the range, fly to Tucson for a shopping trip, and be back in the mountains in time for lunch. The poor tired businessman could live at home beneath the pines and be at his office or store for the full eight- or ten-hour shift.

The *Citizen* ridicules the *Star's* aeronautical reverie and presses for a highway up the mountain. "Experts" parade daily across the front page, predicting economic calamity unless the road is built. The *Citizen* even recruits the local Roman Catholic bishop for its cause, publishing a pro-highway interview with him under the ominous headline:

TUCSON DOOMED TO BE 8 MONTH TOWN
UNLESS MOUNTAIN ROAD BUILT

But cost-conscious voters balk, rebuffing $500,000 bond issues in 1928 and again in 1930. The *Citizen's* publisher, Gen. Frank H. Hitchcock, won't give up. In 1933 he hears that the director of the federal Bureau of Prisons wants to experiment with employing prisoners on highway construction to help "rehabilitate" them. A flurry of meetings ensues, and work begins on the highway within three months.

The Mt. Lemmon Highway turns out to be a more daunting project than anyone imagines. By the time the 25-mile (40 km) road punches into the cool Ponderosa pine country, it has taken 18 years, 8,003 federal prisoners, and—even with all that free labor—nearly $1 million. But the result is a road that, mile for mile, is arguably Arizona's most scenic—and one that remains controversial even today.

■ AN ARCHIPELAGO OF ROCKS

The popular image of Arizona is that of a parched, wrinkled landscape of hostile desert plants set off by a distant backdrop of cardboard-cutout mountains propped against the sky. The nature of those mountains, in this image, remains something elusive and mysterious. This is as it always has been. In the theology of many of Arizona's Native Americans, the spirits dwell in the mountains.

In less mystical terms, the mountains are the reason for Arizona's great environmental diversity. Biologists call them "sky islands," a fitting metaphor. The environment at the summit of a 10,000-foot (3,048-m) Arizona mountain is as radically different from that of the desert floor 7,000 feet (2,134 m) below as that of Hawaii from the water around it. Early boosters of the Mt. Lemmon Highway liked to tout it as being the equivalent of driving from Mexico to Canada in an hour.

On an average Arizona mountain, the temperature falls three to four degrees F, while precipitation increases four to five inches (10 to13 cm) for every 1,000-foot (305-m) gain in elevation. These profound variations create dramatically evolving laminations of biotic communities on the mountains. As many as six of these distinct life zones occupy the sky islands of southern and central Arizona. Biologists sometimes disagree on the names and boundaries of these zones, but here is an attempt to sort them out:

Desert Shrub, 2,000-3,500 feet (610-1,067 m), essentially an extension of the plant and animal communities of the desert floor rising into the mountain foothills. Generous rainfall and runoff from higher elevations, however, produce more lush growth than in the flat basins. Forests of saguaro, mesquite and paloverde dominate, and in years of above-average winter precipitation, these elevations wear spring carpets of wild poppies, mustard flowers and other colorful blooms.

Chaparral, 3,500-6,000 feet (1,067-1,829 m). This is a temperate zone dominated by tall grasses, tough-leafed evergreen shrubs and one remarkably unfriendly succulent, the self-descriptive shindagger agave. The manzanita is its signature plant, a shrublike tree that grows only five or six feet high and sports a distinctive and lovely glossy, cherry-red bark.

Oak woodland, 4,500-6,000 feet (1,372-1,829 m). The dominant species is Emory oak with some Arizona oak and Mexican oak—and still the occasional yucca and prickly pear cactus—interspersed. Not yet dense enough to be considered forest, the trees are fairly sparse except in riparian habitats.

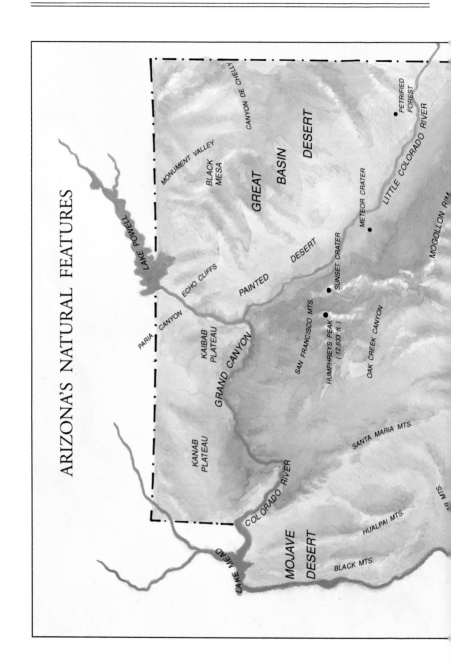

ARIZONA'S NATURAL FEATURES

GREAT BASIN DESERT

MONUMENT VALLEY

BLACK MESA

CANYON DE CHELLY

PETRIFIED FOREST

LITTLE COLORADO RIVER

METEOR CRATER

SUNSET CRATER

PAINTED DESERT

LAKE POWELL

ECHO CLIFFS

PARIA CANYON

KAIBAB PLATEAU

GRAND CANYON

SAN FRANCISCO MTS.

HUMPHREYS PEAK (12,633 ft.)

OAK CREEK CANYON

MOGOLLON RIM

KANAB PLATEAU

SANTA MARIA MTS.

COLORADO RIVER

LAKE MEAD

MOJAVE DESERT

HUALPAI MTS.

BLACK MTS.

MTS.

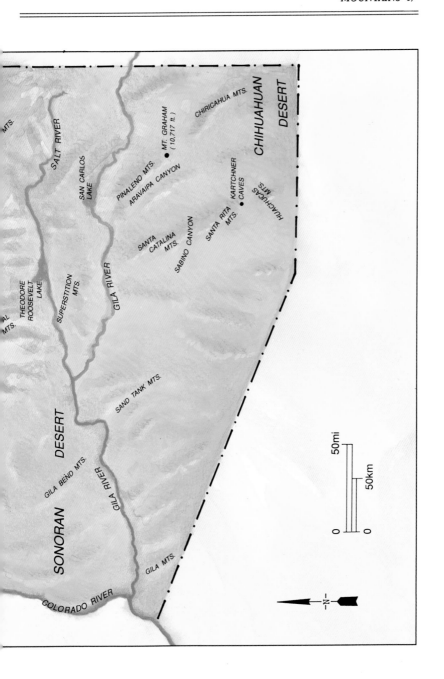

Piñon-juniper woodland, 5,000-7,000 feet (1,524-2,134 m). Substantial snow falls at these elevations even in the southernmost ranges. The piñon, or Mexican pine, is a tree too diminutive and gnarled to be of interest to the timber industry, but its abundant nuts provide food for large communities of birds. The Clark's nutcracker, a jay that has evolved a special nut pouch under its tongue, has been found flying with as many as 95 piñon nuts at a time.

Ponderosa pine forest, 7,000-9000 feet (2,134-2,743 m). These are authentic forests, dominated by the gigantic ponderosa. Mature trees probe up to 125 feet (38 m) into the sky, fighting for sunlight, and the winners live 200 to 400 years. The world's largest stand of ponderosas is in northern Arizona, girdling the San Francisco Mountains, but the forests are profuse enough in the desert sky islands to the south that logging operations have been carried out since the 1880s.

Canadian life zone, 7,500-10,000 feet (2,286-3,048 m). The common name of this zone is not at all misleading; its dark, mossy forests of Douglas fir, white fir and quaking aspen—and its abundant black bears—closely mimic the biology of Canada's forests 2,000 miles (3,200 km) to the north.

The higher one ascends through these life zones, the more compelling the "island" analogy becomes. A squirrel happily adapted to crunching nuts at 9,000 feet (2,743 m) will spend its entire life on that one mountain, as will its extended family. Even if something were to happen on that mountain that threatened its survival (such as a forest fire), it would have no options; it could not survive a 50-mile (80-km) trek through open desert to another "island."

This is true of most other mountain-dwelling creatures, although bears, provoked by the intervention of *Homo sapiens*, have tried it, and periodically the Arizona Game & Fish Department will try moving a "problem bear" from one mountain to another. The extradited bear, guided by an amazing homing instinct, may strike out for his old home, crossing deserts, highways and suburban back yards en route. One such bear was discovered in a tree in a Tucson yard a few years ago; it had been trying to return to the Huachuca Mountains from the Santa Catalinas—a trek of 80 miles (128 km).

For many plants and animals, confinement to one mountain island means that the species inbreeds. As long as the pool of available mates is large, this by no means spells trouble for it. Over time, however, it may well become a unique subspecies, different in important characteristics from its relatives on the next mountain over. If the gene pool is too small, however, the animal will edge toward extinction: the Mexican gray wolf and the grizzly bear both have vanished from Arizona's

The trail from Lockett Meadow is a favorite place to view aspens in the San Francisco Peaks.
(Kerrick James)

mountains in this century. As more and more human beings cluster around and increasingly settle in the Arizona mountains, the problem of saving these island environments for their original inhabitants is producing a swarm of controversies.

■ HUMANS AND MOUNTAINS

"The spirit of the mountain is a woman, and she is troubled," Berniece Falling Leaves explained.

Black Mountain is a strange knob of brown granite and black schist that rises abruptly out of the desert 35 miles (56 km) northeast of downtown Phoenix. Two small communities, eccentric Cave Creek and affluent Carefree, curl around it and press into it. Mansions worth as much as $3 million cling to its sides. This was why Berniece Falling Leaves, a half-Sioux mystic/metaphysicist, believed its spirit was troubled: all those houses were unwelcome.

One day in 1987, Falling Leaves and a Canadian medicine man named Buffalo Dreamer invited some sympathetic believers to a ceremonial dance in honor of the mountain's spirit. It was a mild, sunny day, she recalled, without a cloud anywhere in the sky. Suddenly, as the dance drew to a close, an enormous shudder of thunder erupted in the *blue sky* over Black Mountain.

"Everyone's eyes were the size of manhole covers," Falling Leaves recalled. "But we knew our energy had been transferred to the spirit of the mountain."

The concept of mountain spirits is an ancient one in Arizona. Many Native American cultures regard mountains as sacred. Baboquivari Peak, 60 miles (96 km) southwest of Tucson, is one: I'itoi, the protective Elder Brother of the Tohono O'odham people, is said to live there. For a desert people, this is an elegantly logical theology. Rainfall was and is their most vital resource, and in the desert, thunderstorms almost always begin over the mountains.

Likewise in modern Anglo culture, mysteries tend to reside in the mountains. By far the most durable is that of the Lost Dutchman mine in the Superstition Mountains 40 miles (64 km) east of Phoenix.

The legend of the Lost Dutchman dates from the 1870s, when two German-born prospectors named Jacob Waltz and Jacob Weiser supposedly made a sensational strike somewhere deep in the craggy Superstitions. Every time they showed up in Florence, the little desert town to the south, they paid for their supplies from pouches bulging with gold nuggets—or so the story goes. Somehow, Weiser met with an untimely demise. One account suggests that Waltz did it; another, suspiciously colorful, reports him crawling out of the mountains stuck full of Apache arrows and dying in a doctor's office. Waltz continued mining, eventually retired to Phoenix, and, shortly before he died, dictated some enigmatic directions to the mine to a bakery woman who had become his close friend. That was in 1891, and people have been combing the Superstitions in search of the Lost Dutchman for an entire century since.

Some of the fortune hunters are kooks, some are casual hobbyists, some are serious and indefatigable. Among the latter is the state's recently retired attorney general, Bob Corbin, who has been systematically searching for the mine since 1957. The Superstitions, however, seem determined to preserve their secret. A curiously large number of people have died in these mountains. Some have been weekend hikers and climbers who simply fell to their deaths, but many others were on the trail of the Lost Dutchman when they were mysteriously shot or just disappeared. One ghostly corollary to the mine legend says that Waltz is doing it. More likely—in fact, this has been documented—at least some of the murders have been committed by prospectors who feared that a rival would find the mine first. For whatever reason, according to *Arizona Highways*, at least 36 people are known to have perished in the Superstitions since Jacob Waltz departed with his terrible and compelling mystery.

Environmentalists sometimes like to say—and they are not really joking—that the death toll on these and other mountains is no surprise. The mountains, they say, are only trying to get people off their backs. In 1936, one Arizona mountain literally did just that.

Ever since its founding 60 years earlier, the copper mining town of Jerome had been assaulted by floods, fires and epidemics, but the wealth buried under it in Mingus Mountain kept it booming. Finally the tormented mountain responded. A combination of abnormally wet weather, continuous blasting and a honeycomb of more than 100 miles of mine shafts under the town caused a piece of the mountain to collapse in a colossal mud slide that swept away hundreds of structures. A quaint fraction of Jerome, some 300 buildings, still clings to the mountainside today. At its peak, Jerome had been home to 15,000 people.

In the 1970s and 1980s, a movement to protect Arizona's mountains gained considerable public support. Mining, logging, roadbuilding and virtually every other human development that could scar the mountains or alter their wildlife habitats have been challenged.

In 1975, Pima County and the city of Scottsdale passed the state's first hillside ordinances to halt the steady creep of subdivisions up the suburban mountain slopes. Other communities soon followed suit. Developers sued Scottsdale, however, and the case slogged through courtrooms for a decade. The eventual ruling: developers could still build houses even on the steepest, most exposed mountain slopes—but only for the very rich who could afford to buy 40 acres of mountain and then, typically, build a palatial home. Preservationists saw this as no victory for the mountains.

They did find other causes for cheer. Rep. Morris K. Udall, once dean of Arizona's congressional delegation, managed to jam 3,750 square miles (9,713 sq. km) of pristine Arizona land, much of it mountainous, into a 1990 wilderness bill. It will join 3,125 square miles (8,094 sq. km) of Arizona wilderness already locked up from development pressure, theoretically forever. Udall, who served 15 terms in Congress, once said that wilderness protection for his home state was one of the achievements of which he was most proud.

Fewer than 300 Victorian buildings remain in the mountainside mining town of Jerome, but slowly, entrepreneurs are restoring them.

Outside the wilderness areas, the battles grind on. In 1980, the University of Arizona first approached the U.S. Forest Service about leasing a few acres on top of 10,717-foot (3,267-m) Mt. Graham (near Safford) for a cluster of new observatories. When environmental studies commenced, scientists found a unique rodent inhabiting the site—the Mt. Graham red squirrel, one of those subspecies that had been evolving in isolation for an estimated 10,000 years. A 10-year-long string of studies ensued, accompanied by lawsuits and demonstrations that stretched from the university's mall to the Washington Mall. By 1990 the entire red squirrel population was estimated at 300, the university and environmentalists had become bitter enemies, and construction of the observatories began. The interminable battle illustrated the depth of the passions that now swirl around Arizona's mountains.

There is another interesting example. *Frog Mountain Blues,* a 1987 book by environmentalist Charles Bowden, argued from beginning to end to close that most spectacular of Arizona roads, the Mt. Lemmon Highway.

Politically, it is unlikely the highway ever will be closed. It has many defenders and caretakers, and all it takes is a clear summer day, a good friend, a picnic basket and a convertible with the top peeled back to convince most of us that the mountain may be asked, gently, to please suffer this one intrusion. However, it is even more unlikely that were this highway just being proposed today that it would ever be built. The mountain would remain wild, and would almost surely be the better for it.

■ VISITING THE MOUNTAINS

The **Santa Catalinas** on Tucson's north edge are one of the few major Arizona ranges to be probed by a paved road, the Mt. Lemmon Highway. Picnic grounds, campgrounds and awesome geologic spectacles occur every couple of miles along the two-lane road, which climbs 5,293 feet (1,613 m) in 25 miles (40 km). At the end is Ski Valley, the southernmost developed ski area in the U.S., and Summerhaven, a community with a few unpretentious inns and boutiques. On holiday weekends in summer, the Mt. Lemmon Highway is best avoided.

A road also curls to the summit of 6,882-foot (2,098-m) **Kitt Peak** 55 miles (88 km) southwest of Tucson. This is the nexus of astronomical research in Ari-

On the Mt. Lemmon Highway

The mountain I have described will not be something like hot water or cold beer, an indulgence instantly available to everyone. To go there will call for more than a tank of gas and a machine. . . . It is no longer 1880, and we do not need to flee to the high country to escape summer heat. We do not need to bulldoze a mountain so that we can have a picnic and throw down a six-pack. We can no longer defend slaughtered groves of trees 500 years old so that people can try their luck at skiing in those random years when enough snow comes to the peaks. We hack the mountain down to our size for very trivial reasons, and in doing so we risk losing something that has grown increasingly rare, wild ground that questions the way we live. The only way to make our peace with the mountain is to get off it.

The land I have come to love is in many ways a ruin left me by my ancestors, and as I stand in this lonely canyon on the Catalina [Mountains'] backside I am viewing an invalid struggling to come back from a savage illness. I would not know this fact except for the books and pamphlets that track this orgy of greed and enterprise. I accept the landscape as I see it and find it not wanting. But still, I must consider that it once was lusher, more diverse, and more teeming. Down below me on the flats, antelope once ran.

Now they are gone. Above me on the peaks, bighorns once dominated, and now they are refugees on one isolated ridge of the range. The black bear clings in small numbers; the grizzly has not been seen for more than half a century. The jaguar no longer visits. No one hears the cry of the wolf.

—Charles Bowden, *Frog Mountain Blues*,
1987

zona, with more than a dozen telescopes clustered on the mountaintop. There is a visitor center and small museum open daily (free) with guided tours of the observatories given on weekends and holidays.

The **Chiricahua Mountains** in Arizona's southeastern corner are rich both in history and scenery. These were the ancestral homelands of the Chiricahua Apaches, and when their leader, Cochise, negotiated peace with the Army in 1872, he was promised the mountain range as a reservation. Cochise died two years later, and in 1875 the promise evaporated and his people were herded north to the San Carlos

Reservation. In 1924, President Calvin Coolidge designated the most spectacular part of the range as a national monument.

A graded road, Bonita Canyon Drive, crosses over the north end of the Chiricahuas, but the best way to appreciate them is on foot. There are more than 111 miles (178 km) of developed trails in the Chiricahua Wilderness, and maps are available in the monument visitor center. The most ambitious can take the Morse Canyon Trail to 9,357-foot (2,852-m) Monte Vista Peak and 9,795-foot (2,986-m) Chiricahua Peak. One of the most interesting features in the Chiricahuas is erosion-sculpted volcanic rocks bearing names such as "Duck on a Rock." The other is black bears, which, thanks to the Chiricahuas' protected status, thrive in this range. There are bears on most of Arizona's high mountains, but in the Chiricahuas there is a mob of them.

Arizona's least-known high-country scenery lies in the **Apache-Sitgreaves National Forest**, whose peaks range up to 10,995-foot (3,351-m) Escudilla Mountain. For an introduction, take US Route 666 from Clifton to Alpine, a federally designated Scenic Byway. There is not one town along the 95-mile (152-km) route, but wildlife is abundant: deer, elk, wild turkeys, mountain lions, black bears.

The **White Mountains**, 120 miles (192 km) northeast of Phoenix, comprise Arizona's best-known and most intensively developed mountain vacationland. Recreation is the strong suit in these mountains, not solitude.

Twenty-five lakes are scattered around the mountains. Most are small, but are generously stocked with fish, rainbow and brown trout being most common. Cross-country skiing and snowmobiling are everywhere. Downhill skiers can choose from 61 trails laced across three mountains at the Sunrise Ski Resort, owned and operated by the White Mountain Apache Tribe. The incorporated community of Pinetop-Lakeside (pop. 2,395) offers community theater, guided full-moon ski tours, and frequent golf tournaments; the nearby town of Show Low also has such recreational oddities as a summer Grand Prix for bathtubs on wheels.

The most sublime natural attraction running northwest of the White Mountains is the **Mogollon Rim**, a weird and spellbinding escarpment that plunges 2,000 feet (609 m) in one vertical slash from the undulating mountain country to the Tonto Basin. Spectacular and vertiginous views are best from the Rim Drive (Arizona State Route 300), a good but lonely gravel road closely paralleling the rim for 43 miles (69 km).

More than 400 Arizona mountains are the remnants of volcanic activity. The

most recent known eruption was in the winter of A.D. 1064-65, when a volcano 10 miles (16 km) north of present-day Flagstaff blanketed 120 square miles (311 sq. km) of countryside with lava, cinders, and ash. The most prominent memento of that drama is **Sunset Crater,** a 1,000-foot-high (304-m) cinder cone that is now a national monument. Trails lead among the lava flows, but not up the cone.

Just to its west are the **San Francisco Peaks,** Arizona's highest mountain range at 12,643 feet (3,854 m). This is a "stratovolcano," composed of alternating layers of lava and ash. It is also Arizona's most formidable mountaineering challenge. Snow usually blocks the trail to the summit from October through May, and lightning is a constant hazard in July and August.

Fairfield Snowbowl Ski Resort, off US 180 north of Flagstaff, has four chairlifts and 32 trails slicing down the peaks. Between Phoenix and Tucson, **Picacho Peak** masquerades very effectively as a volcanic cone, but it actually is only the eroded remains of other lava flows. The precipitous climb up Hunter Trail to the summit, a 1500-foot (457-m) elevation gain, erodes the remains of many hikers' courage. The view, however, is spectacular.

The 235-square-mile (609-sq.-km) **Superstition Wilderness** is Phoenix's nearest great, wild mountain. A jagged, forbidding range, the Superstitions can be admired from the base at Lost Dutchman State Park or attacked on trails. The Superstitions are not a remarkably high range; the tallest peak is Mound Mountain at 6,266 feet (1,910 m). This is, however, a truly intimidating range; after scouring it for the Lost Dutchman for more than 30 years Attorney General Bob Corbin confessed to the *Arizona Daily Star* that he had vast canyons left to search. "You'd need ropes to get into some of these areas," Corbin said. "The place we're messing with now, I can't get a horse within half a mile of it."

Snow on San Francisco Peaks north of Flagstaff. (Peter Bloomer)

KARTCHNER CAVERNS

For most of their adult lives, Randy Tufts and Gary Tenen secretly have cared for a baby—a helpless creature more than two miles (three km) long and Lord knows how many millions of years old. A *baby?* Yes: the metaphor surfaces again and again in any conversation with Tufts and Tenen, who discovered Arizona's largest known cave near Benson in 1974 and didn't tell anyone until 1988. "The cave is defenseless," explains Tufts. "It can't speak for itself. It can't make decisions for itself. It's like a child that's forever two years old. It has to have people who will love it, who will protect it, who will argue on its behalf."

Balanced against the straining engines of full-throttle development in Arizona are people such as Tufts and Tenen, people whose dreams are not to transmute the land's resources into personal wealth, but to preserve those resources for future generations. These people are no longer rare, but the state's unexploited treasures are.

Kartchner Caverns will be one of Arizona's most spectacular attractions when it opens as a state park. One of its rooms could swallow a football field. There are calcium carbonate drapes that look like thin-sliced bacon or billowing waves of translucent rice noodles. Some stalactites are several feet long and yet thin as a pencil. Tufts believes it is the most pristine wet cave in the country. And the way he and his friend have worked to keep it that way is as unusual as the cave itself.

The two businessmen have been avid cavers most of their lives. "When I was a freshman at the University of Arizona," recalls Tufts, "my idea of a good time was going to the library on Saturday afternoons and scanning dissertations about Arizona geology for mentions of limestone. Then I'd go out with a topo map to areas that seemed like good prospects for caves to see if I could find anything."

One day in 1974, the two were out on one of these prospecting forays when they discovered an intriguing opening. They tossed in a rock, checking for rattlesnakes, then slithered in.

"Imagine a passage about 10 by 24 inches [25 by 61 cm], surrounded by boulders that weren't quite nested together," Tenen says. "Our legs were out at one angle and our bodies at another, and we squirmed about 20 feet [6.1 m] while the boulders wobbled around us. I guess there's a period in your life when you're young that you have no fear."

This rocky passage opened onto a succession of small, dry rooms, typical of Arizona caves. Then they came to another crawlway, and at its end was a small hole. Moist air was squirting through it. They chiseled at the hole for two hours until they could scrape through. Then, as Tenen recalls, "with every step we took, the fantasy unfolded. The dream of every caver was coming through. The third room was better than the first two, and it was wet."

They explored 500 feet (152 m) of the cave that day, so enraptured that they were ignoring caving's prime rule. "Suddenly we realized that nobody knew where we were," says Tenen. "In an unexplored cave you can get lost, or you can step on a floor that's nothing but a crust with a pit below it . . . ."

They systematically explored the cave over the next six months, never finding any sign that other humans had preceded them. They corked the entrance with a removable concrete plug to conceal it. They traced the land ownership to the J. A. Kartchner family of nearby St. David, then quietly investigated the Kartchners. They feared two things for the cave. One, that its owners might turn it into a tourist trap, slicing stalactites into souvenir ashtrays. Or two, that news of its existence might seep out, and people would start "exploring" it without regulation. A cave not far away is full of trash, and visitors such as "FRANKIE" and "DANNY" have autographed its walls. But the Kartchners, an extended family of Mormon farmers, seemed like people who could be trusted. When Tufts and Tenen finally approached them and took them on a tour of the unsuspected cave on their own property, the family immediately saw themselves as trustees of an environmental treasure.

Tufts and Tenen prepared a detailed proposal for the Kartchners to operate the cave as a private park. The family considered it for two years and finally decided they didn't have the resources. Then the discoverers wrote a plan to move the cave into state hands. In 1988, the Kartchners sold the property to the State Parks Board.

The state now seems equally determined to care for the baby. "It's a live cave, and we need to make sure we know exactly what keeps it alive," says Parks Board Director Ken Travous. "I like to use this analogy: when we go in, we're like a virus invading a living organism, and we need to be certain we don't do irreparable damage to that organism."

Tufts and Tenen say it will be a state-of-the-art cave development with airlock doors and sensitively routed trails. Yet, even as they describe it, one senses that they regret it has to be "developed" at all. It is like caging an animal: inevitably, its wild character is lost forever.

"The entrance is close enough to a major highway that you can hear the cars, so we knew early on that the cave was in trouble," explains Tenen. "We made a choice between controlled change of its environment and the probability of uncontrolled, haphazard, and probably spiraling destruction. If one factor had been different—if it had been hidden deep in the mountains, or if it had a thousand-foot (305-m) rappel to get into it—there would still be a concrete plug in it, and we'd still be keeping it secret."

C A N Y O N S

SHORTLY AFTER THE END OF WORLD WAR I, Marshal Ferdinand Foch, the Allies' supreme commander, visited the Grand Canyon as a guest of Jack Greenway, former Rough Rider and Arizona mining magnate. A contingent of reporters hovered around, waiting to record Foch's reaction. He stared into the great chasm for a moment, then turned to Greenway and said something in French. Greenway turned to the reporters and translated: "Marshal Foch says that the canyon is the most beautiful manifestation of God's presence on the entire earth." What Foch actually had said was, "Let's have a cup of coffee."

Former Arizona Governor Bruce Babbitt recounts this story in his excellent *Grand Canyon: An Anthology*. As Babbitt interprets it, Foch wasn't being indifferent; he just wasn't comprehending what he was seeing. His brain had no precedent for processing visual information on this scale. John Muir, who had visited the canyon in 1898, articulated the problem perfectly:

> No matter how far you have wandered hitherto, or how many famous gorges and valleys you have seen, this one, the Grand Canyon of the Colorado, will seem as novel to you, as unearthly in the color and grandeur and quantity of its architecture, as if you had found it after death, on some other star . . . .

I have been to, and into, the Grand Canyon many times, and my senses, too, keep failing me. My notes, scribbled in a hip pocket notebook, always seem later as limp and banal as a televangelist's sermon. I am irritated with myself, but also consoled by the observation that many other people fail to come to terms with the canyon: in its presence, all human endeavor seems banal.

Almost four million people now visit Grand Canyon National Park in a year, a figure that has doubled in the last 15 years. In summer the more accessible South Rim seems more like a colossal state fair, or even a Disney attraction, than a natural wonder. Weekend athletes employ the canyon as a personal proving ground, whittling away at the record for a rim-to-rim run (three hours, nine minutes). Trading posts, airplane and helicopter overflights ("pilot narrated with stereo music"), Golden Arches, an IMAX theater and even a singing "human jukebox" compete for a share of the tourist dollars. Park officials have begun to worry

FROM THE DIARY OF JOHN WESLEY POWELL, GRAND CANYON

Clouds are playing in the cañon today. Sometimes they roll down in great masses, filling the gorge with gloom; sometimes they hang above, from wall to wall, and cover the cañon with a roof of impending storm; and we can peer long distances up and down this cañon corridor, with its cloud roof overhead, its walls of black granite, and its river bright with the sheen of broken waters. Then, a gust of wind sweeps down a side gulch, and, making a rift in the clouds, reveals the blue heavens, and a stream of sunlight pours in. Then, the clouds drift away into the distance, and hang around crags, and peaks, and pinnacles, and towers, and walls, and cover them with a mantle, that lifts from time to time, and sets them all in sharp relief. Then, baby clouds creep out of side cañons, glide around points, and creep back again, into more distant gorges. Then, clouds, set in strata, across the cañon, with intervening vista views, to cliffs and rocks beyond. The clouds are children of the heavens, and when they play among the rocks, they lift them to the region above.

❖ ❖ ❖

[In the following excerpt, Powell has climbed an escarpment to reconnoiter the rapids ahead.]

In my eagerness to reach a point where I can see the roaring fall below, I go too far on the wall, and can neither advance nor retreat. I stand with one foot on a little projecting rock, and cling with my hand fixed in a little crevice. Finding I am caught here, suspended 400 feet [122 m] above the river, into which I should fall if my footing fails, I call for help. The men come, and pass me a line, but I cannot let go of the rock long enough to take hold of it. Then they bring two or three of the largest oars. All this takes time which seems very precious to me; but at last they arrive. The blade of one of the oars is pushed into a little crevice in the rock beyond me, in such a manner that they can hold me pressed against the wall. Then another is fixed in such a way that I can step on it, and thus I am extricated.

❖ ❖ ❖

And now we go on through this solemn, mysterious way. The river is very deep, the canyon very narrow, and still obstructed, so that there is no steady flow of the stream; but the waters wheel, and roll, and boil, and we are scarcely able to determine where we can go. Now, the boat is carried to the right, perhaps close to the wall; again, she is shot into the stream, and perhaps is dragged over to the other where, caught in a whirlpool, she spins about. We can neither land nor run as we please. The boats are entirely unmanageable; no order in their running can be preserved; now one, now another, is ahead, each crew laboring for its own preservation. In such a place we come to another rapid. Two of the boats run it perforce. One succeeds in landing, but there is no foothold by which to make a portage, and she is pushed out again into the stream. The next minute a great reflex wave fills the open compartment; she is water-logged, and drifts unmanageable. Breaker after breaker rolls over her, and one capsizes her. The men are thrown out; but they cling to the boat, and she drifts down some distance, alongside of us, and we are able to catch her. She is soon bailed out, and the men are aboard once more; but the oars are lost, so a pair from the *Emma Dean* is spared. Then for two miles we find smooth water.

—John Wesley Powell, 1869

openly about the "quality of the experience," as do I. People even lug boom boxes down the crowded Bright Angel Trail, trying—this is my theory—to reduce the experience to familiar terms because they are unable to deal with the Grand Canyon on *its* terms.

Once, rounding a bend on the Bright Angel Trail, I encountered a teenager standing at the edge of a 2,000-foot (610-m) drop. A monstrous boom box was beside him, serenading a vast panorama of Kaibab limestone with music of vanishingly low quality. As he bobbed to this sorry beat, two other hikers stood a few feet behind him, conferring.

"All it would take is one little kick," one hissed.

"Yeah, and a grateful world would have one less boom box to endure."

"I wasn't talking about the boom box."

The Grand Canyon has been forming for at least 2.6 million years, and possibly as much as 10 million—geologists are uncertain. Human beings have lived around and inside it for at least 4,000 years. But humans have changed it drastically in less than the last hundred years.

John Wesley Powell, a courageous and fascinating man who had lost his right arm in the Civil War, led the first thorough expedition through the canyon in 1869. He set out from the Colorado tributary of Green River in Wyoming on May 24 with 10 men and a flotilla of four 16- and 21-foot rowboats. The tattered remains of the expedition—two boats, seven men—arrived more than three months later at the mouth of the Virgin River (now somewhere under Lake Mead in Nevada's southeastern corner). Powell's dramatic and meticulous chronicle, published by the U.S. Government Printing Office in 1875, ranks among the most compelling and literate explorers' journals ever written.

Three of Powell's companions died on the expedition—the ones, ironically, who balked at running the stupefying Separation Rapid (also now inundated by Lake Mead) and tried to walk out of the canyon. Three days later, Shivwits Paiute Indians encountered them on the North Rim and killed them.

Powell's reports from this and a subsequent expedition in 1871 introduced the Grand Canyon to an astonished country, but tourism took hold slowly. Even to settlers in Utah and Arizona Territory, the canyon seemed remote and inaccessible. However, John Hance, an itinerant miner and raconteur, built a log cabin on the South Rim about 1883, and soon began leading paying guests into the canyon on trails. Hance, it could be said, was the father of Grand Canyon marketing. In 1886 he advertised in the Flagstaff newspaper:

> Being thoroughly conversant with all the trails leading to the Grand Canyon of the Colorado, I am prepared to conduct parties thereto at any time. I have a fine spring of water near my house on the rim of the Canyon, and can furnish accommodations for tourists and their animals.

It wasn't until 1901, when the 64-mile (102-km) railroad punched through from Williams to the South Rim, that tourists began flocking to the canyon in serious numbers. By 1905 the luxurious El Tovar Hotel was complete, and in 1922 Phantom Ranch—then as now the only accommodation on the canyon floor— opened for guests. Today's routine amusement of river running, however, remained an exotic and frequently deadly venture for a long time: After Powell's first successful river trip through the canyon in 1869, it was 80 years before 100 people, including the Powell parties, had done the same. What turned the Colorado into the relatively benign stream it is today was the completion of Glen Canyon dam in 1963. Environmentalists still consider the dam an unspeakable outrage, a crime against nature. Interestingly, Theodore Roosevelt, who visited the Grand Canyon in 1903 and proclaimed it a national monument five years later, would surely have agreed. In a speech he made at the South Rim during that 1903 visit, he said:

(following pages) "The prudent keep silent"—John Muir

*I*n the Grand Canyon, Arizona has a natural wonder which, so far as I know, is in kind absolutely unparalleled throughout the rest of the world. I want to ask you to do one thing . . . . to keep this great wonder of nature as it now is . . . . I hope you will not have a building of any kind, not a summer cottage, a hotel or anything else, to mar the wonderful grandeur, the sublimity, the great loveliness and beauty of the Canyon. Leave it as it is. You cannot improve on it. The ages have been at work on it, and man can only mar it. What you can do is keep it for your children, your children's children, and for all who come after you, as the one great sight which every American . . . should see.

■ SEEING THE CANYON

No single mode of exploring the Grand Canyon is enough to fully appreciate and comprehend it, and standing on the rim and staring in is the most inadequate of all. One needs to engage the canyon with all the senses. Hike its trails, feel its walls, challenge its river. Fly over it—at twilight, if possible, when its vivid afternoon colors of auburns, greens, purples and browns slowly converge into a deep, mistlike, saturating blue, and its sharp edges melt away in the faint light, the sensation of mystery growing as bottomless as the gulch itself.

How, when and where to go? The first decision is a fundamental one: North Rim or South? Few people manage both on one visit: the closest road link, which bridges the Colorado at Marble Canyon, is a 216-mile (346-km) journey. There is commercial air service to the South Rim, but not to the North.

A growing number of Grand Canyon enthusiasts, this one included, no longer can tolerate the South Rim's crowds and commercialization at all. The North Rim, with its single hotel and (relatively) modest crush of 350,000 visitors a year, is much quieter, more isolated, more intimate, and seems to have a more favorable ratio of adults to children. A 1990 article in *Condé Nast Traveler* magazine noted that the North Rim "has long been the connoisseur's side of the canyon," while at the same time sounding an alarm: plans to build a second hotel, under legal challenge at this writing, would inexorably begin to turn the North Rim into a mirror image of the South.

Because of the North Rim's higher elevation (8,200 feet/2,438 m vs. 6,876 feet/2,096 m at the South Rim), it is open to visitors only mid-May through mid-October. The only North Rim lodging inside the park is the Grand Canyon Lodge, which incorporates a surprisingly good restaurant (with views overlooking the canyon, of course). Five miles (eight km) outside the park is Kaibab Lodge; 34 miles (54 km) outside is Jacob Lake Lodge. This is about it—for now.

The South Rim is open all year, and frankly is best avoided in summer and on all holiday weekends.

Since 1989, South Rim visitors have had the intriguing option of driving to Williams, then riding a vintage steam locomotive to the South Rim. The Grand Canyon Railway ceased regular service in 1953, but now after restoration and a very popular revival, it slices through 64 miles (102 km) of scenic high plateau country and the Kaibab National Forest. Reservations are strongly advised. Another alternative to squeezing through South Rim traffic is to arrive by air: several commercial airlines serve Grand Canyon Airport with connections from Phoenix, Flagstaff, and Las Vegas.

Accommodations at the South Rim are far more varied than at the North, and most are more expensive. The historic El Tovar, Bright Angel Lodge, Thunderbird Lodge and Kachina Lodge perch on the rim itself, with some rooms offering spectacular views. Many more motels are available in Tusayan, seven miles (11 km) south of the rim.

Overnight camping is permitted only in designated campgrounds on both rims, and reservations and fees are required. Overnight camping inside the canyon also requires a permit, since the Park Service restricts the number of campers to prevent overuse of the wilderness. (For reservation information on all Grand Canyon activities, see "PRACTICAL INFORMATION.")

Hikers have a (literally) dizzying variety of options for exploring the canyon. There are nine rim-to-river trails from the South Rim and four from the North. Unfortunately, on all three of the most popular canyon trails (Bright Angel, South Kaibab and North Kaibab), hikers must share the narrow paths with mules—*a lot* of mules. A 1988 article on Grand Canyon mule pollution in Tucson's *City Magazine* reported that there are more than 35,000 mule trips per year down Bright Angel and South Kaibab, and that the average 1,000-pound (454-kg) mule manufactures about 44 pounds (20 kg) of manure and six quarts (5.6 liters) of urine per day. This is not a pleasant subject, but neither, in all honesty, are these trails.

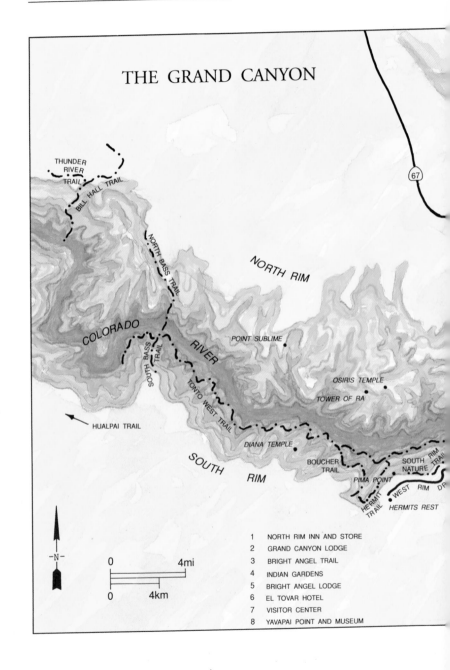

THE GRAND CANYON

THUNDER RIVER TRAIL
BILL HALL TRAIL
NORTH BASS TRAIL
NORTH RIM
67
COLORADO
RIVER
POINT SUBLIME
SOUTH BASS TRAIL
OSIRIS TEMPLE
TOWER OF RA
TONTO WEST TRAIL
HUALPAI TRAIL
DIANA TEMPLE
SOUTH
RIM
BOUCHER TRAIL
SOUTH RIM NATURE TRAIL
PIMA POINT
WEST RIM DR
HERMIT TRAIL
HERMITS REST

−N−

| 0 | | 4mi |
| 0 | | 4km |

1 NORTH RIM INN AND STORE
2 GRAND CANYON LODGE
3 BRIGHT ANGEL TRAIL
4 INDIAN GARDENS
5 BRIGHT ANGEL LODGE
6 EL TOVAR HOTEL
7 VISITOR CENTER
8 YAVAPAI POINT AND MUSEUM

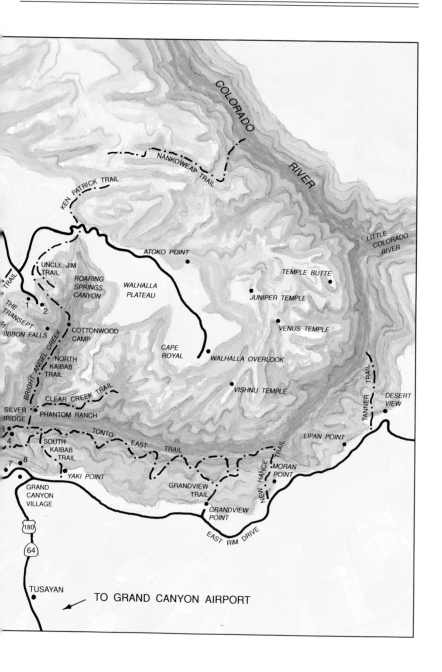

The alternatives are the "secondary trails," which are not maintained by the Park Service: Hermit, Grandview, Tanner, Boucher, New Hance, Thunder River and others. They range from moderately difficult to very difficult; some may require route-finding skills. It goes without saying that they also are more rewarding. Hikers or mule riders staying overnight at Phantom Ranch may want to reserve an extra day for the lovely Clear Creek trail (18 miles/29 km round trip), which passes Anasazi ruins and 1,000-foot (305-m) Cheyava Falls, the canyon's highest (usually a trickle, however, except during spring runoff). Clear Creek is relatively level and easy.

Trail maps and guidebooks are sold in most shops around the canyon. No permit is needed for day hiking on any canyon trail. The most important caveat, however, is to be aware of water availability and weather; too many canyon hikers have died from heatstroke and dehydration. The *average* daily July high at Phantom Ranch is 106.1 degrees F (41.2° C). Consider this as one more reason to stay away from the canyon in summer.

Hikers wanting to avoid the stench of the main trails but who are nervous about negotiating the secondary routes alone might consider professionally guided overnighters with Grand Canyon Trail Guides, a private concessionaire. The final alternative, of course, is to join 'em—that is, to ride a mule train into the canyon. Wrangler-guided trips ranging from seven hours to three days are available. The concessionaire requires that riders weigh less than 200 pounds (91 kg) and be fluent in English. Warns the brochure, "Those who are disturbed by heights or large animals should reconsider."

Running the river is still an adventure, but it isn't a wilderness experience: 21 operators offer Grand Canyon river trips, both motorized and oar-propelled, ranging from three days to two weeks. Write the Park Service for a list of companies or pick up brochures in Flagstaff or Page.

Finally, consider a helicopter or airplane tour—with another important caveat: Grand Canyon Airport is now Arizona's third busiest, and the canyon's airspace is hazardous. An inordinate number of people have died in crashes in canyon airspace or at the airport since 1964. The FAA now prohibits flying *in* the canyon, much to the relief of the Park Service, hikers, and resident Havasupai Indians. Tour operators may fly no lower than the rims, and all other aircraft must stay above 14,500 feet (4,420 m) in most flight corridors.

In truth, any human interaction with the Grand Canyon carries some element of risk; the landscape is awe-inspiring precisely because it is forbidding. This is no reason not to make its acquaintance. Let the canyon scare you a little; you will then understand it better.

■ OTHER CANYONS OF ARIZONA

"I swore I would never come back here," says Bob Kittredge, canyon man.

He is relaxing in the cheerfully cluttered log house his father built in Oak Creek Canyon between Flagstaff and Sedona in the 1930s. He lives here now, and feels comfortable, but it has been a long emotional journey. The canyon was a desperately lonely and frightening place in which to grow up.

To a little kid, he explains, the canyon was overpowering. The scale of everything was too large. Once the sight of a bear cub, a plump furball hardly larger than a dog, scared him out of his wits. At night, the pines were shadowy monsters threatening to reach out and snatch him. He remembers falling off a horse while crossing Oak Creek, and it seemed like a river 60 feet (18 m) wide.

He grew up and moved away, and when he returned, in his thirties, a new emotion arose. He felt confined, even claustrophobic. There were no horizons, only canyon walls squeezing away the skies.

"I finally came to feel the canyon as a place of refuge, but it's been a long process," Kittredge says. "And I find it interesting that none of the kids who grew up here at the time I did today lives in the canyon—or, for that matter, in *any* canyon."

Kittredge's story illustrates the power that canyons can exert on the emotions, which is even greater than that of mountains. Canyons enclose and define worlds. They nourish unique biosystems and work unpredictable magic on the pliant human mind. A canyon can fill one with wonder or fright, or both at once.

There are literally thousands of canyons in Arizona, far too many to canvass here. There are V-shaped mountain canyons, formed more by volcanic upheavals than by erosion. There are sandstone "slot canyons" on the Colorado Plateau only a few feet wide and hundreds of feet deep. There are urban canyons that flood with people every weekend, and canyons so remote that only the most determined backpackers ever get into them.

These are the best canyons I know:

Canyon de Chelly (pronounced "d'shay") in northeast Arizona earned its pseudo-Spanish name from the inability of early nineteenth-century Spaniards to pronounce the Navajo word *tsegi*, which means "rock canyon." A more elegant solution might have been for them simply to call it *el cañón exquisitó*, for it is arguably Arizona's most exquisite canyon.

There actually are several adjoining canyons here, with the largest tributary—Canyon del Muerto—stretching nearly as long as Canyon de Chelly's 27 miles (43 km). While the greatest depth is only about 1,000 feet (305 m), the walls themselves form an astonishing spectacle. Generally even steeper and sheerer than the Grand Canyon's walls, some appear to have eroded in layers, like a flaking biscuit, while others look as though they were sliced by a 600-foot (183-m) knife. One remarkable feature is Spider Rock, a needle-like sandstone monolith shooting 800 feet (244 m) out of the canyon floor. In autumn, particularly, Canyon de Chelly is a festival of color, with the auburn walls playing off the lime-green and golden cottonwoods snaking along the river at the bottom.

Humans have occupied Canyon de Chelly for almost 2,000 years. The Anasazi left some 400 ruins beginning with primitive pit houses and ending with the construction of a three-story masonry high-rise around A.D. 1284. They also left thousands of paintings on the canyon walls, and when their Navajo successors

Bear Wallow—one of the many lush upland canyons surrounding Sedona.
(opposite) Some 400 Anasazi ruins huddle under the walls of Canyon De Chelly. This, the White House Ruin, is the only one accessible without a Navajo guide.

began to move into the canyon in the mid-1700s, they added their pictorial stories. One Navajo canyon painting quite literally depicts the Spanish military expedition of Antonio Narbona in 1804-05, and behind it lies a tragic story.

On a chilly January morning in 1805 Narbona and his men discovered more than a hundred Navajos hiding in a remote cave 600 feet (183 m) above the canyon floor. Narbona later claimed that after a battle "with the greatest ardor and effort," his valiant troops killed "90 warriors" along with a few women and children holed up in the cave, but Navajo oral history holds that the victims were *all* women, children and old men. The Navajo version has more of the resonance of truth: the first Spaniard to climb to the cave that day was attacked by a *woman* defender armed with a knife. The massacre gave Canyon del Muerto its haunting Spanish name: it means "Canyon of Death."

Canyon de Chelly became a national monument in 1931, although the Navajos, who still farm the canyon floors, restrict access to much of it. Plan to take a half-day or full-day tour of the canyon floor with a Navajo guide. (See "THE FIRST ARIZONANS" and "PRACTICAL INFORMATION" for visitor information.)

Oak Creek Canyon, like the Grand Canyon, is to be avoided during peak vacation times—its top attraction, Slide Rock State Park (so named for a natural sandstone slide leading into a pool on Oak Creek) draws crowds like a Southern California beach on a warm summer afternoon. Fall is the best season in the canyon anyway, because of the color show staged by its forests of oak, mountain mahogany, sycamore, and sumac. From mid-October to early November, Oak Creek Canyon near Sedona is the most colorful place in Arizona.

The U.S. Forest Service maintains about 10 hiking trails into Oak Creek's tributary canyons, all of which are spectacular. One deserves special mention: the **West Fork of Oak Creek**, poetically and accurately described in an *Arizona Highways* article by William E. Hafford as "the canyon the moon cannot find." Even in the daytime, West Fork can seem dark. Some of its walls are actually concave, sculpted by a creek into forms that look like frozen ocean waves. The trail crosses the creek repeatedly, so expect to get wet.

Paria Canyon, a water-tortured gash in the Paria Plateau just west of Lake Powell, may offer the most spectacular canyon trek of any in the state—but it's not for the timid, inexperienced or claustrophobic. In places, Paria is 1,100 feet (335 m) deep and 10 feet (three m) wide. Late summer hiking (July-September) is discouraged because a heavy thunderstorm could quickly flood the canyon. The trailhead lies in Utah on US Highway 89 just east of the Paria River, and there are 35 miles (56 km) of canyon to the end at Lee's Ferry.

The rugged Santa Catalina Mountains on the north edge of Tucson include seven major canyons—Bear, Sabino, Esperero, Ventana, Finger Rock, Pima and Romero. Sabino, highly accessible by roadgoing tram, is by far the best known. Most visitors walk or ride along the canyon bottom, although the easy 4.2-mile (6-7-km) Phoneline Trail, which is in effect a man-made ledge 400 feet (122 m) up on the canyon's south wall, is much more engaging. The Esperero Canyon Trail leads 5.5 miles (8.8 km) to a lovely seasonal waterfall named **Bridalveil Falls**; unfortunately the trail rises about 3,500 feet (1,066 m) en route. On a warm day, Esperero feels rather more like a death march than a day hike.

Aravaipa is the connoisseur's canyon of southern Arizona, an enclosed wilderness whose lush riparian habitat harbors seven species of fish, eight amphibians, 46 reptiles, 46 mammals and more than 200 species of birds. To preserve them, the U.S. Bureau of Land Management strictly regulates the number of humans allowed in. For a hiking permit, contact the BLM Safford District Office (425 E. 4th St., Safford, AZ 85546; 602-428-4040); I have not known anyone who doesn't think this lovely canyon is worth that small bother.

(following pages) One of northern Arizona's water-sculpted "slot canyons," hundreds of feet deep and only a few feet wide.

THE FIRST ARIZONANS

HE WAS A CONSTRUCTION WORKER, SHORT BUT WITH a mountain-man build, a sand-colored beard, and a direct, guileless manner of speaking. He seemed mildly intrigued that I had spent two days tracking him down, so he agreed to tell me firsthand what happened to him one night at an 800-year-old Sinagua Indian ruin near Sedona—so long as I would identify him only by his nickname, "Ropes."

He had worked occasionally as a wilderness guide, and had poked around this little-known cliffside ruin for 15 years. Twice he had lingered after dark, and had found that the place spooked him. "I got a real uneasy feeling," he said. "Like I was intruding."

Finally, he packed in with a sleeping bag, determined to spend the night. He watched the red mountains turn violet in the twilight, then a smoky purple, then black against an indigo sky. He was about to drift into sleep. And then he began to hear crying.

"At first I tried to tell myself it was bats. Then I thought, well, it's jackrabbits. Finally I realized I was hearing children. Crying, in *this room*. I kind of chilled out, let the hair come back down on my neck, tried to go to sleep again. And every time I was on the verge of sleep, I'd be awakened by these ungodly sounds. Children crying. It felt like tears in there. All night, it felt like tears."

In the next morning's light, Ropes investigated the room. He found tiny fingerprints that had been pressed into wet mortar nearly a millenium ago. He traced the sun's path and realized that this room would have been the first to receive the winter light and the last to relinquish it, so it would have been the warmest room in the village. It had been some kind of a nursery.

I did not scoff at Ropes' story. I had heard too many others. An *Arizona Highways* editor told me about a night near Sycamore Canyon, 20 miles (32 km) south of Sedona, when a little Indian kid materialized inside his camper and stared at him through the darkness for several minutes. Indians haven't lived in Sycamore Canyon for hundreds of years. A Tucson restaurant owner, also a credible source, was hiking in Anasazi land when he spotted a crow that seemed to be trying to get his attention. He followed the bird, which eventually fluttered down beside a prehistoric stone ax. The restaurateur took the ax home and began to suffer an inexplicable string of misfortunes. His health unraveled. Business at his little crêperie, for no apparent reason, fell off 70 percent. Then one night at home he got out of bed in the dark, stumbled over the ax, and it severed a tendon in his foot. There was, he said, *a lot* of blood. Yet the ax had been wrapped securely in plastic and stashed *on top* of a table. The next week he took it back.

■ PALEO-ARIZONA

Arizona's prehistory lies literally on the surface of the land, exposed to view in the abundant ruins and potsherds and skeletons and ancient trash dumps. It tempts the imagination.

Possibly the spiritual residue of these civilizations still abides. If not, we may be excused for imagining it. We are steeped in prehistoric mystery.

The place we now call Arizona has been populated for about 12,000 years. The first 10,000 did not produce anything we would recognize as civilization. The original Arizonans, whom archaeologists call Paleo-Indians, were nomadic big-game hunters who roamed what then were grasslands, killing mammoths, bison, bears and other big game with stone-tipped spears. They probably had some form

Streamlined coatis—Sonoran Desert natives, relatives of the raccoon—streak around a Hohokam pot.

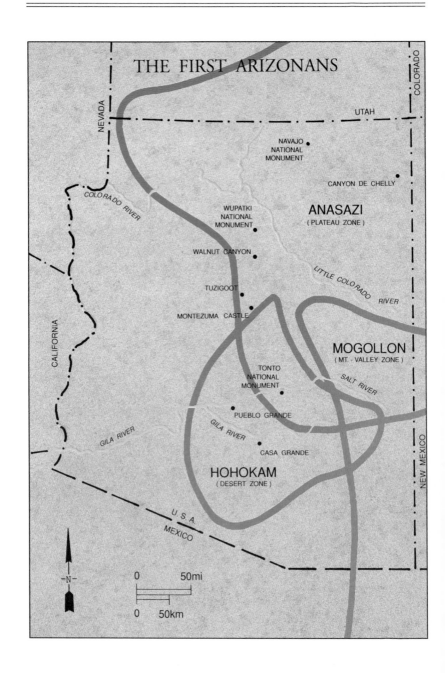

THE FIRST ARIZONANS

NEVADA

COLORADO

UTAH

NAVAJO
NATIONAL
MONUMENT

CANYON DE CHELLY

COLORADO RIVER

WUPATKI
NATIONAL
MONUMENT

ANASAZI
(PLATEAU ZONE)

WALNUT CANYON

LITTLE COLORADO RIVER

TUZIGOOT

MONTEZUMA CASTLE

CALIFORNIA

MOGOLLON
(MT. - VALLEY ZONE)

TONTO
NATIONAL
MONUMENT

SALT RIVER

PUEBLO GRANDE

GILA RIVER

GILA RIVER

CASA GRANDE

NEW MEXICO

HOHOKAM
(DESERT ZONE)

U. S. A.

MEXICO

–N–

0   50mi

0   50km

of social organization based on cooperative hunting. A pile of mammoth bones found on a southeastern Arizona ranch in 1955 had more than a dozen chipped flint projectile points in it, confirming what archaeologists had suspected: a lone Paleo-Indian could only have irritated a mammoth by flinging one spear at it. Not much more is known about these people. Living in nomadic bands, probably on the ragged edge of survival, they left no art, no architecture, no ritual objects for our examination. Looking at the monstrous bones of the slain mammoth, we can imagine that they had steely nerves.

By 6000 B.C. the big game had begun to thin out because the climate was drying, and a new people, the Archaic, either evolved from or replaced the Paleo-Indian culture. They were small game hunters and foragers, and their trash dumps ("middens" to archaeologists) suggest that they were more resourceful than their predecessors. They made fishhooks and awls from bones and armed their spears with sharp antler tips—an intriguing *offensive* recycling of their own quarry's *defensive* arsenal.

The turning point in Arizona prehistory was not the employment of increasingly clever tools, however, but agriculture.

The idea of cultivating food arrived in southern Arizona from Mexico about 300 B.C. It was a revolutionary change from hunting and gathering, and eventually it triggered profound changes in primitive society. It required that people live communally and stay in one place, which led to the dawn of architecture and villages and, presumably, some system of managing those villages—in other words, government. It was accompanied by new, more complex rituals to coax rainfall and productive crops—that is, religion. It provided people with more security and leisure time, which finally allowed art and recreation to flourish. It yielded foods that could be stored and transported, such as beans and corn, and that meant they could be traded. Ideas could travel with the traders, so the pace of technological development quickened: one culture, for example, might learn from another how to weave yucca fiber into sandals. By A.D. 1000, the archaeological record tells us, prehistoric Arizona was undergoing an information revolution.

By this time several important cultures lived in Arizona: the low-desert Hohokam, the mountain Mogollon, the high-desert Anasazi, and the Sinagua of the Verde Valley and southern Colorado Plateau. In every case, their art, architecture and perseverance astonish us.

■ "ALL USED UP"

One November day in 1867, a prospector and speculator named Jack Swilling rode into the Salt River Valley of Arizona and saw something that must have astounded him: the windswept remnants of a vast system of irrigation canals, tendrils probing into the desert as far as 15 miles from the mother river. Swilling couldn't have had any idea how old they were, nor who had dredged them, but he understood their implication: people had successfully farmed this desert before, on an enormous scale, and therefore it could be done again—profitably. He organized the Swilling Irrigation and Canal Company, dredged one of the prehistoric ditches, and began attracting homesteading farmers. Thus the city of Phoenix was born, inspired by the successes of the Hohokam a thousand years earlier.

Most archaeologists think the Hohokam migrated up from Mexico, bringing the knowledge of irrigated desert farming with them. Eventually the Hohokam world sprawled across a third of Arizona, from the San Pedro River in the southeast to the central Verde Valley. Wherever they settled, they adapted. Around what is now Phoenix, where the Salt River provided a reliable year-around water source, they irrigated their corn, beans and squash by canals. In the Tucson basin, which probably received more rain but had no major river, they farmed the flood plains of the arroyos and built small check dams on slopes to manage runoff. Everywhere they built pit houses, constructed by digging a pit one to two feet deep, then raising a wood frame above the pit and filling in the walls with brush and sticks and a plaster of mud.

Not all their architecture was so modest, however. Around A.D. 1000 they began to build platform mounds, some as large as football fields and 10 to 20 feet (three to six m) high, with storage rooms inside and free-standing houses on top. Around 1350 they began to build high-rises. The ruin of just one remains outside the modern town of Coolidge; it is a four-story building made of solid adobe. When the Spaniards discovered it, they called it the *Casa Grande*, or Big House. Its purpose is still in dispute, but it seems to offer some tantalizing clues to the great Hohokam mystery—about which there will be more later.

The Hohokam arts were, if anything, even more impressive than their architecture and engineering. Their pottery sizzles with life. Scorpions, fish, lizards, turtles, snakes, birds, rabbits and deer parade in tight formation around ceramic vessels of all forms and sizes. Some are so highly stylized they look like animals molting into geometry, such as a bird in flight that resembles the Greek letter Σ with a bow tie. They made primitive trumpets by cutting off the spires of large conch shells. They turned other shells into jewelry by etching patterns on them, probably by using the mild acid of fermented saguaro cactus fruit. This was centuries before Europeans thought they invented acid etching in the 1400s.

And then something cataclysmic happened in the Hohokam world. Around A.D. 1400, its archaeological record begins to evaporate. Datable artifacts, such as pottery, become rare. By A.D. 1450, the line goes flat. The Hohokam literally vanish. A century later, when the first Spanish expeditions trek into Arizona, the explorers find the Pima Indians, a more modest culture of desert farmers, occupying the Hohokam lands. The Pimas supply the word for their predecessors. "Hohokam," in the Piman language, means "all used up."

"Used up" how? And why? All the theories are perforated with holes. And when we consider the contemporaneous neighbors of the Hohokam, the mystery only deepens.

The Hohokam ruin of Casa Grande has the air of a fortress.

■ "ENEMY ANCESTORS"

The high badlands of northeastern Arizona are gouged by canyons where immense ocher and auburn sandstone cliffs soar hundreds of feet over long-dry riverbeds. Here and there huge alcoves lie at the bases of the cliffs, scooped out by water and wind. In these shelters huddle the Anasazi cities, the most scalp-tingling prehistoric ruins in North America.

The Anasazi first appeared as a coherent culture in the Four Corners area (where Arizona, New Mexico, Colorado and Utah now meet) some 2,500 years ago. Today, more than any other prehistoric culture, it is these people who command our fascination. Their architecture is the prime reason. The cities—yes, cities, because these are dense, complex, urban habitats—seem like a metaphor for a relationship of perfect harmony between man and nature: they borrow protection from the cliffs, but do not deface their dramatic sites. No architecture in modern Arizona evokes the mood and power of the land so thoroughly. Half a millenium after the Anasazi, Frank Lloyd Wright developed his philosophy of "organic architecture," buildings with forms and colors and textures inspired by their sites. But Wright never designed anything so organic as did the Anasazi.

And their spirits seem restless. The Navajo, who presumably moved later into Arizona, never occupied abandoned Anasazi sites; they had the forbidding air of ghost towns. Archaeologist Alfred V. Kidder originally picked up the word "Anasazi" from the Navajo language back in 1936, believing it meant "the ancient ones." The more accurate translation is also a more ominous one: "enemy ancestors."

Given all this, it is easy to romanticize Anasazi culture, but the cold evidence is that their lives were hard and short. Their physical environment, for all its beauty, was more difficult than anything faced by the Hohokam—hot in summer, dismally cold in winter, with unpredictable rainfall and unreliable running water. Anthropologists analyzing Anasazi remains have found pitting of some bones, which suggests poor nutrition and anemia. They were short people, the men no taller than about five feet three inches, (1.6 m) and they rarely lived more than 35 years. The cliffside pueblos, hauntingly beautiful in ruin, would have been decidedly less engaging as actual dwelling places—dark, cold, claustrophobic, and smoky.

But the social and artistic achievements of the Anasazi are a legitimate source of wonder. The architecture suggests that an entire pueblo of hundreds of people functioned as an extended family. Quite probably they were able to make a primeval form of communism work. Wrote New Mexico anthropologist Linda S. Cordell, "Our notions of personal independence and privacy would be completely foreign to the Anasazi."

The detached, single-family dwelling disappeared from Anasazi society after A.D. 1000, and the apartment-like pueblos were built in compact plans to make the most efficient use of space. Most Anasazi pueblos have multiple kivas—large, circular rooms—which implies that a different communal activity took place in each one: religious ritual here, social gatherings there. Or maybe concerts. Anasazi wood flutes as old as 1,400 years have been found in playing condition in Arizona caves. (For those into Anasazi arcana, their musical scale was A#, C, C#, D, F, G, A. Improvise on this strange scale and the music seems hauntingly open-ended; it never wants to conclude.)

Like the Hohokam, the Anasazi cultivated corn and squash, although their arid land may have given it reluctant nourishment. To supplement their diet, they devised remarkably inventive hunting techniques. Nets as long as 200 feet (61 m) were woven from yucca fiber and human hair, then stretched across gulches by a few people while others chased rabbits toward them. If it wasn't the most dignified style of hunting, it must have been effective. The laboriously woven nets attest to that.

The Anasazi culture was strong enough to influence its neighbors. The Mogollon, who inhabited the mountain lands of eastern Arizona and western New Mexico, learned stone masonry and pueblo-style architecture from them. Some of the pueblos of the Sinagua, who staked out the Verde Valley and parts of the Colorado Plateau, look strikingly like the Anasazi's. Yet the Anasazi did not endure.

The peak of Anasazi civilization, the period of its most ambitious buildings and strongest trade with other cultures, spanned only two centuries—from about 1100 to 1300. Then they abandoned their canyon cities and drifted away, gradually mingling into the Pueblo people occupying the high mesas of northern Arizona and New Mexico. There is little doubt that the modern Hopi are the descendants of those Anasazi.

The mystery is *why* the Anasazi left their traditional lands. And then why did the Sinagua and Mogollon follow them into that same black hole of lost civilizations, along with the Hohokam, only a century later?

■ THE ABANDONMENT

Archaeologists term it "the abandonment." Between A.D. 1300 and 1450, every one of the dominant cultures of prehistoric Arizona either straggled away, died off or reverted to simpler, less urban lives. This does not have the whiff of random coincidence.

The lifeline of any civilization is water. When an arid-land people disappear, archaeologists logically focus their first suspicions on the water supply.

And in northern Arizona, these suspicions pay off. Tree-ring studies reveal a devastating drought that lasted from 1276 to 1299—more than half an Anasazi lifetime.

Tree trunks cut and used for ceiling beams in the houses at Betatakin, one of those Anasazi cities on today's Navajo reservation, form a story line that meshes precisely with the cataclysmic-drought theory. The first three suites at Betatakin were built in 1267. The population expanded to a peak of about 125 in the mid-1280s. The last tree used in construction at Betatakin was cut down in 1286. By 1300, the settlement was abandoned to the spirits.

The Hohokam present a much thornier problem. There is no way to tell whether this drought affected their lands as severely; the desert trees they used in their building provide no reliable ring calendar. In any event, the Hohokam persisted for another 150 years after most Anasazi cities were deserted. Water, or the lack of it, does not explain their disappearance.

What about an epidemic? One anthropologist has wondered whether some European disease, such as smallpox, leapfrogged up the trade routes from Mexico ahead of the Spaniards' march into Arizona. Not likely, since Cortes, the original *conquistador,* was born 35 years after the Arizona abandonment was complete.

Warfare? The evidence itself is in conflict. For hundreds of years, the entire Southwest and northern Mexico was a vast melting pot, with the different cultures all trading, learning from each other and even adopting each other's customs. Hohokam ballcourts, for example, began turning up in Sinagua settlements around 1100. Some archaeologists have speculated that Anasazi intermarried and merged with Mogollon. There is much more evidence suggesting interdependence than large-scale conflict.

By about 1200, though, some kind of unease appeared to be spreading across the land. Anasazi and Sinagua settlements from this period onward clearly show a

Sinagua sandstone masonry has endured for 800 years at Wupatki National Monument.

defensive posture. Look at the ruin of Tuzigoot, whose 86 rooms sprawl over a Verde Valley hilltop. They have no windows or doors; the Sinagua who lived in them would have climbed ladders to drop through the roofs into dismal, pitch-dark rooms. Still, a team of archaeologists who in 1933-34 excavated 411 Tuzigoot burials found little evidence of violent deaths.

Further south in Hohokam lands, villages after 1300 tended to be larger, more urban, and apparently defended by rings of rockpile walls called *trincheras*. Casa Grande has the unmistakable air of a primitive fortress. One archaeologist has wondered, rather exotically, whether this and the other Hohokam high-rises were the castles of conquering warlords ruling over Hohokam villages. Not likely: the problem, said archaeologist David R. Wilcox of the Museum of Northern Arizona, is that no iconography of Hohokam warfare—that is, rock art or images on pottery—has ever been found. Why wouldn't the extravagantly expressive Hohokam have left some hint of epic war in their art? Since they regularly drew pictures of people hunting, dancing and making love, wouldn't they also have left some pictorial record of fighting and killing?

Question archaeologists about the abandonment late into the night, and eventually you'll hear an interesting but elusive phrase: "worn cultural patterns." Press for elaboration, and you may hear something like this:

Think about the Hohokam irrigation system, which as time wore on became increasingly extended and complex. A 15-mile-long (4.5-m) canal would have served numerous settlements, and that would require some sort of centralized authority to control and maintain it. Over time a network of authorities might have developed special status and knowledge, passing it on from generation to generation, guarding its privilege through mystic ritual, and living apart from the proles atop mounds or in the big houses. The parallel with the Roman Catholic priesthood on another continent at the same time, the Middle Ages, is exact.

There is an engaging sliver of evidence at Casa Grande: a small hole in a wall on the fourth story aligns precisely with the sunset on the summer solstice. Knowledge of the seasons would have been critically important to the Hohokam farmers, yet this information was kept in a special and probably well-guarded place.

Now stir in a second speculative ingredient, which might be termed the USSR Analogue. Centralized authorities, aloof and isolated from the real world in their kremlins or *casas grandes*, almost always prove poor at responding to problems.

They resist change. When they make a mistake, it's a grand one, affecting a large population.

Consider this scenario. It is the mid-fourteenth century at Casa Grande, the big house by the Gila River. The Gila is drying up because of several years of poor rainfall in its watershed to the east. The farmers approach the tsar in the big house, recommending some action—perhaps a move to the nearby Superstition Mountain foothills where more rain is likely to fall. The ruling family, thinking about the years they would have to spend sleeping on the ground with the scorpions until a new big house could be built, drag their feet. They claim that the positions of the sun and moon now presage rain. But the crops fail, and the people starve— or revolt, or both.

As this pattern repeats itself in more and more villages, old trading patterns fall apart. Hohokam trade with other cultures, particularly the Sinagua and Mogollon, breaks down. And thus the very complexity and interdependence of all these Arizona cultures lead directly to their extinction. Now that they have grown too advanced to be self-sufficient, the unforgiving environment snuffs them out.

This complicated theory may never be proven, but it is the one that seems to explain everything.

Where did the Hohokam go? Nowhere, most archaeologists agree. Those who survived stepped backward in time, so to speak, and became the Pima and Tohono O'odham that the Spaniards found inhabiting the Sonoran Desert a century later. The Hohokam threw off their worn cultural patterns, retreating into a simpler, more self-sufficient, more marginal lifestyle. The evidence for this continuity is persuasive—for example, some twentieth-century Pima houses resemble thousand-year-old Hohokam dwellings excavated in the same villages. But those Hohokam villages shrank, authority disintegrated, the great canals shut down, the big houses slowly weathered into dust. Life surely became harder: by 1450, decorated pottery was no longer made, which suggests there was no longer the luxury of leisure time. This was a prehistoric perestroika, the only way a suffering, beleaguered people could think of to survive. The complex lifeway was considered *hohokam*, all used up, and therefore expunged from its peoples' cultural memory.

The fascinating question: will this same desert land support *our* way of life in modern Arizona for another millenium?

■ MUSEUMS, RUINS, AND FELONIES

While Arizona's prehistory teems with unsolved mysteries, there is no shortage of museums and accessible ruins in which to ponder these ancient civilizations.

The world-class **Heard Museum** in Phoenix has a staggering collection of more than 75,000 artifacts and art works that document both prehistoric and modern Native American cultures. The changing exhibits are consistently first-rate.

The **Arizona State Museum** in Tucson also has enormous holdings of Native Americana and an excellent research staff of archaeologists and ethnologists. Changing exhibits are open to the public.

The **Museum of Northern Arizona** near Flagstaff has staked out a special turf interpreting the natural and cultural history of the Colorado Plateau. Its quarterly magazine, *Plateau*, is well worth the subscription price. Changing exhibits are open to the public.

The **Museum of Anthropology** at tiny Eastern Arizona College in Thatcher, a small town in southeastern Arizona, has a fine permanent exhibit of Mogollon, Salado and Hohokam pottery. Not large, but worth a visit.

The best remaining Hohokam mound, along with excavations and interpretive exhibits, can be seen at the **Pueblo Grande Museum** in Phoenix. The one "big house" ruin is at **Casa Grande Ruins National Monument** near Coolidge, and is indispensable to anyone struggling to understand the Hohokam.

The Sinagua, a mysterious culture that may have been a composite of Anasazi and Hohokam, left hundreds of dramatic ruins scattered throughout the Verde Valley and the southern edges of the Colorado Plateau. **Montezuma Castle National Monument** is the most engaging, an astonishingly graceful pueblo with smooth, concave facades that fill in much of a huge cave high in a limestone cliff. It does not, by the way, have anything to do with Montezuma; nineteenth-century Verde Valley settlers gave it this name, blithely assuming that the Aztecs had preceded them. **Tuzigoot National Monument** is a very different sort of development, demonstrating Sinagua adaptability; its 86 rock-walled rooms flow over the crest of a low hill in the lee of Mingus Mountain. **Wupatki National Monument** north of Flagstaff exhibits still another architectural style. These soft, red sandstone houses bud from rocky outcroppings with such grace and logic that nature and architecture seem to become one.

Navajo petroglyphs chronicle the Spanish invasion (top, photo by Paul Chesley), while more enigmatic prehistoric rock paintings decorate Newspaper Rock in the Petrified Forest (bottom).

Walnut Canyon National Monument just east of Flagstaff is unusual in that visitors are welcome to walk inside any of the 24 Sinagua ruins in this gorge. A few moments inside one of the cramped, dark dwellings offers memorable insight into the lives of the people who once lived there. Finally, private jeep-tour firms in Sedona offer visits to little-known Sinagua ruins around the Red Rocks, and the guides generally are knowledgeable and entertaining.

Anasazi ruins are scattered throughout the deep and forbidding canyons of northern Arizona, particularly on the Navajo Reservation. Most abundant both in ruins and astounding scenery is **Canyon de Chelly National Monument** adjacent to the town of Chinle. Visitors may hike unescorted to only one of the ruins in the canyon, the White House, but Navajo guides offer horseback and four-wheel-drive tours to others.

Navajo National Monument near Kayenta includes the huge and poetically graceful 135-room **Betatakin**, a three-hour guided walking tour from the monument headquarters, and the 160-room **Keet Seel**, a 16-mile (26-km) round-trip hike or horseback ride from headquarters. Though not the most easily accessible, these are the two most spectacular prehistoric ruins in Arizona.

Amerind Foundation in Dragoon in southern Arizona was founded in 1937 by archaeologist William Fulton to do research in Southwestern and Mexican archaeology. Housed in Spanish-colonial revival buildings built among the rock formations of Texas Canyon, the museum exhibits an outstanding artifact collection.

Casa Malpais, a Mogollon ruin at Springerville, startled the archaeological community in 1991 when word went out that there was a complex of catacombs for burials under the pueblo. Nothing of the sort has been found at any other site in the Southwest. The above-ground ruins are open to visitors, but the catacombs are absolutely off-limits.

Finally, some law: don't scavenge ruins for souvenirs. The Arizona Antiquities Act of 1960 makes it a felony to remove or damage prehistoric artifacts from state-owned land without a permit. The U.S. Archaeological Resources Protection Act of 1979 likewise protects artifacts on federal lands. Yet for the cause of archaeology, these laws have come almost too late; pothunters have raided thousands of sites, erasing part of the record of prehistoric Arizona. In archaeology, context is what tells stories. A prehistoric ax stashed in someone's drawer is meaningless. An ax in a scattering of Anasazi skull fragments could fill in one more blank in this sprawling web of mystery.

HISPANIC ARIZONA

ONE SPRING MORNING IN 1981 A DELEGATION of Mexican journalists arrived in Tucson bearing a startling gift to commemorate our international friendship: a 14-foot-high (4.2-m) bronze equestrian statue of Pancho Villa, guerrilla general of the second Mexican Revolution. A controversial figure even in Mexico, Villa is best remembered north of the border for leading the only invasion of the United States mainland in this century. On March 9, 1916, Villa and his band sacked the small town of Columbus, New Mexico, killing 19 American citizens. President Wilson, probably overreacting, sent 10,000 troops into Mexico to chase him. They never caught him, but the failed manhunt elevated Villa into a hero in the eyes of some Mexicans.

Pancho Villa. (Arizona Historical Society)

Back in Tucson, City Hall checked the diplomatic wind, concluded it would be bad form to reject the gift, and nervously installed Villa and his mount in a small but prominent downtown park. Tucsonans reacted as if it were the statue from hell. The mayor himself boycotted the dedication ceremony. Historians growled that Villa was hardly a revolutionary Robin Hood, but a bandit and terrorist who also massacred his own people on whim. One midnight commentator slipped into the park with a can of paint and left a yellow stripe cleaving Villa's back.

But the statue stayed, and eventually the uproar subsided. Four years later, the *Tucson Citizen*, the evening newspaper, polled its readers on the best public sculpture in Tucson. The winner: Pancho Villa. Following that, however, a local anthropologist began an annual one-man protest, pounding 19 white crosses into the grass beside the statue on every anniversary of the Columbus raid. Several Tucsonans of Mexican ancestry now regularly turn out to protest his protest. A story in *The Arizona Daily Star* quoted one of them as saying it was proper to honor Villa in Tucson, because Tucson ought still to be a part of Mexico.

"This was all our land," she told a reporter. "Your people stole it."

■ SPANISH ROOTS

The first Spaniards entered Arizona around 1540, lured by fables of the Seven Cities of Cibola, legends redolent of riches. Francisco Vásquez de Coronado, the most persistent of the early explorers, probably led his party north along the San Pedro River and around the Mogollon Rim to the Hopi villages of the Colorado Plateau. There they learned that the rumored cities were made of sun-dried mud and not gold. Worse still, two Franciscan missionaries who stayed behind among the natives were murdered, beginning a pattern that would endure for more than a century between the persistent Franciscans and recalcitrant Hopis.

More than 300 miles (480 km) to the south, Jesuit missionaries led by the tireless Italian-born Father Eusebio Kino temporarily found a warmer reception among the Pimas and Papagos (now called the Tohono O'odham). In 1701 Kino established missions at Guevavi, near modern Nogales, and at Bac, eight miles (13 km) south of today's downtown Tucson. These were the northernmost outposts in a chain of 22 missions he stretched across the deserts and grasslands of the *Pimería Alta* of New Spain, the Land of the Upper Pimans. Kino had no further successes

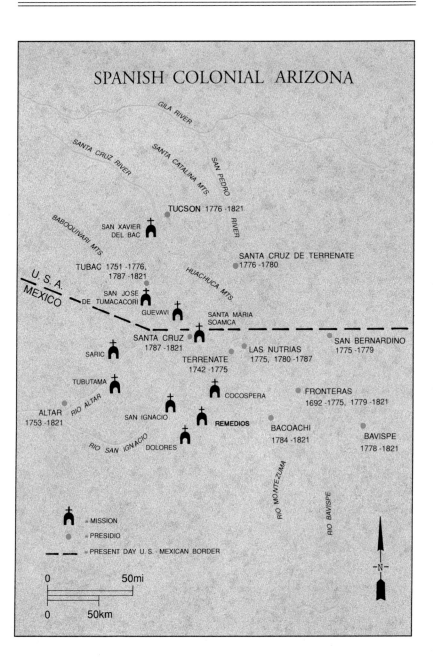

SPANISH COLONIAL ARIZONA

GILA RIVER

SANTA CRUZ RIVER

SANTA CATALINA MTS.

SAN PEDRO RIVER

BABOQUIVARI MTS.

TUCSON 1776 -1821

SAN XAVIER DEL BAC

SANTA CRUZ DE TERRENATE 1776 -1780

TUBAC 1751 -1776, 1787 -1821

HUACHUCA MTS.

U. S. A.
MEXICO

SAN JOSE DE TUMACACORI

GUEVAVI

SANTA MARIA SOAMCA

SANTA CRUZ 1787 -1821

SARIC

LAS NUTRIAS 1775, 1780 -1787

SAN BERNARDINO 1775 -1779

TERRENATE 1742 -1775

TUBUTAMA

RIO ALTAR

COCOSPERA

FRONTERAS 1692 -1775, 1779 -1821

ALTAR 1753 -1821

SAN IGNACIO

REMEDIOS

BACOACHI 1784 -1821

BAVISPE 1778 -1821

RIO SAN IGNACIO DOLORES

RIO MONTEZUMA

RIO BAVISPE

= MISSION

= PRESIDIO

= PRESENT DAY U.S.- MEXICAN BORDER

0   50mi

0   50km

-N-in Arizona, but some 80 years after his death in 1711 the great church of San Xavier del Bac would be completed, and to Kino would go the credit both of introducing Christianity and European civilization to Arizona.

Kino is venerated today in Arizona and our neighbor Mexican state of Sonora. Many Catholics on both sides of the border are campaigning for his canonization. He appears to have been a man of boundless endurance, great charisma and principle. His contemporary, Capt. Juan Mateo Manje, left a profile of him that in our century could as easily describe Gandhi:

> When [Kino] publicly reprimanded a sinner, he was choleric. But if anyone showed him personal disrespect, he controlled his temper to such an extent that he made it a habit to exalt whosoever maltreated him. . . . He was so austere that he never took wine except to celebrate Mass, nor had any other bed than the sweat blankets of his horse. . . . He never had more than two coarse shirts, because he gave everything as alms to the Indians.

There is a statue of Kino in modern Tucson, as well as a Kino Boulevard, Kino Hospital, Kino Paving Repairs and Kino Termite & Pest Control. There is no controversy around him today.

Possibly there should be. In the *Pimería Alta* of the eighteenth century the growing Spanish presence was a dubious blessing. The Spaniards introduced cattle ranching and improved agriculture, but also exotic European diseases such as measles and smallpox. And the more Spaniards that trickled in, the more the natives seemed to grasp the implications. In 1751 the normally peaceful Pimans rebelled, killing more than 100 Spanish ranchers, miners and priests in an astonishing uprising that ranged from Caborca, near the Sonoran coast, to Bac, near present-day Tucson. The Spanish government responded with a show of force, beginning by building a presidio (fort) at Tubac, 40 miles (64 km) south of Bac. What followed was grimly precursive of the U.S. Cavalry campaigns that would follow a century later. As Juan Bautista de Anza, the captain of Tubac, reported in 1767:

> When I took over my present command in 1760, my section of the frontier was faced with an uprising of over a thousand Papagos [Pimans]. After launching various campaigns to subjugate them, I attacked them personally . . . and took the lives of Ciprian, their captain, and nine others. All the rest then capitulated and renounced the inconstancy that has been plaguing the Piman nation.

The Apaches were still more "inconstant," staging hit-and-run raids and ambushes on Spaniards and Pimans alike. They never did come fully under Spanish control, despite long and bloody warfare. In another eerie foreshadowing of the American struggles, the Spaniards resorted to trickery. In 1776, Spain's new Minister of the Indies, José de Galvéz, ordered that Apaches who agreed to make peace were to be rewarded with "defective firearms, strong liquor, and other such commodities as would render them militarily and economically dependent."

In our modern Southwest, we love to romanticize the Spanish Colonial era, recalling it as a time when simple Indians learned civilized ways under the tutelage of kindly priests, and manly dons ruled over their vast *rancheros* from tiled and arcaded *haciendas* recalling the great mansions of baroque Iberia. This is such nonsense that it qualifies as hallucination. For all the respect showered on Kino, and the rich cultural heritage left in Arizona by its Hispanic past, the raw truth is that the seventeenth and eighteenth centuries were ugly times in what is now Arizona. The Spaniards, even those marching in alleged humility under the cross, were not welcomed guests, but invaders.

■ THAT "MOSTLY MEXICAN" TOWN

Sam Hughes, a Welsh immigrant who had been working as a baker in gold-rush California, clattered into the southern Arizona desert aboard a stage one spring day in 1856. Hughes had tuberculosis and was desperately trying to make Texas, where he hoped the warm, dry air might prolong his life. The driver, afraid that Hughes would cause him the annoyance of dying en route, kicked him out in Tucson. Hughes must have felt like he was being abandoned in Neverland. Of the 500 or so people living in this isolated desert town, the driver assured him, five spoke English.

Tucson, along with the rest of Arizona, had flown the Mexican flag since 1810, the year Mexico began its violent break from Spain. Then in a dozen bloody years, 1836 to 1848, the Texas Revolution and Mexican War severed Texas, California, Nevada, Utah, and most of Arizona and New Mexico from Mexico's upper body. In 1853, the United States, strong-arming its hemorrhaged rival, bought the southern third of Arizona and the last sliver of New Mexico for a fire-sale price of $10 million and incorporated them into a U.S. territory the following year.

Despite all this, the heart and soul of Tucson, the largest and most important town in the Gadsden Purchase, would remain essentially Mexican until the first trains rumbled into town in 1880. Until then, nearly all of Tucson's cultural ties, communication and trade clung to Mexico.

Gringos who stumbled through Tucson in those days were not enchanted. The most frequently quoted description of Tucson, which dogs the Chamber of Commerce even today, is that of journalist J. Ross Browne in 1864. Modern travel writing is pallid fluff compared with this:

> . . . [The traveler] emerges to find himself on the verge of the most wonderful scatteration of human habitations his eye ever beheld—a city of mud-boxes, dingy and dilapidated, cracked and baked into a composite of dust and filth; littered about with broken corrals, sheds, bake-ovens, carcasses of dead animals, and broken pottery; barren of verdure, parched, naked, and grimly desolate in the glare of a southern sun. Adobe walls without whitewash, inside or out, baked and dried Mexicans, sore-backed burros, coyote dogs, and terra-cotta children . . . .

It's easy to dismiss Browne's raving as gringo bigotry. Yet, other early descriptions are not very different. The Tucson of the 1860s, though the largest settlement in Arizona, was severely isolated, still under periodic assault by Apaches, and simple survival, not civic beautification, headed the priorities. It was not a charming place.

It began to change with the arrival of Anglos who would become entrepreneurs, such as Hughes, and professional-class Mexicans fleeing the political tumult to the south, such as Federico Ronstadt. We can sketch the cultural history of pre-1880 Tucson through these two men.

Hughes had no formal education but a deep reservoir of determination. In photos from throughout his long life—he died in 1917, at the age of 88—his eyes, shadowed by bushy, steel-woolly brows, glow with confidence and intensity. Such a man could improvise without a blueprint in Tucson; his career eventually comprised ranching, real estate, banking, and politics.

There was one problem for men such as Hughes: women. The 1860 census of Tucson on the opposite page graphically explains.

Four years after he was dumped in Tucson, Hughes married a Mexican girl named Atanacia Santa Cruz. Eyebrows surely arched skyward all over town. Sam was 32 years old, Atanacia 12.

TUCSON'S 1860 CENSUS

	AGE	NUMBER
Mexican males	15-39	168
Mexican females	15-39	163
Anglo males	15-39	132
Anglo females	15-39	6

While the bride's age was unusual, the union across the ethnic line wasn't. Until the railroad came, there was a chronic dearth of Anglo females. The list of Anglo men who took Mexican brides reads like a who's who of territorial Tucson; it includes most of the successful merchants, ranchers and politicians. Hiram Stevens, who became the territorial delegate to Congress, married Atanacia's sister, Petra. It is unimaginable that the Mexican men weren't angered, yet oddly there is no record, not even an oral history, of trouble. One reason, suggested by University of Arizona anthropologist James E. Officer, is that the spurned Mexican men of Tucson simply brought in a fresh supply of young women from Sonora. However, none of the pre-1880 Spanish-language newspapers of Tucson survive—and if there had been resentment against the gringos, this was one outlet where it might have been vented.

In fact, Anglos and Mexicans lived in remarkable harmony in territorial Tucson. They went into business together, fought Apaches together and partied together—more so than in any other old town in the Southwest. One reason was that the Hispanic *Tucsonenses* were not mainly peasants and laborers, as they were in early Los Angeles and Phoenix. Many came from ambitious, upper-class families in Sonora.

Ronstadt, an engineer's son, was one of them. He arrived in Tucson in 1882, when he was only 14, signed on as an apprentice wainwright with the firm of Dalton and Vásquez, and eventually built up a coachworks of his own that employed 65 people. The business enjoyed a fine regional reputation; Ronstadt supplied wagons and carriages to ranchers from Colorado to the Sonoran capital of Hermosillo. While Sam Hughes endowed schools, Ronstadt generated culture. He founded the *Club Filarmónico*, one of Tucson's earliest orchestras, and launched a family musical dynasty. His daughter, Luisa Ronstadt Espinel, went on to an international career singing both opera and Spanish folk music. His great-great granddaughter, who started her career singing in Tucson coffeehouses in the 1960s, is Linda Ronstadt.

The dominance of Mexican culture in Tucson began to shrivel the day the first train wheezed into town. We can still read the story today in the architecture of the two oldest neighborhoods, El Presidio and Barrio Histórico, which huddle immediately north and south, respectively, of downtown's modern towers. The oldest houses, dating from the 1860s and 1870s, are pure Sonoran: simple, box-like shapes with plastered adobe walls two feet (half a meter) thick, a wide entry hall called a *zaguán*, and ceilings fashioned of saguaro or ocotillo ribs. By 1880, some of these adobes began to sport porches and peaked roofs of corrugated steel, the Anglo newcomers' stopgap efforts to make traditional Mexican architecture into something that felt more like home to them.

Luisa Ronstadt Espinel, great aunt of Linda Ronstadt. (Arizona Historical Society)

By the late 1880s, all but the poorest Anglos had abandoned the adobe neighborhoods and were building modest Victorian houses with yards and fences on tree-lined streets. In Florence, another essentially Sonoran town 70 miles (112 km) north of Tucson, a newspaper editor in 1887 seemed to sum up Anglo attitudes—and not only about architecture—in an editorial: "The adobe does not make an attractive or a clean building, and Eastern people (that is, eastern U.S.) find it somewhat repulsive in appearance. . . . It is hoped that all new building of any pretensions will be built of brick and the unsightly adobe discarded."

With the discarding came discrimination. University of Arizona ethnohistorian Thomas E. Sheridan studied courthouse records in Tucson from 1882-89 and found that convicted murderers with Spanish surnames drew average sentences of 3.58 years; Anglos one year. Mexicans convicted of grand larceny served 3.9 years; Anglos 1.88. (The fact that stealing was punished more severely than killing, whatever one's ethnic persuasion, says something else about life in frontier Arizona.) As late as the 1950s, speaking Spanish in some Tucson schools was

(From left) Hiram and Petra Stevens, Samuel and Atanacia Hughes. (Arizona Historical Society)

punished with a soapy rinse of the offender's mouth—a sad irony in a town that owed its founding and first hundred years to Spanish-speaking people.

Yet after the railroad and even to the present, prominent Hispanic businesspeople, journalists and artists retained their status, Anglos and Hispanics continued to marry each other, and Tucson avoided the worst of the ethnic segregation that plagued so many other cities.

Those early days had set the stage. As James Officer once put it, "How were you going to tell a Ronstadt that his kid can't go to your school?"

■ HISPANIC ARIZONA TODAY

Every year on September 16, a crowd gathers at sunset on the still-hot concrete of the Phoenix Civic Plaza. *Ballet Folklórico* dancers swirl across a stage, the aroma of *carne asada*, flame-broiled beef, drifts through the air, and here and there Mexican flags flutter in celebration. The party leans on well into the night, until all at once the merriment abates and a speaker takes the stage. In Spanish, he recites the *Grito de Dolores*, that spine-prickling call to arms from a parish priest on September 16, 1810, that launched the Mexican Revolution: "My children, a new dispensation comes to us this day. Are you ready to receive it? Will you be free?" As he finishes, fireworks streak through the Phoenix sky, the national anthems of Mexico and the United States swell, and the revelers shout *¡Viva México!* The celebration of *el dieciseis de septiembre*, the Sixteenth of September, Mexico's independence day, is as colorful, noisy and passionate in Arizona as anywhere in Mexico.

About 18 percent of Arizona's population is Hispanic, and these 688,000 people celebrate their heritage with pride. Not everyone embraces the troubling Pancho Villa, but certain traditions, such as the *quinceañera*, seem to be observed more faithfully now than ever. The *quinceañera* is a special Mass to bless a girl turning 15, followed by an elaborate coming-out party. In Phoenix, some priests have started to complain that their churches' schedules are being overrun with *quinceañeras*.

Some of the more internal aspects of Hispanic culture also remain firmly rooted —for one, the tradition of closely entwined, extended families. There is no shortage of Hispanic yuppies in Phoenix and Tucson, but it is still a little unusual even for well-educated, professional young Hispanics to bounce from city to city to pump up their careers. In Tucson, a city where Anglos joke that anyone who's been around at least ten years qualifies as a native, fifth- and sixth-generation Hispanic natives are not uncommon.

Anglos like to immerse themselves in the more colorful, accessible aspects of Hispanic culture; it is a way of loosening the jacket of our stiffer Puritan heritage. Mexican food is a virtual Arizona religion. Once a year the Phoenix weekly *New Times* and the *Tucson Weekly* poll their readers, not even asking which is the best local Mexican restaurant—the question seems too epic to face—but which has the best *fajitas*, best *salsa*, best *enchilada*, even the best beans. Tucson's former mayor, Lewis C. Murphy, officially trumpeted the city as the "Mexican Food Capital of the World," apparently not pausing to consider how such a proclamation might play to the south. For years, Phoenix, Tucson, El Paso and Santa Fe sent their top chefs to battle in an intercity Mexican Food Cookoff. When Santa Fe won in 1987, irritated Arizonans wrote letters to their editors complaining, in all seriousness, that the godless New Mexicans had used revisionist ingredients such as crab meat in their *chiles rellenos*.

But when Arizona joined the Official English movement in 1988, with a majority of voters approving a law that required all government and legal business to be conducted in English, Hispanics generally saw it as an effort to keep their culture in its place—that is, under the Anglo heel—and as a signal that the gringos, at heart, didn't want to understand or absorb anything more significant than what distinguishes a good *chile relleno*. If Arizona is good because it is multicultural, they wondered, why isn't it good that it is multilingual?

In practice, the law had hardly any effect, and two years later it was found constitutionally defective and thrown out by the courts. A little damage, however, had been done. A little more acrimony was left hanging in the air, and a few more Arizonans of Mexican lineage seemed willing to say out loud what had been held locked in their hearts before: this, after all, had been their land.

■ EXPLORING HISPANIC CULTURE

Most of the "Spanish" architecture the visitor sees in Arizona is the product of Anglo* architects unearthing and romanticizing the state's past. (See a more detailed discussion in "ARTS.") Two authentic Spanish missions survive south of

* The term "Anglos" is used for convenience, and comprises all non-Hispanic Arizonans.

Experts began restoring the interior of San Xavier in 1990, a project expected to consume several years and a million dollars (top left). A winged angel resides under San Xavier's great dome (top left). San Xavier's baroque retalbo: the Virgin Mary at top center, San Francisco Xavier below (above). The dome crowning San Xavier's east tower was never completed; the best theory is that the builders simply ran out of money (opposite).

Tucson, however: **San José de Tumacácori** and **San Xavier del Bac** (see "ARTS"). Although some gentrification has occurred in Tucson's **Barrio Histórico**, a stroll along Meyer or Convent streets offers a remarkably intact impression of pre-1880 Hispanic Tucson; just mentally blot out the power lines and parked cars.

Every Arizona town and city that has a substantial Mexican-American population also has public fiestas on both September 16 and *cinco de mayo* (May 5), the latter celebrating Mexico's rout of the French occupation force at Puebla in 1862. These festivals are wonderful introductions both to Hispanic culture and Mexican history.

Mariachi music traces its roots to the *son*, a sometimes ribald or seditious Spanish song-and-dance form of the eighteenth century. Today the mariachi band is a virtual national emblem of Mexico, and it has gathered in ethnic influences from European classicism to American pop and country. A good mariachi band knows a thousand songs and will stamp its personal imprint on anything from one of Brahms' Hungarian Dances to that famous love anthem to Guadalajara, "*Ay, Jalisco no te rajes.*" The best Mariachi bands in the Americas can be heard annually at the **International Mariachi Conference**, held each April in Tucson. (For information, see "PRACTICAL INFORMATION.")

Two galleries in downtown Phoenix are devoted to Hispanic art: the **Museo Chicano**, 641 E. Van Buren (in the Mercado), and MARS **Gallery**, 130 N. Central. Other museums around the state frequently schedule exhibits of Mexican or Hispanic-American art. Finally, to contemplate the checkered history of Mexican-U.S. relations, park at the fringe of downtown Tucson and walk to *Veinte de agosto* Park at Church and Broadway: there, atop a prancing horse, is that concomitant hero and villain, **Francisco "Pancho" Villa.**

(below) San Jose de Tumacácori, constructed 1773–1822. The mission's roof and walls are sealed with mortar of sand, lime, and cactus juice. (opposite)

MODERN INDIANS

NEARLY EVERYONE WHO VISITS CHINLE, A TOWN OF 3,360 people in the high desert badlands of the Navajo Nation, has come to see the natural spectacle yawning at its back door: Canyon de Chelly, a two-pronged gash in the earth whose sculptured sandstone walls and soft, ruddy coloring rival parts of the Grand Canyon in mesmerizing beauty. Few give a second thought to the town, which appears at a glance to be a scruffy huddle of government-issue houses and utilitarian stores in need of landscaping.

But in a way, Chinle is the more interesting phenomenon. The canyon will abide, barely changed in a human lifetime. The town is a collision taking place in slow motion, a metaphoric head-on between a careening modern behemoth and an ancient, fragile wagon. Chinle's people are Navajos, but their lives are increasingly imprinted with the ways of mainstream America.

"The culture is dying; the language is dying," Marjorie Thomas told me. I had come to Chinle for a week in 1987 as a writer for *Arizona Highways* to learn what was happening to the Navajo, and much of what I was hearing seemed both poignant and painful.

We walked atop a red mesa overlooking Chinle, talking, while her seven dogs swirled around herding her sheep back to their pen for the night. Thomas had recently retired from a long career as a teacher and principal, and had returned to this cold, treeless, windswept rise to do what fewer and fewer of her people were choosing: to live as a Navajo.

It had not been an easy journey back to the mesa. She was raised in Christian boarding schools where she was taught that the whole Navajo culture was something best discarded, like an obsolete appliance. Navajo religion was incorrect, Navajo ritual meaningless. Only her grandmother persisted in teaching her something of her people's tradition.

The pivotal incident in her life came years later, when she was teaching in Tuba City, another Navajo town 115 miles (184 km) west of Chinle. Another teacher asked her if a certain Navajo belief were true. Thomas said she didn't know.

The other teacher responded, "Aren't you Navajo?"

So she began going to Navajo ceremonies, gradually learning about her own culture. Slowly she realized the wisdom of her grandmother's words: to live as a

Navajo woman displays her jewelry.

Navajo, rather than as an imitation of an Anglo, keeps one strong. You go out in the frigid dawn and chop wood for a fire. You herd your sheep. You weave blankets from their wool. None of this is incompatible with having a modern education; it only augments one's character.

"When I compare myself with my grandchild, I see how really weak she is," Marjorie Thomas said. "All she wants to do is ride everywhere in the pickup. She turns on a switch and gets light. She is not strong."

Down in town, I heard stories, wistful and regretfully told, describing the inexorable erosion of Navajo ways. Only a generation ago children would come home from school, do their homework, then spend the rest of the evening being entertained by their grandparents telling stories—Navajo stories. But not now. One family living a few miles out of Chinle on the canyon's south rim finally got electricity—from a car battery. It powered a television, but the charge was only good for two programs a night. Then the power lines at last arrived, and the children, predictably enough, began watching TV all evening. And it was white people's TV. Although the Navajo nation comprises 165,065 people in 22,610 square miles (58,560 sq. km), an area 40 percent larger than Switzerland, only one station broadcasts programming in Navajo—for one day a week.

The faculty at the Many Farms Elementary School 15 miles north of Chinle was making an honorable effort to preserve Navajo tradition, while at the same time trying to outfit the students for survival in a white people's land. But straddling the two cultures at once did not appear easy.

The issue of language was (and is) a thorny one. Tribal policy is to have the children grow up fully bilingual, but this requires a delicate balancing act in the classroom. Non-Indian teachers may be reluctant to let the students speak Navajo at all, fearful that it will impede their progress in English. Navajo teachers, who live with bitter memories of having their own mouths lathered with soap at school for speaking their native language, may lean too far in the other direction. And then, sadly, a few parents do not want their children taught Navajo at all: they equate it with backwardness and poverty.

Once a week, the Many Farms students in kindergarten through sixth grade filed into a traditional eight-sided hogan next to their modern school building for 45 minutes of instruction in Navajo history, culture and art. It seemed not nearly enough—and yet it was much more than the old BIA (Bureau of Indian Affairs) boarding schools provided. (Their philosophy dated from the mid-nineteenth century, when the government believed that Indians would achieve "civilization" only when they were stripped of their own culture.) Even in this sanctuary, however, the intrusions of the society surrounding the reservation were unavoidable. The children colored Navajo landscapes with crayons; they built model hogans with ice-cream sticks; they practiced weaving by making woolen covers for Kleenex boxes.

One 10-year-old in the class had dyed her hair in a triad of red, blue and silver. Beside her was a boy wearing his hair in a traditional Navajo bun. A Navajo school administrator pointed out the latter in admiration. "It takes guts to wear that today," he explained. "If he went to Window Rock, nearer the edge of the reservation, the other Navajo kids would really put him down. They'd call him a bushman, a sheepherder. In a few more years, that's probably the way it'll be here, too."

The cultural shock waves reverberating across Navajo lands today are not very different from those buffeting other tribes. The ways of the white world spill across the reservation borders and collide violently with traditional values and customs. Sometimes the consequences are tragic: alcoholism has bedeviled the reservations for generations; now drugs do, too. At other times the fusion only causes the native culture to do something not necessarily destructive, but antithetical to its nature—and perhaps thereby humiliating.

One such story was that of the Baboquivari High School football team on the Tohono O'odham reservation. In 1987 the Warriors won some embarrassing publicity when a few newspapers observed that its football team had been outscored a cumulative 118-0 in the first three games of that season. The previous season had been even worse, with a margin of 494-0 in nine games. Baboquivari had played 23 consecutive games without scoring. *The Arizona Republic* quoted tribal officials as saying that the Tohono O'odham simply were not by nature aggressive. The team's coach disagreed, telling *The Wall Street Journal* that his boys displayed no shortage of aggression in practice. But because of the school's isolation deep in reservation lands, they were naturally shy and inhibited in dealing with outsiders. "When they go against other teams, their timidity takes over and they don't hit," he said.

In certain ways, life on the reservations is better because of outside influence. A 40-year-old man in Chinle explained that as recently as his high school days, everyone's diet was monotonous and stuffed with carbohydrates: flour, potatoes, beans, corn and mutton. "Anything beyond that was hard to get, and we kids were kind of chunky." In the 1980s a Phoenix supermarket chain opened a store in

Chinle, and in just a few years, he said, he noticed that the kids appeared taller and slimmer and their complexions looked better. There was a catch, of course: for the first time they also had to worry about cavities.

Indians who move off the reservation face different problems. Some assimilate successfully, but for many, the cultural chasm is too deep to be bridged. A letter written by a Tohono O'odham and published in the *Tucson Citizen* in 1971 explains this so poignantly that it demands to be reproduced in full. Although today's anti-discrimination statutes might save the writer from losing his job, the misunderstandings would be the same.

> *I* am a Papago Indian (former name for the Tohono O'odham) very proud to be one, and what I want to say I hope you'll understand for I don't know much about the so-called English grammar.
>
> The main problem I'm concerned with is unemployment for Papago Indians. Some of the problems I have in keeping a job I will discuss. I have worked with white people, but couldn't get along with them or maybe they didn't get along with me.
>
> The people I worked with were all non-Indians. They talked behind my back (luckily I had a nosey friend to tell me all this).
>
> They criticized the way I dressed. A great many Papagos disapprove of the white shirt and necktie bit. This is one reason why the Papago turns away clerical jobs, or vice versa. The Papago tries to be neat in every way —if he can afford it.
>
> They criticized how quiet I was. They wished they hired someone else who'd be a little more lively. Well, this Indian isn't concerned about how much he should open his mouth, but rather how he should get his work done.
>
> They criticized how rude I was not to say: good morning, good afternoon, hi, goodbye, etc., to every one of them. To the Papago it is silly to greet each other with the same word day after day after day, because it will only become meaningless.
>
> The Papago, when greeting on a morning or anytime, will say what he wants to, but it is no greeting like "good morning." At times he will ask "Are you feeling fine," which I think has a little more meaning than the word, "Hi."

They criticized how rude it was not to introduce myself to a new person on the job. If a Papago wants to know who somebody is, he will ask someone else or he'll hear his name mentioned. You know, to the Papago it's quite funny to see people shake hands when introduced. Shaking hands is done only for religious purposes. When meeting a new person a smile shows the person is already accepted as a friend.

They criticized how rude I was not to say thank you when done a favor. To the Papago there is no such word. When a favor is done or a gift is given, he shows appreciation by returning something of equal value to the giver. (Those people never saw the favors I returned which meant thank you.)

These are some of the reasons I was told to quit my job. So now I'm looking for another, knowing I'll face the same problems in the white society.

Along with the problems have come successes, however. The people of the 15 tribes that inhabit Arizona have contributed immeasurably to the life of the state and the nation. The Navajos, for example, take justifiable pride in their unique role in World War II.

A California engineer who had grown up in a missionary family on the reservation first had the idea of using the Navajo language as a code. He was certain that no Japanese had ever been exposed to enough Navajo to learn it, and equally confident that unlike codes that merely rearranged English, the enemy would have no linguistic foundation for cracking it. To confound the enemy cryptologists still further, the 400 young Navajos who enlisted in the program scrambled words around in their own language, devising a crypto-Navajo that not even their own mothers could understand. It worked flawlessly. The entire invasion of Iwo Jima, for one, was directed by orders that crackled over shortwave radios in Navajo. More than 800 messages were transmitted and translated for the Marines, not one was in error, and the Japanese never deciphered the code. Years after the war, when the Japanese chief of intelligence finally was told that the code had been based on a Native American language, he reportedly sighed and said, "Thank you. That is a puzzle I thought would never be solved."

What Native Arizonans still are contributing is an understanding and respect for the natural world that is as alien to us as Navajo speech was to Japanese cryptologists. A newspaper reporter from Tucson learned about it one scorching August day as he walked across the desert with a Tohono O'odham friend.

The Tohono O'odham noticed that the white man was wheezing from asthma, and he mentioned that his people successfully treated the problem by drinking a hot tea made from the leaves of the creosote bush. But first, he said, you must ask the plant for permission to use its leaves. And then, he said, you must pray to the Great Spirit, offering appreciation for his kindness in sending such a wonderful plant. And there was one more thing, the Tohono O'odham said:

"It's also better if you find one special tree to use most of the time. In this way you get to know each other and become friends."

■ ARIZONA TRIBES

The first of the lands to be established as a trust for Arizona's native people was the Gila River reservation 40 miles (64 km) south of Phoenix. This was in 1859. Today there are 20 reservations covering about 31,000 square miles (51,800 sq. km), or more than a quarter of Arizona's land. There are 14 distinct tribes using a total of 18 languages, some of which are as unrelated to each other as French is to Russian. There is no monolithic "Indian culture" in Arizona.

The **Navajos** are the most populous, and their reservation (they prefer the term "Navajo Nation") extends into

"Old Washie," a Navajo medicine woman. (Arizona Historical Society)

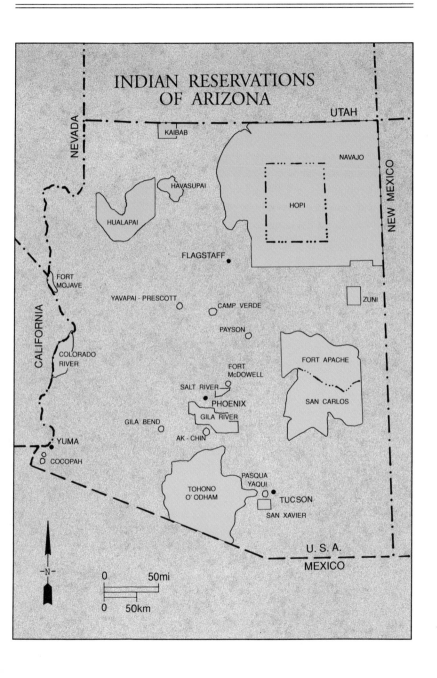

INDIAN RESERVATIONS
OF ARIZONA

New Mexico and Utah. This high desert land, though hardly suited for supporting a large number of people, includes Arizona's most spectacular prehistoric ruins (see "THE FIRST ARIZONANS") and many of its most dramatic land forms, including Canyon de Chelly and Monument Valley. Ethnically, the Navajos are related to the Apache: both came from the same Athapaskan stock that migrated from western Canada and Alaska to the Southwest sometime around A.D. 1400-1500.

The **Apaches** are divided into a number of subtribal families—San Carlos, White Mountain, Tonto, etc.—and these inhabit several Arizona reservations. Despite their long and very prominent moments in Arizona history, they remain poorly understood by non-Indians; their blood-stained past has encouraged more imagination than it has straightforward scholarship. The complete transformation of Apache society over the last 120 years is one of the most fascinating but untold cultural stories in Arizona, for no other tribe has changed as radically. As an *Arizona Highways* publication noted, the once-nomadic Apaches now "excel as cowboys, ranchers, farmers, lumbermen, artisans [and] businesspeople." Little of that is found in their history.

The **Yavapais** are scattered about three reservations: Fort McDowell, Prescott and Camp Verde. Originally a Yuman-speaking people culturally related to the Havasupais and Hualapais, Yavapai history became entwined with Apache in the 1860s as the two fought the white man together in the Verde Valley. In 1870, however, the starving Yavapais surrendered to the U.S. Army and began working as scouts for the white men. This gave the Army a decided edge, and by 1873 the defeated Apache and Yavapai were herded onto reservations together. Today pure Yavapai blood has virtually disappeared, and much of their culture essentially has

RIGHTS AND RIFLES

. . . To Americans generally, the aborigine is a nonentity except when he is on the war-path. The moment he concludes to live at peace with the whites, that moment all his troubles begin. Never was there a truer remark than that made by [Gen. George] Crook [commander of the U.S. Army campaign against the Apaches in 1871-72]: "The American Indian commands respect for his rights only so long as he inspires terror for his rifle."

—John G. Bourke, *On the Border With Crook,* 1892

Apache boys, in a photo likely dating from the 1880s. (Arizona Historical Society)

merged with the Apache.

The **Hualapais** and **Havasupais** are the people of the Grand Canyon. The Hualapai, whose name derives from a Yuman word meaning "pine-tree people," live on 1,551 square miles (40,179 sq. km) of forest and high plateau land abutting the canyon's south rim. The Havasupais ("People of the blue-green water") number only about 600, and are the most isolated of any Arizona tribe: to reach their one village, Supai, drive 60 miles (96 km) north of Arizona State Highway 66 through the Hualapai Reservation, park at Hualapai Hilltop and either walk or ride a mule 11 miles (18 km) farther into Havasu Canyon, a tributary of the Grand Canyon (or else charter a helicopter). The scenery is grand indeed, with three waterfalls within two miles (three km) of the village. Edward Abbey once noted that the Havasupais were an unusually wise people, having rejected a BIA scheme to blast a million-dollar road into the village to funnel in mass tourism. (There is, however, a small guest lodge at Supai.)

The **Hopis**, defying meteorological odds and conventional horticultural wisdom, have successfully raised corn, squash and melons on the arid mesas of north-

HOPI CULTURE

Not so many years ago, a team of archaeologists excavating a Sinagua burial site near Flagstaff were astonished to discover the remains of an ancient Sinagua shaman interred with a dozen wooden wands carved and painted to resemble hoofs and hands. The find paled, however, in the light of what happened next. A modern Hopi, taken to view the remains, could not only identify the uses of the millennium-old paraphernalia, but also tell from them which clan the magician had belonged to.

For archaeologists, the incident was more proof of the long-suspected Sinagua-Anasazi-Hopi linkages. But it also illuminated something else: the phenomenal endurance of Hopi tradition and culture. No other tribe in Arizona has resisted the encroachment of the outside world so successfully.

All Hopi life, religion, and society is organized around an all-encompassing belief system called *Hopivotskwani,* the Hopi Path of Life. According to legend, it began when the first ancestors of the Hopi emerged from the spirit Underworld to wander until they arrived at the arid mesas that would become their home. The Bear Clan, so called because they found a dead bear during their pilgrimage, became the founder upon their arrival at Shungopovi, in northeastern Arizona. As other groups arrived, they were given land to farm and accepted into Hopi society once they could demonstrate their acceptance of *Hopivotskwani.*

The concept of the Hopi Path is extremely difficult for an outsider to grasp, but it has to do with the presence of the spirit world in virtually everything. Every plant and animal has a spirit; every summer thunderstorm is generated in the spirit universe—those storms being critical to Hopi farming. Every winter solstice marks the beginning of ceremonial kachina dancing, which continues until mid-July. The kachinas, which appear to outsiders to be men dressed in elaborate and astounding costumes, are in Hopi belief the spirits of departed ancestors. They sing songs of admonition and perfected life, and they take the Hopis' prayers for rain, health and fertility back to the spirit world.

Most of today's 10,000 Hopis live on a reservation surrounded by Navajo lands. Hopis are at best ambivalent about tourism; some of their villages do not welcome visitors at all, and those that do generally ask outsiders to register at the local community office. As tribal spokeswoman Kim Secakuku told a *Los Angeles Daily News* reporter, "[Our] people felt like they were living in a museum." At the same time, however, Hopi prosperity is increasingly linked to the sales of their crafts, particularly their distinctive black-and-yellow pottery and kachina dolls.

The Hopi dilemma is similar to that of the Navajo, Tohono O'odham, and others: they do not want to be stirred into the American melting pot, yet the realities of modern transportation, communication, and economics are pulling them mightily. If the unique Hopi Path of Life fades into oblivion, it will be one of the great tragedies of American cultural history.

Hopi potter Marilyn Sakewa of Polacca decorates her pots with paint made from wild spinach and applies it with a yucca spine brush. (Kerrick James)

eastern Arizona for at least 600 years. Not surprisingly, many of their sacred ceremonies center around the need for rain. Most astonishing is the snake dance, in
which Hopi priests carry live snakes—including rattlesnakes—in their mouths.
Since they live underground, the snakes are viewed as the logical intercessors to the
gods, which in Hopi theology inhabit the Underworld. Hopi arts, along with their
rituals, are highly developed: their contemporary pottery and kachina dolls are the
most refined of all the Native American arts in Arizona today. The Hopi villages
are fascinating to visit, particularly Walpi, the "sky village" appearing to bud right
out of the top of a mesa; and Old Oraibi, the oldest continuously inhabited town
in the U.S. (since A.D. 1150).

The **Tohono O'odham** are the quintessential desert people: they believe, no
doubt correctly, that their culture will abide in the arid heart of the Sonoran
Desert long after we have squandered what we understand of its usable resources
and gone on. Before the encroachment of Anglo culture, the O'odham successfully grew corn, squash and beans on the dry ground and harvested the native
saguaro fruit for dessert. Except for the "Papago Bingo" parlors on the San Xavier
Reservation just south of Tucson, the O'odham have done little to generate
tourism. They are not in the least hostile to outsiders, but neither are they as outgoing as, say, the Navajo and Apache. The **Pimas**, closely related to the O'odham,
live with the **Maricopas** on the Gila River Reservation just south of Phoenix.

The remaining Arizona tribes are much less well-known than the above:

The **Kaibab Paiutes** and **Chemehuevis**, two descendants of the Southern
Paiutes of the Great Basin, have very few members today. The Kaibab Paiutes in-
habit the 188-square-mile (487-sq.-km) Kaibab reservation on the Utah border.
The Chemehuevis, who saw their farmlands become Lake Havasu when Parker
Dam backed up the Colorado River in 1938, moved downstream to the Colorado
River Reservation.

The **Mohaves**, a tribe of Yuman speakers, straddle the Colorado on the Fort
Mohave Reservation just south of Bullhead City.

Still farther downstream, near the Mexican border, are the related **Cocopahs**
and **Quechan** (Yuman) people. Both small tribes depend heavily on agriculture.

The **Yaquis**, nineteenth-century refugees from Mexican persecution, inhabit
tiny reservations just southwest of Tucson and the incorporated Phoenix suburb of
Guadalupe. The U.S. Government officially designated them an American tribe
only in 1978; since then they have adopted a tribal constitution and transcribed

their language into written form. Though small—about 5,300 members in Arizona— they seem more determined than ever to preserve their heritage.

Few if any **Zuni** Indians reside in Arizona, but the official state map shows a tiny Zuni reservation a few miles northwest of St. Johns, near the New Mexico border. This 17-square-mile (44-sq.-km) "reservation" is in Zuni belief the ceiling of heaven, and it was given to the tribe as part of a complicated land swap in 1985.

Once every four years, immediately after the summer solstice, the Zunis make a 45-mile (72-km) pilgrimage from their New Mexico reservation to this Arizona annex. They follow the Zuni River to a spring where they bathe, then proceed on to Kolhuwalawa, a dry Arizona lake bed that spreads over their underground spiritual afterworld. There they conduct ceremonies that are believed to date back at least a thousand years.

There are no roads or travelers' facilities on this tiny reservation, but visitors can drive to Zuni Pueblo on the Zuni reservation in New Mexico. This pueblo was one of Coronado's fabled Seven Cities of Cibola. From St. Johns, head northeast on Arizona State Route 61, continuing 10 miles (16 km) into New Mexico.

■ VISITING THE RESERVATIONS

Outsiders are welcome on all of Arizona's 20 reservations, but there are some restrictions. Possession of alcohol is illegal on all except the Colorado River Reservation and the towns of Whiteriver and Cocopah. Hunting, fishing and camping all require a tribal permit. In some areas, such as the Navajos' Monument Valley, even hiking is forbidden. Where anything is forbidden, signs will be abundant.

Photography and videotaping also are unwelcome in many situations. Hopi villages and ceremonies may not be photographed, sketched or their sounds recorded. Visitors to Guadalupe will see many signs outside people's homes asking that their outdoor shrines not be photographed. Navajos, however, do a thriving business with photographers, charging a dollar or two for a pose—and lately, even photographing some hogans has begun to carry a fee.

A few of the reservations have visitor centers with museums and craft shops. The **Yavapai-Apache Center** (east off I-17 at exit 289, en route to Montezuma Castle National Monument) is particularly good; the building, designed by Hopi architect Dennis Numkena, is a stunning abstract reinterpretation of prehistoric

Only a few Navajos still live in a traditional eight-sided hogan, but their use in ceremony remains important.

forms. The **Hopi Cultural Center** on Second Mesa has fascinating exhibits on Hopi arts and culture. The **Gila River Arts and Crafts Center** belongs to the Pimas and Maricopas, but its gift shop is an omnium-gatherum of crafts from many different cultures. (Take exit 175 off I-10 south of Phoenix.) Nearly all the reservations have trading posts in the larger towns. On the Navajo Reservation, hundreds of roadside stands selling jewelry and other crafts line the highways.

When driving across either the vast Navajo or Tohono O'odham reservations, take spare water and watch your fuel: filling stations can be as much as 100 miles (161 km) apart.

Corn has been a staple crop on the Colorado Plateau for 2,000 years. (Paul Chesley)

VIKKI STEVENS

If this were Scottsdale . . .

It is not. It is San Carlos, the largest town on the San Carlos Apache Reservation, inside the Indian Health Service hospital. It is a Friday afternoon, and Dr. Victoria Stevens begins many of her observations with this same clause. "If this were Scottsdale, you'd write a prescription and this patient would be making daily trips to a physical therapist . . . ."

"If this were Scottsdale and you treated somebody the way the Indian people are treated medically, there'd be so many lawsuits it'd be ridiculous . . . ."

Victoria Stevens—she goes by Vikki—runs a biweekly orthopedic clinic in San Carlos, a 16-mile drive (26-km) from her office and conventional medical practice in the Central Arizona mining town of Globe. She calls the clinic "my M*A*S*H unit." Spend an hour in it, and you understand why. Medicine is improvised here. "The reason I do it is I love the people." Stevens is half Apache herself, brought up on a ranch on this reservation.

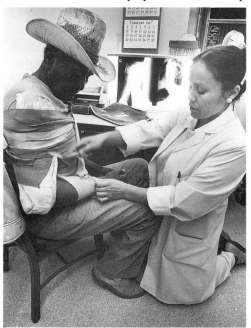

She was the first Native American to graduate from the University of Arizona College of Medicine.

She is a tiny woman with a gorgeous, softly contoured face, an infectious smile and the characteristic coarse, black hair of the Apaches. That face is a moving catalog of expressions; her thick, short fingers constantly weave and stab the air in punctuation for her words. They are working fingers. "People ask me, how can you be an orthopedic surgeon? But I grew up on a ranch. I did physically difficult things — helping build fences,

Dr. Vikki Stevens works on an ailing arm. (P.K. Weis)

castrating calves, helping my dad butcher animals. Maybe growing up like I did, I didn't feel a lot of limitations. My parents never said, 'Oh, little girls don't do that.'"

After graduating, she married another orthopedic surgeon and returned to the small town where she had gone to high school. "It still has values that are missing from the mainstream of life. People are concerned about each other. They want to know whose house burned down last week and who's helping out with that. They're not as materially oriented—they can't be; we don't have that much money up here.

"The advantage for a physician is that you have a very personal relationship with your patients, and when you practice you practice a lot by word of mouth. In a larger setting, sometimes you're treating a patient in a void. You see him once a month. Here, I go to the Safeway and I see so-and-so on his crutches, and I say 'How're you doing?' And he'll say, 'Well, I'm fine, but look at this sore on my calf.' And I'll say, 'Well, come on into the office.'"

The disadvantage is painfully obvious in the San Carlos clinic. The first patient is an elderly woman with a broken ankle. Her cast has been on for months too long, and in desperation she has tried to remove it herself, first with a knife, then with a saw. She lives in Bylas, 24 miles (38 km) away, and for four months hasn't been able to get a ride to Vikki Stevens' clinic. Another patient still suffers from a three-year-old leg fracture. Stevens had attached a plate to it; it had broken again. Now she is urging the bone to heal itself. "You could put the leg on an osteostimulator, which will stimulate bone growth with electrical current," she says. "Ideally, I'd send him over to the store to plunk down $500 for one. If this were Scottsdale . . . ."

Another also hurts from an old injury, a dislocated shoulder he acquired while hauling an elk carcass up a hill. He needs physical therapy, but the best Stevens can do is coach him on exercising his arm. The exercise is painful, and she is not at all certain he will tough it out on his own. All these patients are suffering from complications that wouldn't exist if they had had Scottsdale care at the time of their injuries, she says. The San Carlos hospital tries, and does an excellent job with the resources it has, but "some days it looks like Vietnam out there."

Is medical care on the reservation growing worse, not better? "I think so," Stevens says. "And the sad thing is that these are people without a voice. These people don't complain. Somebody who's got a crooked leg and lives out on the Apache or Navajo reservation is never going to be as noticeable as somebody in Scottsdale. Here we are, spending billions on weapons, and here are all these people with horrible deformities. It just makes you want to cry."

MAKING ARIZONA

CHARLES DEBRILLE POSTON LIKED TO CALL HIMSELF the "Father of Arizona." Spiritually if not literally, he appears to have been exactly that. Were he alive today, however, he would find that the grown-up state little resembles the strange community he created at the old Spanish *presidio* of Tubac.

Poston was toiling as an obscure law clerk in gold-rush California when he read about the Gadsden Purchase in 1853. He must have sniffed opportunity, because he quickly organized a party of fellow adventurers and set out for the silver-veined hills of southern Arizona. His company moved into the ghost fort of Tubac, began rebuilding it, and commenced lucrative mining operations in the Santa Rita mountains nearby. Before long, Mexican miners and unmarried women drifted up from Mexico, and Poston installed himself as the town's *alcalde*. The Spanish word literally translates as "mayor," but Poston was more like a potentate. He ran the mines, performed marriages and granted divorces, baptized children and dispensed justice. Still, he appears to have been no dictator, but a Utopian and a precursor of modern libertarians.

"We had no law but love and no occupation but labor," Poston wrote, "no government, no taxes, no public debt, no politics. It was a community in a perfect state of nature."

This was true in still other ways, in Poston's mind. All the women in Tubac had come from Sonora, which, Poston wrote, "has always been famous for the beauty and gracefulness of its señoritas . . . . They are exceedingly dainty in their underclothing, wear the finest linen when they can afford it, and spend half their lives over the washing machine."

If the barest tint of condescension seems to color Poston's admiration, well, he was not to be the last Anglo pioneer who held such contradictions. In any event, his Utopia was short-lived. In 1861 Apaches reduced Tubac to rubble, and Poston fled for his life, later observing bitterly that "The Government of the United States abandoned the first settlers of Arizona to the merciless Apaches."

Still, Poston never ceased to dream—another quirk of character that would appear in so many pioneers and developers that followed him. He successfully lobbied Washington in 1863 to have Arizona separated from the Territory of New Mexico. He founded serious historical societies in Tucson and Phoenix. He proposed irrigation projects. Then he made a pilgrimage to Asia and became a Zoroastrian, returned to Arizona and tried in vain to establish a sun-worshiping sect in the land he loved. He died impoverished in Phoenix in 1902.

It was not long after Poston's experiment at Tubac that larger waves of Anglo settlers came rolling in. They were mostly of three types: the cattle ranchers, the agrarian Mormons spilling down from Utah, and the miners. While few of these had such exotic ideas as Poston, they were, like him, following their dreams and questing in some form for personal freedom. They all faced the same headaches: a shortage of water, a surplus of Apaches.

■ THE APACHE WARS, 1871-86

No ethnic tribe on the planet has bounced so far and so often from utter vilification to romantic glorification as have the Apaches. A researcher from some other world flying in to comb through the voluminous histories, novels and movies about the Apaches would learn, for example, that they were "blood-drunk and beast-hot . . . fetid-breathed and shrieking . . . lecherous and without honor or mercy . . . the Apaches hate life and they are the enemy of all mankind." (All this from the 1950s novels of James Warner Bellah.) And then he would hear agent Tom Jeffords in a contemporary novel, *Blood Brother*, explaining that among the Apaches "there is no private hoarding, no cheating. Whatever they have is divided equally. . . . There's no caste system, and no aristocrats and no commoners. . . . I wonder by what standards we have arrogated to ourselves the right to call Indians savages?"

There is universal agreement on one fact regarding the nineteenth-century Apaches: they were incredible individual fighters. "There were 23 different Apache groups in Arizona, and there was no communication among them," explained historian David Faust, curator of the Fort Lowell Park Museum in Tucson. "Everybody was fighting his own war, essentially. If they had waged a coordinated war, they probably would have been able to hold out into the twentieth century."

In purely objective terms, the Apaches were undeniably aggressors. When they emigrated into the Southwest, probably in the sixteenth century, they found much of the territory already occupied by farmers such as the Hopi and Pima. To survive, they raided when necessary. But the advent of truly bloody, vengeance-driven war came only after Spaniards and Anglos arrived.

The Camp Grant Massacre set the savage tone for the war with Anglo Arizona. In April of 1871, a motley posse of Anglos, Mexican-Americans and Papagos organized in Tucson rode the 60 miles (96 km) northeast to Camp Grant, where a cluster of Arivaipa Apaches were living under an informal treaty with the Army. The Tucsonans, led by former mayor William S. Oury, suspected the Arivaipas of the incessant hit-and-run raids plaguing southern Arizona ranchers and supply wagons— which may indeed have been an accurate suspicion. But when the posse attacked at dawn on April 30, they found hardly any Apache men in the camp; most were out hunting. No matter: the raiders had come to exterminate Apaches. They killed between 85 and 100—the number is still disputed—and all but a handful of them were women and children.

"The attack was so swift and fierce," Oury later boasted, "that within half an hour the whole work was ended and not an adult Indian left to tell the tale."

The massacre focused national attention on the "Indian problem" in Arizona, although the consequences hardly did the Apaches any good. The raiders were tried for murder in Tucson and acquitted. Then President Ulysses S. Grant launched a carrot-and-bayonet effort to coax the Apaches into peace treaties and reservations, or, if they refused, to wage full-scale war against them. Gen. George Crook, a brilliant military strategist who thoroughly understood his enemy, directed the campaign of 1872-73 and came close to quelling the "problem" in those two years.

A network of 16 army forts laced through Arizona, providing a base for Crook's troops. The Apaches never attacked the forts directly—that would have been suicidal—but ambushed the troops in small scouting parties well away from the forts. The Army employed friendly or "tame" Apaches as scouts to lead them through unfamiliar terrain in pursuit of the enemy. Neither side practiced much charity. If the Apaches captured a soldier alive, they would execute him either by lashing him to a convenient tree or cactus and perforating his torso with arrows; or by suspending him head down over a slow fire. Crook ordered his troops to make "every effort to avoid the killing of women and children," but women and children sometimes accompanied the warriors into caves or canyons from which the Apaches staged a last-ditch defense—and then the Army bullets were hardly selective.

Nor did the atrocities end with surrender. In 1873, the Verde Valley Apaches and Yavapais surrendered to Crook at Fort Verde. The U.S. Government promised them an 800-square-mile (2,072-sq.-km) reservation stretching 10 miles (16 km) on either side of the river for a distance of 40 miles (64 km). This land would be theirs, they were promised, "for as long as the rivers run, the grass grows, and the hills endure." But this temperate, fertile valley was worth more to Territorial settlers than the honor of keeping the promise. After only two years, 1,476 Indians literally were herded 180 miles (288 km) southeast to the arid San Carlos reservation. As described by Yavapai scout Rim-Ma-Ke-Na, in an unpublished history of the Yavapai-Apache tribes:

> They drive them like cattles [sic], they have no pity. Some have to be left and die. Those that can't go any farther. Even when it's rainy day and floody they have to drive them in the flood. And many are drowned. And that was one of the saddest thing that I ever saw.

Even with most of the Apaches installed on reservations, sporadic fighting and raiding erupted. The Chiricahua Apaches, led by Geronimo, held out in the mountains of southeastern Arizona until they also surrendered to Crook in 1886. They were then shipped by train to a prison camp in Florida.

Geronimo himself provided a pathetic epilogue to the Apache wars in the years following his detention. He reinvented himself as an exotic celebrity, making the rounds of fairs and conventions, selling autographs, buttons off his clothes, and other trinkets to amuse white Americans. There is an extant photo of him taken at

Geronimo (right) and his warriors were as well armed as the U.S. Army, and they knew the land much better, 1886. (Arizona Historical Society)

the St. Louis World's Fair in 1904. He is wearing an ill-fitting wool coat, short hair and a stoic yet vacant gaze, and he is selling bows and arrows—a caricature Indian now, lurching gracelessly between two worlds. In that picture he appears as a prescient metaphor for much that would happen to Native Americans in the twentieth century.

In the 1980s an Apache man set up shop in a teepee on the west outskirts of Tucson, charging people a dollar each to take his picture. He claimed to be Geronimo's grandson.

■ GRAZING, FARMING AND MINING

The cattlemen, who established their herds in the high desert grasslands of the southeast and the temperate meadows of north-central Arizona, contributed an enduring romance to the frontier. They also created its first modern environmental disaster: not many of those grasslands survived. In 1870, an estimated 5,000 cattle grazed Arizona; by 1891 there were 1.5 million. The fragile land could not support them. In 1892 and '93 a devastating drought appeared—as it periodically does in the arid Southwest. The range was already overgrazed and overtrampled, and something between 50 and 75 percent of the animals died. When the rains finally returned, thousands of square miles, gnawed bare by the starving cows, was exposed to erosion. Raw desert replaced many of the grasslands, and ranching dwindled to a minor role in the state's future.

The Mormons proved to be better custodians of the land, but their welcome was checkered. Mormon expeditions into Arizona had begun as early as 1846, when the Mormon Battalion, a force of 500 pseudo-military volunteers under the command of Captain Philip St. George Cooke, punched a wagon trail through the uncharted land to California. This was no missionary or colonialist adventure; Cooke saw no good use for Arizona. It was, he wrote, ". . . a wilderness where nothing but savages and wild beasts are found, or deserts where, for lack of water, there is no living creature."

This land of "wild beasts" and, alternately, "no living creature" proved compelling enough to later Mormons who began spilling down from Utah in the 1870s. They came for three reasons: to colonize new farmlands, to try to convert Indians—specifically the Hopis—and to find refuges isolated enough to discourage the U.S. Government from harassing the polygamists among them. They founded settlements along the Little Colorado River in east-central Arizona, where they were harassed instead by floods, and established several more communities in the desert farther south, including Lehi (now the Phoenix suburb of Mesa), Thatcher and St. David.

Despite unforgiving and unfamiliar environmental conditions, Mormons in Arizona, as elsewhere, became successful farmers. A correspondent of the *Prescott Miner*, writing in 1878, probably pointed out the reason: "The work done by these people is simply astounding," he wrote. "The alacrity and vim with which they go at it is decidedly in favor of co-operation or communism." Still, polygamy was as unwelcome in Arizona as it was elsewhere. The Territorial Legislature of 1885 disenfranchised polygamists, and Mormon skirmishes with gentile neighbors —ranchers, mainly—were not uncommon. The church ended sanctioned polygamy in 1890, although a handful of wildcat fundamentalists continue the practice in deepest northern Arizona even today. The more significant legacy of Mormons in Arizona, however, is this: the public schools in virtually every community they established remain among the state's best.

Mining formed the third territorial boom, and it reshaped the state's physical and political landscape in a far more profound way than anything else. The treasure buried in Arizona's mountains attracted a different breed of dreamer than the range or farmlands, because it offered the lure of quick and dramatic wealth.

Arizona's gold rush, a short-lived phenomenon, began in 1857 when an itinerant Texan named Jack Snively swished a pan through the Gila River and saw some residue glinting in the desert sun. Gila City, the town hastily assembled on the site, was a metaphor for the rush itself. After a year it had a teeming population of 1,200 prospectors, gamblers, prostitutes and assorted other merchants. In another two years the gold began to dwindle. In 1862 the Gila River, as if in moral outrage, went on a rampage and wiped out what was left of the town. When journalist J. Ross Browne passed through in 1864, he noted with finely tuned sarcasm that "the promising Metropolis of Arizona consisted of three chimneys and a coyote." Much the same fate befell other mining camps.

The silver boom followed gold, and it was not much more durable. The most famous lode was discovered in 1877 by a wandering miner named Ed Schieffelin, who had traveled with a U.S. Cavalry troop from California to establish Arizona's new Fort Huachuca. This was hostile land, controlled by the Chiricahua Apaches.

(following page) The carcass of an abandoned mining operation rots slowly in the sun.

At first Schieffelin tried to do his prospecting in the company of scouting parties dispatched from the fort, but he soon realized he would have to follow his own instincts in search of ore. As he left the safety of the fort alone, someone warned him, "All you'll ever find out there will be your tombstone."

Schieffelin lived to have the last laugh, and it was one energized by considerable wealth. He indeed found silver ore, and wryly named his first stake "Tombstone." In 10 years, the hills around the boom town that adopted that name yielded $19 million worth of silver. In 1886, however, the mines flooded and even Tombstone —which truly had been a metropolis, the largest town in the territory—collapsed into the role of historic artifact.

It was copper that finally etched Arizona onto the global mineralogical map. The copper boom also forged a permanent change in Arizona's character, one that persists today: copper transformed the territory from a frontier to an economic colony, a place largely owned and controlled by outsiders.

Copper mining had little in common with the small-scale, nickel-and-dime operations of men like Poston and Schieffelin. Anywhere between 20 and 100 pounds (nine to 45 kg) of ore has to be processed to yield a pound of copper, and a mine has to produce hundreds of tons a copper a day to pay off. This requires gigantic investments in land, equipment, personnel and science. Since no individual in Arizona Territory had such deep pockets, the boom was financed by corporations from back East. And while they brought considerable prosperity to Arizona, they also extracted a painful social price.

Jerome, Clifton, Globe, Bisbee—these copper-mining capitals of turn-of-the-century Arizona appear quaintly picturesque today, with their neighborhoods of pint-sized Victorian homes snaking up and down precipitous hillsides and gulches. In the middle of a Bisbee intersection stands a smashing socialist-realist-era copper statue of a miner stripped to the waist, bristling with muscle and wearing an expression of world-dominating confidence. The inscription reads: "Dedicated to those virile men—the copper miners." Viewing artifacts such as these from the safe distance of the 1990s, it is easy to romanticize the copper boom. In truth, it was an ugly business.

The miners worked in stopes, or pits hundreds of feet underground, drilling holes for dynamite and blasting the ore into rubble to be carted to the surface. There might be water up to their ankles, the temperature would be well over 100 degrees, and the humid air would be fouled by the stench of carbon dioxide and

(previous page) Copper miners thousands of feet below Bisbee, c. 1910.
(Bisbee Mining & Historical Museum)

human excrement. Until well into the twentieth century, safety records were not encouraging; in 1913, according to Phelps Dodge records, a laborer in the Copper Queen operation at Bisbee could expect to have a "lost-time" accident once every 474 shifts. There were many ways to die: quickly, in fires or cave-ins or untimely explosions, or slowly, from silicosis caused by breathing the fine quartz dust produced by the drilling. An article in the *Tombstone Epitaph*, even if written in the florid style of the era, describes in graphic terms the death of one Copper Queen smelter worker:

> *Joe* Bailey of Bisbee is dead. . . . While pursuing his daily vocation, unmindful that death lurked nigh, a pot containing one ton of molten slag came detached from the crane that was conveying it, and fell to the ground below, a distance of twelve or fifteen feet, lighting squarely upon the man. There were no cries of pain, no shrieks of anguish, no pleading for mercy or assistance. The spirit of Joe Bailey had taken its flight.

Above ground, the miners and their families—those lucky ones who had families—lived in company towns built and owned by the mine operators. On the surface the companies seemed benevolently paternalistic; they provided baseball fields, hospitals, schools, housing at below-market rent and plenty of credit. A retired Phelps Dodge geologist in Bisbee recently recalled that the company even gave $50 "Christmas bonuses" to all the ministers in town. But all this was also calculated to insure obedience to the company. "They used the carrot more than the stick," said mining historian James W. Byrkit, "but the fear of losing these things was always present in the background."

The event that illustrates the political muscle that the mine companies came to have was the bizarre Bisbee Deportation of 1917. To this day it remains controversial in Bisbee; some long-time residents don't even like outsiders asking questions about it.

On June 27, 1917, a radical labor union, the Industrial Workers of the World (IWW, or "Wobblies") called a strike. Although fewer than 400 were card-carrying Wobblies, about half of Bisbee's 4,700 miners walked out. Mine management responded with a public relations blitz painting the IWW as German sympathizers sabotaging the Allies' wartime copper supplies.

At 6:30 on the morning of July 17, Cochise County Sheriff Harry Wheeler and a colossal posse of 2,000 "loyal Americans" fanned through Bisbee and arrested an equal number of strikers in their homes. The vigilantes marched the captives under armed guard two miles (three km) to the suburb of Warren. Those who agreed to return to work were freed; the other 1,186 were crammed into 23 boxcars and railroaded to a camp at Columbus, New Mexico. Few ever returned to Bisbee, and union power in Arizona was emasculated.

Thus the script for offstage control of Arizona was forged in copper. As a territory and then an adolescent state after 1912, Arizona never found the means to sort out its own destiny. This remains the story today. Most of Arizona's banks (and the desolate remains of its S&Ls) are owned out of state. Many of the most ambitious development projects are planned and financed out of state. This is the result of unchained growth: there is money waiting to be made here. The story of Phoenix explains how.

Visitors to Canyon de Chelly pay their respects.

MARTIN LUTHER KING, JR. IN ARIZONA

At the polls on November 6, 1990, Arizonans were greeted by a slate of initiatives so long and complicated that the official voters' guide ran for 224 pages. Two of those proposals, either of which would have created a paid state holiday honoring Martin Luther King Jr., proved more fateful than voters anticipated. After the election, Arizona skidded into the nation's doghouse, weathered a hurricane of abuse, lost an estimated $11 million in convention cancellations over the next two months alone, and inspired the NFL to snatch the 1993 Super Bowl away from Phoenix. Within the state, no political fray save the impeachment of Governor Evan Mecham has ever been as divisive.

Mecham, not surprisingly, played a role in it.

In 1986 the Arizona Legislature declined to join most of the nation in honoring King. After the session ended, outgoing Gov. Bruce Babbitt declared the holiday anyway, which he apparently had no constitutional authority to do. Mecham, who followed him, voided it. A couple of years later, with Mecham sidelined, the legislature did pass the King holiday, substituting it for Columbus Day. That enraged Italian-Americans. Finally two different King holiday measures went before voters: one to swap Columbus for King, the other to add King to the 10 paid holidays state workers already enjoyed. Both failed.

Analysts and critics have floated various explanations: (1) Voters were disgusted or confused by the history of the bungled holiday, and voted "no" to signal their frustration. (2) Taxpayers didn't want to bloat the state budget with another paid holiday. (3) On the eve of the vote, the NFL had threatened to pull the Super Bowl if the holiday failed, so Arizonans voted "no" to show they can't be shoved around. (4) Arizona harbors more racists than other states.

The view from here is that the first three reasons all influenced voters. The last is a crimson herring. Of course some Arizonans are racists, as are some humans everywhere. But the suggestion that hundreds of thousands of Arizonans refused to honor King because he advanced the cause of civil rights is too absurd to take seriously.

In the 1992 election Arizonans finally approved a proposition to honor King with a holiday; the vote was 61 to 39 percent. The nation's caning of Arizona ended, and convention hotel phones began ringing again. However they voted, Arizonans still resent the lingering label of racism. As King himself might have said, self-righteousness is no substitute for hard work on the real agenda of building a fair and equal society for everybody.

ARIZONA POLITICS

Many an outsider who ventures to write about Arizona politics is visited by a ghostly spasm that causes the fingers to type the words ". . . frontier mentality . . ." Normally they appear not far from the beginning of the commentary, and if the writer is in good form, the reader will be treated to supporting anecdotage: the bill perennially introduced in the state legislature to let every Arizonan carry a concealed weapon, for example, or the governor's education lobbyist who in 1987 proclaimed that "if a student wants to say that the world is flat, the teacher doesn't have the right to try to prove otherwise."

Such stories have great entertainment value (except among grimacing Arizonans), but prove nothing except that crackpots sometimes stumble into public service here, as they do in every state. If Arizona truly had a "frontier mentality," the concealed weapons bill would pass—which it hasn't—and the governor who appointed the flat-earth man wouldn't have been impeached and removed from office—which he was.

What Arizonans do have is a tenacious distrust of governing bodies and a ready resolve to take political matters into their own hands. There is an element of the frontier's self-reliance in this, but it is not mere backwardness or arch conservatism. It is more complicated than that, and it has made the temperament of Arizona politics rowdy and unpredictable.

President William Taft was among the first to notice this. Troubled by the populist tilt of Arizona's proposed constitution, with its provisions for voter initiative, referendum and recall, he refused to approve statehood until recall for judges was removed. (Taft, incidentally, had been a judge.) Once inducted into the union, the first legislature of the new state immediately placed judicial recall on the ballot, and Arizona voters ordered it right back in.

From statehood in 1912 to the early 1950s, Arizona was essentially a one-party state, and that party was Democratic. It was more populist than liberal, however, as most citizens seemed to distrust big government as well as big business. The dramatic shift toward a two-party state, and then the dominance of the GOP, began in 1950 with the election of a Republican governor, Howard Pyle. By the end of that decade, registered Democrats still outnumbered Republicans by 68 to 32 percent—yet Republicans were consistently sweeping Democrats out of offices at every level. One explanation, among many advanced by historians, was that conservatives were registering as Democrats in order to have a voice in the dominant party's primaries, then voting for Republicans in the general elections.

Air conditioning was the prime reason for the rightward swing of Arizona. With the Valley of the Sun newly rendered fit for human habitation, metropolitan Phoenix rapidly attracted major industries and swarms of retirees. Between 1950 and 1960, Phoenix's population ballooned from 106,818 to 439,170, and more were streaming in from the Republican Midwest than from the Democratic South. The Phoenix newspapers, *The Arizona Republic* and the *Phoenix Gazette*, became relentless boosters of economic growth and conservative causes. As the state's most influential news media, they certainly helped build the GOP's power.

Tucson, which since 1950 has languished in Phoenix's economic shadow, has remained the state's Democratic stronghold, returning—as one example—the unabashedly liberal Morris K. Udall to Congress for 15 terms. But even Tucson is slowly turning more conservative, a trend that can be discerned in the voters' consistent rejection of municipal bond issues and budget increases for the public schools. Phoenix today has emerged as Republican and progressive; Tucson remains Democratic but more wary of taxing and spending than Phoenix.

Confused? So is the political theater of Arizona today. Or perhaps "contentious" is the better description.

We are at least true to our history. Through voter initiative, liberal Arizonans enacted women's suffrage in 1912, and conservatives inflicted Prohibition two years later. We gave ourselves the death penalty in 1914 and revoked it in 1916 and revived it in 1918. Today most of the issues are less profound than these but the list seems endless. Arizonans fight over everything. A county board of supervisors rezones a square mile of desert for a housing development, and opponents fan out through the shopping malls waving petitions to force a referendum. The legislature, after years of acrimonious debate, at last enacts a Martin Luther King Jr. holiday, only to be greeted by an initiative drive by critics who claim the lawmakers took "the people's voice" away. John Kromko, a long-lived Democratic state representative, who always has trouble propelling his programs through the Republican-dominated legislature, has become adept at mounting initiative drives himself, using the public to confound the very body it elected.

Most remarkable of all is that Arizonans emerge from this turbulent atmosphere to achieve national political prominence that is out of all proportion to the state's population. In fewer than 30 years, three Arizonans have made a serious run at the presidency: Sen. Barry Goldwater (1964), Udall (1976), and former Gov. Bruce Babbitt (1988). Two Arizonans now sit on the U.S. Supreme Court: William Rehnquist and Sandra Day O'Connor. Carl Hayden, who was first elected to Congress in

1912 and retired as Senate president pro tem in 1969, served Congress longer than any other American in history. There are numerous theories to explain all this, but the most logical is that of a former congressman from Tucson, James F. McNulty: "I suppose any 'frontier' state probably encourages the more ambitious," he says. "New growth is where things happen."

In other words, it's the frontier mentality.

THE MECHAM ADVENTURE

Too bad the recall voting is confined to Arizona.
—The Atlanta Constitution

In the darkest hours of Arizona's modern political nightmare, it seemed as if the entire nation ached to join the pursuit of Gov. Evan Mecham, like sharks flocking to a thrashing prey. Most Arizonans simply prayed for a quick end to the ordeal, whether it came in the form of impeachment or recall: Evan Mecham was the only governor in American history ever to face both at once. A *Tucson Citizen* reporter, whose parents lived in Philadelphia, spoke for many Arizonans' embarrassment when she said, in all seriousness, "I'm not calling home till this is over."

In 1986 Mecham, a Republican, was running for governor for the fifth time. He already had been rejected four times. He was regarded not only as a perennial loser but as an outsider, a man whose reactionary political views and religious affiliation —Mormon—coincided to place him outside the orbit of the presumably electable mainstream. But that year his opposition committed political suicide. Carolyn Warner, the Democratic nominee, seemed so unpopular that another nominal Democrat, Bill Schulz, leapt into the contest as an independent. That split the moderate and liberal vote, and Mecham squeezed into office.

A normal politician's instinct is to avoid alienating significant blocs of voters, even if in his heart he finds them personally repugnant. Evan Mecham was driven by ideology and the fire of religious righteousness, not political pragmatism. He manufactured enemies daily. He declared war on homosexuals and the news media, attacked the political establishment and, probably most damaging, constantly made slips that insulted various ethnic groups. Trying to defend himself against charges of racism, he said: "I'm not a racist. I've got black friends. I employ black people. I don't employ them because they're black. I employ them because they are the best people who applied for the cotton-picking job." He told a Jewish businessmen's club that because America follows "Christian principles," it is "a great land for everyone, allowing great freedom of religion for Jews. . . ." In October 1987, 10 months after Mecham's inauguration, with the state's government writhing in chaos, even GOP patriarch Barry Goldwater publicly called for his resignation. Mecham ignored him.

By November, the Mecham Recall Committee had more than enough petition signatures to force a recall election. But by this time, reports of financial misdeeds in the Mecham campaign had surfaced, and both the state House of Representatives and a statewide grand jury were conducting separate investigations. In January 1988, the grand jury indicted him for failing to disclose a $350,000 loan to the campaign. Accusations of obstruction of justice also emerged. Mecham allegedly had ordered the Department of Public Safety not to cooperate in an investigation of a death threat by one of his staff members against another. In February, Mecham became the first American governor in 59 years to be impeached. In April the Senate removed him from office, and the now-moot recall election was cancelled. The criminal trial followed in June, and the ex-governor was found not guilty of all six counts brought against him.

Had Mecham truly been guilty of "high crimes, misdemeanors or malfeasance in office," as charged in the articles of impeachment? An iron-hard core of Mecham loyalists, still estimated at 20 percent of Arizona voters, still insists not—he was driven from office, they say, because he alone had the courage to stand against amorality and corruption. Less partisan observers, many of whom watched the televised impeachment proceedings in rapt fascination, believe there was more than enough evidence of malfeasance. Both sides miss the point. An impeachment is a *political* act; it does not need to be fair to be proper—only essential. Mecham had drawn national ridicule to Arizona, dragged state government to the brink of paralysis, and unleashed unprecedented public hostility (the impeachment proceedings were awash not only in ugly demonstrations but death threats). There seemed no alternative to removing him.

Even after impeachment, Mecham doggedly ran again for governor in 1990, and placed a distant second in a five-man race for the Republican nomination. Late on primary night, as the earth fell in on his political grave, he remained in character to the end. Conceding defeat, he promised to support his fellow Republican, J. Fife Symington III, over the Democratic candidate, Terry Goddard.

"Goddard will be a 100 percent disaster," he said in his endorsement. "Fife will only be an 80 percent disaster."

P H O E N I X

IT WAS A CHARACTERISTICALLY SIMMERING mid-June morning in Phoenix when Mayor Paul Johnson showed up at a groundbreaking ceremony and challenged the businesspeople gathered around to take off those silly coats and ties.

"I do recognize there is a sense of power that relates to that tie," said a tieless Johnson. "But the bottom line is: we need to be different. This needs to be an open and friendly environment. It needs to be one in which we're cognizant of the fact that we live in the desert."

The mayor's good sense went begging. A few days later, *The Arizona Republic's* business section served up a stiff-necked story quoting business consultants and executives who complained that the rest of the country wouldn't take them seriously if they weren't wearing those coats and ties.

"We just think it's appropriate in terms of projecting a proper business image," sniffed one.

Johnson's failed campaign tells more about Phoenix than one might think. First, that it is a city that always has been reluctant to come to terms with its desert environment. Second, that in recent years it has become remarkably self-conscious about its image as a sprawling adolescent, a city full of the laissez-faire good life but without much ambition to be anything but big. And prosperous, of course, but on its own laid-back terms.

All of this is changing.

Phoenix (along with its brood of suburbs, collectively called the Valley of the Sun) has never looked like a desert city. Unlike its downstate rival, Tucson, Phoenix was conceived as an oasis. Agriculture was its original *raison d'etre*, and when in 1911 Roosevelt Dam walled off the Salt River 60 miles (96 km) to the east, the combined watersheds of the Salt and Verde rivers became a 13,000-square-mile (33,670 sq. km) catchment— an area larger than Belgium—to make Phoenix verdant.

The network of irrigation canals expanded across the valley, serving not only cash crops but also a lush urban landscape. Praising a new housing development in 1920, *The Arizona Republican* noted that the "umbrella of elm and ash trees are set so close together along these drives that the sun's rays barely penetrate the dense forest." Such developments forged the pattern for the next 70 years. Golf courses are now the Valley's most ubiquitous landscape. Suburban Fountain Hills boasts the world's highest fountain, a man-made geyser shooting water 560 feet (171 m) high. (This is more than three times the height of Yellowstone's Old Faithful.) So many modern subdivisions were being built around man-made lakes that the Legislature finally outlawed the practice in the 1980s. Scottsdale Mall, admittedly one of the loveliest city parks in the country, is a moist, emerald fantasyland of grassy hummocks, gurgling streams, sculptural fountains, pools and even a pair of municipal swans—swans!—named Winnie and Pooh. In such a setting the desert seems as distant as another planet.

For at least the last couple of decades elsewhere in the state it has been fashionable, even *de rigueur*, to denounce Phoenix's scandalous thirst (in 1988, the metro area used 253 gallons/956 liters of water per person per day, compared with Tucson's 164/620). But Phoenix's attitude toward the desert has its roots deep in its history. Bradford Luckingham, author of *Phoenix: The History of a Southwestern Metropolis*, explains that the American East, not the emerging West, was the early settlement's model. Pilgrims to territorial Phoenix found beauty in the desert not as it was, but in its potential to be an idealized version of the lands they had left behind: no snow, no industrial grime.

Once Roosevelt Dam guaranteed Phoenix a reliable flow of water, idealism and optimism seemed as pervasive as the year-round sunshine. In the 1910s it gained a reputation as a health mecca, particularly for Easterners suffering from lung diseases, and in the 1920s boosters successfully began pushing it as an all-around resort area. Slogans such as "Phoenix, Where Summer Winters" proved enticing to snowbound Easterners. By the 1930s Phoenix's roster of winter residents was quite impressive—it included, for example, William Wrigley, Jr. (the chewing gum magnate), Cornelius Vanderbilt, Jr. and Frank Lloyd Wright. At least in part, it was the influence of names such as these that attracted big-time investment to Phoenix instead of Tucson and made it, by 1940, the dominant city in the state.

Something first had to be done about Phoenix summers, however. Evaporative air conditioning (disaffectionately known as "swamp cooling" to Arizonans today) had been invented in 1908 by one Oscar Palmer at his father's Phoenix sheet metal shop, but amazingly, it was more than two decades before it became commercially available. Into the 1930s, Phoenicians routinely slept outdoors in summer, on their roofs, porches or in screened backyard bedrooms. (The cleverest survivors planted the legs of their outdoor cots in pails of water to dissuade scorpions from crawling into bed with them.) Even after the advent of evaporative cooling,

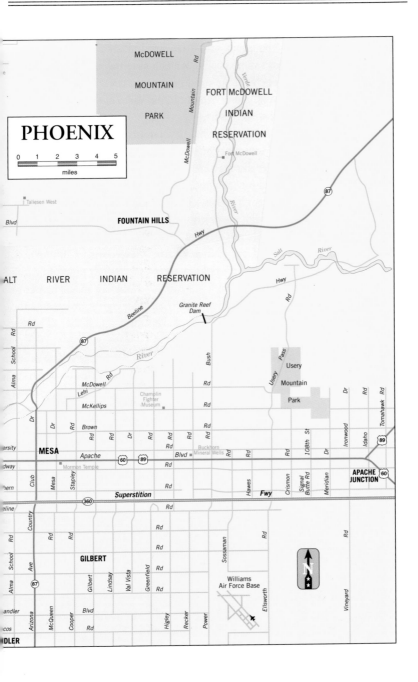

however, the July-August "monsoon" season remained nearly unbearable: during these humid days and nights swamp cooling is about as refreshing as the breath of a panting dog. It was refrigerated air conditioning, in the 1950s, that finally primed Phoenix for its greatest boom. Without it, the Valley of the Sun would still be an agricultural center and winter resort.

Between 1945 and 1960, more than 300 new industries moved to the Valley, most notable among them Motorola. Phoenix successfully pitched its then-clean air, a climate that would never disrupt a manufacturer's operations or transportation, its lifestyle of leisure, and probably most significant of all, Arizona's right-to-work law, passed over the bitter objections of the labor unions in 1946. Phoenix's old city government, infested with inefficiency and cronyism, had been as discouraging to executives eyeing the place as was swamp cooling, but it was frozen out by the conservative but clean and progressive Charter Government Commission. (The CGC launched Barry Goldwater's political career, successfully promoting him as a candidate for the City Council in 1949.) In 1958, the last major barrier to Phoenix's emergence was hurdled when voters statewide agreed to change the name of Arizona State College to Arizona State University. Until then, Phoenix was the only major metro area in the country lacking a university.

During these great boom years, though, Phoenix's character was frequently called into question—a process that continued even into the 1980s. Down in intellectually priggish Tucson, people groused that there was nothing going on in Phoenix except the making of money and the playing of golf. The bigger city seemed like a gawky adolescent whose growth hormones had gone berserk, but whose cultural development was stalled at potty training. Except for the Heard Museum, Phoenix had no nationally recognized cultural resources (it still doesn't), no pro sports until the 1970s, and no tangible urban atmosphere.

The outsider's view is best summed up by the Tucson newspaper editor who, a few years ago, proclaimed that "Phoenix is the turkey who shows up at your cocktail party in green polyester pants, white shoes and white belt." This vivid metaphorist is now editor of *Phoenix* magazine, where he makes more money than he ever could in Tucson.

The engine that drives the Phoenix boom today is the city's raw youth. For practical purposes, Phoenix as an urban entity is less than 50 years old, which means that only energy and determination matter, not bloodlines or connections.

"There's a competitive spirit here that's almost Darwinian," explained Michael

Lacey, editor of the liberal and aggressive *New Times* weekly. "People come out here, they create their own histories, they create their own reputations. It's not based on who your family is. Sure, Phoenix is pretty conservative, politically and morally. But entrepreneurially, things are still up for grabs here. The success of *New Times* is one indication that minds aren't necessarily made up. If what you do you do well, you can sell it to Phoenix."

There is trouble in entrepreneurial paradise, however. Intoxicated by the boom, Phoenix never got around to effectively planning its growth or managing its resources. Consequently:

Air pollution is the among the worst in the nation—so bad that in the winter, Valley motorists have to use EPA-mandated oxygenated gasoline. Even at that, on most mornings a phlegmatic yellow-brown cloud hangs over the Valley like an inverted bowl, obliterating the scenery.

Building on most of the metropolitan area's numerous mountains and buttes has never been effectively controlled. Pretentious houses encrust the slopes of landmarks such as Camelback Mountain, and developers still gouge roadways for eventual subdivisions across ridgelines and into canyons.

Water demand is outstripping the capacity of the Salt and Verde watersheds to supply it, so the metropolitan area is now counting on the Central Arizona Project, which channels water from the Colorado River uphill to Phoenix and Tucson. This may not be enough to ensure either city's survival: the Colorado, already dammed and diverted and drained to within an inch of its life, may not have enough water in it to meet CAP projections. The experts are divided.

Contemporary Phoenix, however, is behaving very much like a city with a future.

And the critical word is, at last, "city." Until the late 1980s, Phoenix never had the sensations of a big city because it had no community focus. Its downtown was a huddle of 20- to 40-story office towers with virtually no street life. Now, suddenly, there's action.

Patriots Square, a new square-block park in the heart of downtown, attracts noonday concerts and swarms of brown-baggers. The park's design, which includes a 115-foot-high (35-m) spire, inspired the most acrimonious architectural debates in Phoenix's history, drawing fusillades such as this by columnist E.J. Montini of *The Arizona Republic:* "It [the spire] will always look like the twisted remains of a fire at a lawn-furniture factory." But the controversy itself was healthy, because it demonstrated that Phoenicians finally were investing emotion in the city's heart.

In 1988, the same year that Phoenicians were hissing at each other over Patriots Square, they voted to pass a $1 billion "quality-of-life" bond issue, the largest publicly funded culture and recreation effort ever undertaken by an American city. Through the 1990s, the bond issue will give birth to a new central library, art museum, community theater, parks, and more—most of this in the central city.

Since Patriots Square in 1988 has come the Mercado, a $15 million downtown marketplace in postmodern Spanish Colonial style; America West Arena, a $90 million, 19,000-seat coliseum for the Phoenix Suns and blockbuster concerts; and Arizona Center, a $200 million downtown shopping mall and office complex with a spectacular (and typically thirsty) three-acre terraced garden.

Downtown Phoenix doesn't yet have the diversity that makes downtown San Francisco or downtown Minneapolis so lively—a great downtown needs both Woolworth's and Victoria's Secret; both fanatic street preachers and street musicians playing Mozart. But the new development has lured people back to the central city, and there is more in the works. Downtown Phoenix at last has a pulse; eventually it will work once again as the city's heart.

The fact that something as complex and important as the downtown of the nation's ninth-largest city can be turned around in just five years says something remarkable about Phoenix. It's a town on the make; it always has been.

■ SUBURBAN PHOENIX

About 15 suburbs huddle around Phoenix; the exact number is slightly vague because some towns that qualify geographically as suburbs are not at all related culturally to the mother city. For example, the little town of **Guadalupe**, squeezed between Tempe and Phoenix's South Mountain Park, is a Yaqui Indian settlement, founded in 1904 as a refugee camp. The Yaquis, indigenous to Mexico, were around that time being conscripted into forced labor by Mexican President Porfirio Diaz, and thousands gained sanctuary in Arizona. Another sanctuary on the opposite corner of the valley is **Sun City**, manufactured in 1965 as one of the first retirement villages in the nation. Sun City's population is now about 65,000, its statutes still prohibit home ownership by anyone younger than 55, and 80 percent of its registered voters are Republican. It has its own professional symphony orchestra.

Phoenix's Valley Center, at 40 stories Arizona's tallest building, mirrors the streetscape around it. But it also reflects the already overabundant sunlight.

The two most interesting suburbs are **Scottsdale** and **Tempe**. Scottsdale is wealth, resorts, sophisticated art galleries, and the most progressive community in the state with regard to preserving its natural beauty. Tempe has Arizona State University, the state's largest with 42,952 students, and a great downtown.

Scottsdale was founded as a farm village in 1888 by Winfield Scott, an Army chaplain. For about 60 years after that it was determinedly bucolic. A 1913 headline in the *Arizona Gazette*—this was classic Arizona boosterism—described it thus: "Scottsdale, [a] lovely oasis where olives and fruit vie with cotton and alfalfa in paying tribute to soil of great richness." The boosters eventually attracted enough attention to the "lovely oasis" that agriculture shrank into eclipse. Frank Lloyd Wright came in 1937 to build his winter home at the foot of the McDowell Mountains. A stream of artists followed. Dude ranches sprang up, eventually to be followed by world-class resorts. Eleanor Roosevelt, among others, came to shop. By the late 1960s, Scottsdale had international fame as a resort and art center.

Students of urban development appreciate Scottsdale for other reasons. Because land in Arizona historically was cheap, and seemingly unlimited, towns and cities typically would ooze into the horizons along spines of strip-zoned commercial development. Garish signs and billboards would line the strip, bleating for attention and generating visual cacophony. Scottsdale was the first Arizona city to attack this blight, enacting a restrictive sign ordinance in 1969. It worked: drive today along Scottsdale Road, the most important artery, and there is visual tranquility unequalled on any other main street in the state.

Scottsdale used to promote itself as "the West's most Western Town." Today, the only remnants of the frontier are the very expensive Western paintings in the galleries clustered along Fifth Avenue. There is contemporary art in the galleries, too, and a cultural center with an impressive concert series. Unfortunately, the new Scottsdale Galleria, a mammoth four-level shopping mall, has begun to change the pedestrian-friendly scale of the downtown streetscape. The numerous destination resorts seem engaged in competition to see which can devise the most exotic water gardens. Undaunted by criticism from downstate, Scottsdale still celebrates its origins as a "lovely oasis."

Tempe started life as a ferry landing on the Salt River in 1871. Its original name was Hayden's Ferry, so designated by the boat operator Charles Trumbull Hayden. A later visitor thought the landscape, punctuated with hulking gray-red buttes and groves of mesquite, reminded him of the Vale of Tempe in Greece.

Tempe's future character was ordained in 1885, when the Territorial Legislature voted to build the state's normal school, or teachers' college, in the town. That future, however, was a very long time in gestation. Tucson and graduates of its University of Arizona lobbied successfully for decades to keep the little Tempe college poor and obscure. Finally in 1958, while the legislature still cowered, a statewide referendum changed the name of the college to Arizona State University. Academic respectability and parity with the old university to the south was then inevitable, given the Valley's political muscle, but it still took another 20 years. This snip of history illustrates just how unfriendly and serious the rivalry between Tucson and metropolitan Phoenix has been.

Thanks to the university, Tempe has a more animated night life and more entertainment options than the other Valley suburbs. It also has a compact downtown district with more life in it than all the other suburbs combined—a rare urban renewal success story.

By the early 1970s, Mill Avenue, the main street, had become a strip of "hippie shops and biker bars," as Tempe residents remember it. City Hall hired a San Francisco consultant, who recommended tearing everything down and starting over. Two local architects, Ernest Nickels and Robert Hershberger, howled in outrage, and as a consequence were awarded the job of plotting a more respectful renovation themselves. They redesigned Mill Avenue, banishing the parallel parking, widening the sidewalks and planting a forest of ficus trees. Three blocks of handsome turn-of-the-century commercial buildings were restored, not demolished. ASU, at downtown's south edge, provided clientele for new businesses ranging from a Rolfing studio to contemporary furniture stores. Now the city is preparing to turn the Salt River and its flood plain, which cuts off downtown on the north, into a five-mile (eight km) linear park that is to include wildlife refuges, bike paths, water sports and even "urban fishing." As longtime mayor Harry Mitchell explained, the reason Tempe has been able to develop such amenities is that it has a sense of direction not always found in fast-growing, transient communities. "There hasn't been any real bickering or infighting in the City Council," he said. "It's been a team effort."

■ VISITING THE VALLEY

Many of the most popular Valley attractions are described in other chapters: for example, the **Desert Botanical Gardens** in "DESERTS," the **Heard Museum** in "THE FIRST ARIZONANS," **Taliesin West** in "ARTS." If a Phoenix visit has to be rushed, I would take in the **Heard Museum** in the morning, browse the galleries clustered in downtown Scottsdale in the afternoon, and climb the well-used trail to the top of **Squaw Peak**, 1,500 feet (457 m) above the valley floor, to watch the sunset and then see the city become a horizon-to-horizon blaze of light. (The latter exercise cannot be recommended in summer.) Given more time. . . .

Several art museums in the Valley are worth a visit. Most eclectic are the **Phoenix Art Museum** and **University Art Museum** at Arizona State University, and the latter is housed in a building that is itself a work of art (see "ARTS"). *New Times*, in its 1990 "Best of Phoenix" issue, bestowed "Best Museum" honors on the little-publicized **Fleischer Museum** in Scottsdale. Its permanent collection features more than 200 paintings from the California Impressionist school. The MARS **Gallery** in downtown Phoenix celebrates Hispanic art, and offers the liveliest

Phoenix bannered its boosterism as early as 1896. (Arizona Historical Society)

openings in town. Other specialized museums include the **Hall of Flame** firefighting museum, the **Champlin Fighter Museum** of combat aircraft from the first two world wars, and the **Arizona Museum of Science and Technology**.

There is more than one zoo in the Valley. Best known is the eclectic **Phoenix Zoo**, but the private **Wildlife World Zoo** in the suburban wilds of Litchfield Park claims the nation's largest collection of kangaroos and wallabies, along with other exotic species. The **Desert Botanical Gardens** features not only desert plants, but a provocative ethnobotany trail demonstrating how pre-refrigeration man coexisted with his Sonoran Desert habitat.

Phoenix's several mountain ranges are not as high as those surrounding Tucson, but they offer entertaining hiking and great views. Besides the aforementioned Squaw Peak, urban hiking enthusiasts most highly recommend the **Echo Canyon Trail** up **Camelback Mountain** (four miles/six km round trip) and the much easier **Hidden Valley Trail** (three miles/five km) in **South Mountain**. Incidentally, South Mountain Park's 16,000 acres of undeveloped desert make it the largest city-owned park in the world.

Water sports, of all things, are popular in Phoenix and environs. A traditional

Phoenix skyline at sunset. (John Drew)

warm-weather pastime is **tubing the Salt**, meaning floating down the gentle Salt River east of Phoenix in an inner tube. Boating and jet skiing also are popular on the chain of lakes created by the dams on the Salt; **Roosevelt Lake**, 50 miles (80 km) east of Phoenix, is the largest. Avoid it on weekends. In the city, there are several surfing waterparks with wave machines. Finally, golf, which in the desert is certainly a water-*using* activity, is unquestionably the Valley's most popular winter sport. At this writing, there are 105 golf courses in metropolitan Phoenix, and more are in the works.

*The 1895 Rosson House is the exuberant remnant of Victorian Phoenix.
Now a museum, it is open for tours at downtown's Heritage Square.*

T U C S O N

THERE IS SOMETHING SPECIAL, EVEN MYSTICAL, in the desert light of Tucson. Lynn Taber-Borcherdt, an artist who moved here from Chicago in 1970, explained:

"In the early works here, I began painting sharp, overexaggerated shadows. You would know what time of day it was in the painting by the shadows. Then I started noticing that sometimes when the sun was setting, and I would be on the other side of a cholla, I could see it glowing. So then I moved into making the objects in the painting glow, or almost pulsate, with light. Now my new thing is to let different colors of light bathe my paintings—the amber of twilight, the blue-green cast of moonlight on the mountainside. I'm fascinated with luminosity and iridescence. If I hadn't come to Tucson, none of this would have found its way into my work. My paintings in Chicago were dark, dark, dark, dark, dark."

Taber-Borcherdt's observation is a fresh twist on an old Tucson aphorism: you get paid in sunshine. It's true enough in economic terms—Tucson is a chronically low-wage city, but there are always plenty of people willing to stick around and take the low-wage jobs, supplementing their paychecks, in a sense, with the psychological rewards of living in a place with a (mostly) benign climate and astounding natural beauty. But the light—constantly changing, toying with the forms and textures of the mountain slopes—is a source of inspiration all by itself.

Nature has not created many more spectacular natural settings for a city. Metropolitan Tucson's 620,000 people sprawl across a desert basin defined by four mountain ranges, each lying in a cardinal direction from the city's midpoint and each exuding a distinctive character. The 9,157-foot (2,789-m) Santa Catalinas on the north are heroic and craggy, a late Beethoven sonata of gneiss and granite. The Rincons, to the east, appear smooth and rounded, as if they had been buffed. The twin peaks of the Santa Ritas, to the south, often wear caps of snow; the summit of Mount Wrightson towers to 9,453 feet (2,879 m). The small Tucson Mountains close off the western horizon like randomly sized sawteeth. Phoenix's much smaller mountains seem to poke up in the middle of the urban area, like geological afterthoughts. Tucson is contained by its mountains.

The city, sorry to report, has not lived up to its stage setting. Strip-zoned arteries six, eight, ten miles long (10, 13, 16 km), choked with billboards and speculative shopping centers, carry rivers of traffic between the mountains. There is little distinguished public architecture. In 1984 the American Institute of Architects' national magazine, *Architecture*, visited Tucson and reported, "With a few exceptions, like the tile-domed Pima County Courthouse, the buildings seem interchangeable with those in Rochester, N.Y., or Knoxville, Tenn."

Tucson's character, however, is not illustrated in its architecture. Its story is more complex than that.

The seminal event in Tucson's history as an American town was a rainstorm a couple of hundred miles away. This was in 1885, and Tucson had dispatched its delegate C. C. Stephens to the Territorial Legislature in Prescott with instructions to bring home some political pork. Stephens' stagecoach got stuck in the mud, and by the time he arrived, the legislature had parceled out the coveted insane asylum to Phoenix and the teacher's college to Tempe, leaving only the university for Tucson. In the crude frontier town this was so widely regarded as the booby prize that when Stephens came home to explain it at a public meeting, he was pelted with eggs, rotten vegetables, and a dead cat.

The University of Arizona opened for business in 1891 with one building, 36 students and six professors. Its curricula tilted heavily in the direction of mining and agriculture, the two sciences that had immediate application in nineteenth-

Sonoran-style adobe buildings still lined Tucson's Stone Avenue in the 1880s.

century Arizona. At this point there was still no high school in the territory, so the professors had to teach prerequisites as well as college courses. With such a modest beginning, it was a decade or two before Tucson forgave poor C. C. Stephens and began to feel the influence of its frontier university.

The University of Arizona today has 35,735 students, a massive research establishment, and, of course, a major intercollegiate sports juggernaut. It shapes the city's character as pervasively as the mountains have shaped its geography. Compared to Phoenix, Tucson is more liberal, more cosmopolitan, more intellectual, and more conceited—and less wealthy. The university is the city's largest employer, and the spine of its economy. When Tucson is mentioned in the national news, it is usually because of the university. The process of dendrochronology—tree-ring dating—was developed on its campus, as was the newer science of garbology—the study of contemporary human cultures by analyzing what they throw away. The university's facilities have attracted everything from a scrap of the Shroud of Turin (for testing) to a new postseason college football game, the Weiser Lock Copper Bowl.

Tucson also distances itself from Phoenix by its attitude toward the Sonoran Desert. Phoenix repudiates the desert; Tucson embraces it. There is relatively little agriculture in Tucson's history, no irrigation, and no river comparable to the Salt.

Tucson (Terrence Moore)

Tucson's "rivers" are its network of arroyos, dry most days out of the year, but periodically tearing through town on a muddy, rain-swollen rampage. Even when dry, however, these arroyos nourish what biologists call a xeroriparian habitat, a word marrying Greek and Latin roots for "dry" and "riverbank." These are linear forests of mesquite and paloverde trees and bird habitats, and they have the effect of extending tendrils of the lushest imaginable desert through the urban landscape. Reminded so frequently of the desert they live in, Tucsonans tend to be more respectful of it.

Grass lawns—a preposterous waste of water in this climate—still grow in the older central part of the city, but in many newer subdivisions grass isn't even allowed. Most Tucsonans, in fact, have learned to *hate* grass. In 1990 an uninformed Houston landscape architect planted an acre of it around the new downtown Main Library, and was immediately engulfed by monsoons of criticism. One letter to the editor, in particular, seemed to encapsulate Tucson's ultimate nightmare:

"Not too long ago Tucson was a unique, special and wonderful place. Now it just gets more like Phoenix every time we see it. . . ."

But Tucson will never be much like Phoenix, and the most important reason is that its people are, and always have been, more individualistic, more contentious, unwilling to agree on any single vision for the city. It seems as though most Tucsonans have not, for the most part, moved here in order to build a great city, but to be left alone and pursue personal dreams. They fight incessantly, and mostly they fight *against* things, such as freeways and rezonings of virgin desert land, rather than *for* things. There are more environmentalists per square mile in Tucson than anywhere else in Arizona, yet there is little support for quality-of-life urban projects. Nothing remotely like Phoenix's billion-dollar bond issue has been proposed in Tucson, and it would not pass if it were.

"I think people have moved here to get away from things: cold weather, families, commitments," former Arizona Theatre Company Director Gary Gisselman once said. He tried to schedule plays that would encourage people to think about community, but there is no evidence so far that this has borne fruit.

But is a city of 620,000 determined individualists an unproductive place? Decidedly not. The sanctuary movement to defy the U.S. Government and protect Central American refugees from deportation was born in Tucson. Biosphere II, a controversial experiment in which eight "bionauts" are spending two years in a sealed ecosystem, is just outside Tucson. And there is Lynn Taber-Borcherdt, who described the other effect Tucson has had on her art:

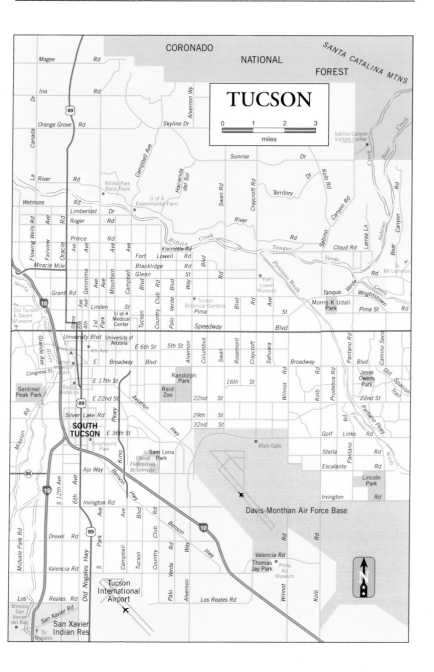

"The other thing that happened is harder to describe. The soul of my work changed. It had something to do with the quiet, the peace, the serenity, listening to the crickets, watching the hawks soar. I read a lot, thought a lot—things like 'who are we?' I turned inward, and that found its way into my paintings. In Chicago, we were always in the midst of a more externally exciting world—what gallery's opening, what's playing tonight. I came to the desert and found myself kind of alone."

■ VISITING TUCSON

Several of Tucson's major attractions are noted in other chapters: among them the **Arizona-Sonora Desert Museum, Saguaro National Monument, Mt. Lemmon,** the dramatic canyons of the **Santa Catalinas,** and **San Xavier del Bac.** If just one day is available for a visit, the two essentials are the **Desert Museum** and **Sabino Canyon** on the city's northeast edge. When more time is available . . . .

Two tiny slices of Tucson as it was in the 1870s and 1880s have survived into the present as historic districts: the **Barrio Histórico,** 13 square blocks just south of downtown on Main, Meyer and Convent avenues; and **El Presidio,** just north of downtown in the Franklin Street and Main Avenue area. Barrio Histórico has some wonderful adobe Sonoran Row houses; El Presidio illustrates, in the space of one block from Meyer to Main, the transformation of Tucson from a Mexican to an American village.

A not-quite-historic re-creation of frontier Tucson can be investigated at **Old Tucson Studios,** a movie set that has served as a Wild West town for hundreds of Westerns and TV shows. Stuntmen stage constant gunfights and robberies for tourists' entertainment; frequently visitors stumble across a movie or commercial being filmed.

Tucson's most unusual shopping street is **4th Avenue,** a five-block stretch of galleries, custom furniture builders, restaurants and oddball shops where stepping inside seems to whisk one into a time warp back to the sixties. There certainly is no better place to buy hippie clothes in Arizona.

The **University of Arizona** has numerous attractions open to the public: **Flandrau Planetarium,** the **University Museum of Art,** the **Center for Creative Photography** and the **Arizona State Museum** are the most interesting. The **UA Artist**

Series is one of the most ambitious performing-arts series in the nation, booking about 20 events annually, from Glen Campbell to major symphony orchestras.

Other museums in Tucson: the **Pima Air Museum** has a great collection of 130 historic aircraft, the most recent addition of which is an SR-71 Blackbird—the fastest jet ever built. The associated **Titan Missile Museum** is the only place in the world where the public can tour a disarmed ICBM in its underground silo. The **Tucson Museum of Art** has changing exhibits and a block of restored historic buildings. The **International Wildlife Museum**, endlessly controversial locally, displays the vast big-game animal collection of hunter C. J. McElroy in a rebarbative building modeled on a French Foreign Legion fort in sub-Saharan Chad. McElroy established the museum here because he retired in Tucson, but given the city's fierce environmentalist tilt, he could not have chosen a less hospitable place.

Twenty miles (32 km) south of Tucson is the Titan Missile Museum, the only place in the world to see a decommissioned ICBM in its original underground silo.

ARIZONA TOWNS

ARIZONA HAS TWO MAJOR CITIES AND A MORE VARIED scattering of small towns than any other state. We have desert towns, mountain towns, Native American towns, Hispanic towns, mining towns, company towns, farm towns, cow towns, border towns, retirement towns, tourist towns and ghost towns. What follows is not an all-inclusive, objective statewide stroll through them, but some personal notes on the more engaging ones.

■ BISBEE

"Bisbee—the city of foul odors and sickening smells," bitched the *Tucson Citizen* at the turn of the century. Brewery Gulch, one of its main streets, was an open sewer, "covered with a slime several inches deep and about four feet wide." Gambling and prostitution were endemic, and beds in the rooming houses were booked in shifts. The classical image of the early Bisbee copper miner is that of a man who spent eight hours underground in the mine, the next eight hours boozing and wenching, and the next eight hours sleeping it off. Certainly not everyone's lifestyle conformed to this scenario, but enough did to solidify Bisbee's status as the quintessential Western mining town.

Serious copper mining began in these hills and gulches six miles (10 km) north of the Mexican border in 1880. By 1900 Bisbee was the largest, most prosperous settlement in Arizona Territory. It was crude but at the same time remarkably cosmopolitan. The copper mines had attracted immigrants from Germany, Serbia, Italy, Ireland, Mexico, even Russia. Each ethnic group clustered in its own "town" or neighborhood. Some longtime Bisbee folk recall the charm of it all—the Germans making wine, the Serbs raising goats (their neighborhood was called "Goat Grove"), the Irish raising hell. Underground, in the mines, these people depended on each other for their lives, so they got along well. Above ground, cosmopolitan Bisbee was tense with ethnic rivalries. "You never went to the show by yourself; you always took someone with you," said Les Williams, a retired miner. "Each 'town' had its own gang. We stole burros from each other, we'd play baseball with each other, then we'd fight after the games."

One group never entered Bisbee's churning ethnic stew: an unwritten law held that no "Chinaman" could stay in town overnight. Behind this lay a morbid reason. In early Bisbee, widows of men killed in mine accidents sometimes would eke out a living by taking in laundry, and the white citizenry feared competition from the Chinese.

The mining era ended in Bisbee in 1975. It had been the town's sole industry, and the economic shock waves were enormous. Houses tumbled onto the market for as little as $800, and that attracted a wave of artists, bohemians, and assorted dropouts. Bisbee's "hippie era," as older townspeople disdainfully called it, lasted about a decade. Eventually one of the "hippies" turned 30, opened a restaurant and became mayor; he now runs a bed and breakfast.

Today the town still has some bohemians, many serious artists, wonderful Italianate Victorian architecture, no industry, and an utterly seductive, delightful spirit. Bisbee is Aspen turned inside-out, kicked into a time warp and trapped in a happy reverse universe devoid of traffic lights, designer labels or pretentious boutiques. Bisbee is a town where one can walk the narrow, decaying, mountainside streets in the evening and hear someone practicing Bach fugues on a piano in questionable tune, or stop into "Bisbee's One-Book Bookstore" downtown, where a retired plasterer named Walter Swan has sold thousands of his self-published memoirs of growing up near Bisbee in the 1920s. Bisbee, more than any other town in Arizona, is a place in which to re-invent oneself; the presence of 6,207 people doing just that makes it the most fascinating small town to visit in Arizona.

Visiting Bisbee: Most visitors will enjoy the tours of the underground **Copper Queen Mine** and the enormous **Lavender Open Pit Mine**, guided by retired miners themselves. Bisbee also hosts an impressive number of annual events. The town's steep hills make April's La Vuelta de Bisbee one of the world's most harrowing professional bicycle races. Spring's Wine at the Mine festival is more a colossal community block party than a serious wine tasting (no one actually spits out the wine). Visitors to Bisbee at any time should bring a camera; the colors, textures, and historic buildings of the town are a photographer's dream.

■ TOMBSTONE

No newspaper ever wore a more memorable masthead than the famous *Tombstone Epitaph*. Tombstone, in its silver-boom prime of the early 1880s, was the West's most notoriously violent town. While its history has been embellished by Hollywood as well as popular historians, it was undeniably a place in which men lived fast and died in trivial quarrels. The killing was common enough that the *Epitaph* ran its accounts of the everyday grim-reaping under a standing headline: "Death's Doings." Lawlessness was abundant enough that in 1882 it even attracted the notice of President Chester Arthur, who threatened to send in the Army. Hearing that, the *Epitaph*, in the finest tradition of Arizona boosterism, ran an editorial ridiculing Arthur and insisting that "We were never in a more peaceable community than Tombstone and law and order is absolute." In the three months preceding that editorial, the Epitaph had chronicled eight killings.

It was a uniquely colorful town, a melange of adventurers, drunks, whores, rustlers, honest working stiffs and wealthy sophisticates. The silver mines were throwing off enough money that Tombstone built ambitious show halls and imported vaudeville and serious theater. At one point there were 110 liquor licenses in town, but Tombstone also boasted, according to historian John Myers, "the best food between New Orleans and San Francisco." The 1887 Thanksgiving menu from the Maison Doree Restaurant listed these entrees:

Papillote
Paté Financiere
Saddle of Lamb à la Milanese
[And, lest anyone forget where he was . . .]
Buffalo Tongue

But Tombstone has secured enduring fame not for its culture, but for all that flying lead. The shootout at the OK Corral in 1881 remains the most notorious gunfight of all time.

The complicated prologue to the shootout was essentially a struggle for political spoils in newly created

Tombstone was one tough town, as the tombstones at Boot Hill explain.

Cochise County. On one side were Sheriff Johnny Behan and the Clanton clan, ranchers who moonlighted as cattle rustlers and harbored stagecoach robbers. The (relatively) good guys were U.S. Marshal Wyatt Earp, his brothers Virgil and Morgan, and the infamous alcoholic gunfighter "Doc" Holliday. On the afternoon of October 26, the Earps and Holliday strode purposefully into the vacant lot at Fremont and 3rd Street, where five young members of the Clanton gang were rumored to be looking for a fight. According to later testimony by Ike Clanton, Wyatt Earp shoved his pistol into Clanton's belly and growled, "You son of a bitch, you can have a fight." Clanton turned white and fled, pistols and shotguns began blazing, and in about 30 seconds—Wyatt Earp's estimate—three of the Clanton men lay dying and Virgil and Morgan Earp had been seriously wounded.

The story doesn't end there, and the aftermath tells much about the nature of life and justice in frontier Tombstone. The Earps and Holliday faced a hearing on murder charges, and were cleared. Two months later, a midnight marksman tried to take out Virgil Earp, but succeeded only in crippling his left arm for life. Three months after that, an assassin did kill Morgan Earp. Wyatt, operating well outside the law on the trail of vengeance, gunned down three of the men he suspected of killing his brother, then left Cochise County for good.

Visiting Tombstone: This is a tourist town today, making a living from its historic infamy. The restored **Crystal Palace Saloon**, among others, is open for business. **Helldorado Days** every October includes a parade, gunfight reenactments, and in several recent years, visits by Edward Earp, cousin of Wyatt. **Allen Street**, once lined with bars, casinos and cathouses, has been beautifully restored; it has served as a set for Japanese crews filming samurai Westerns. The original **Cochise County Courthouse**, built in 1882, is now a state historic park. It is the most sophisticated piece of Victorian neo-classical architecture in

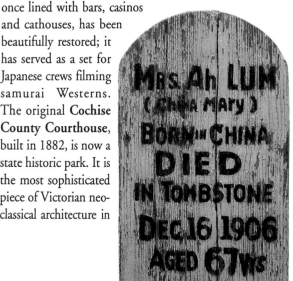

Architecturally, the Cochise County Courthouse exuded order and dignity—qualities hard to find anywhere else in Tombstone.

the state—an anomaly to ponder while listening to the reenacted gunfights echoing in the street two blocks away.

■ TUBAC

This lovely unincorporated village in the lee of the Santa Rita Mountains is the oldest non-Indian settlement in Arizona, a place redolent with history. Several times in its first 150 years of existence it was a locus of the conflict between European and Native American civilization in the New World.

Tubac was established as a *visita*, or chapel served by an itinerant priest, around 1726—that, at any rate, is the date of the first recorded baptisms by one Fr. Agustín de Campos. The next generation was a time of increasing tension in the upper Pima Indian lands (the *Pimería Alta*), however, with not only more Jesuit missionaries but also Spanish silver miners flooding in. The European attitude was summed up in the term *gente de razon*—"people of reason"—which the Spanish used in census documents to describe themselves, as opposed to the unenlightened (even if freshly baptized) native *bárbaros*. In 1751 the Pimas revolted, killing two priests and more than 100 ranchers and miners, and burning churches—including the one at Tubac. The following year the Spanish established the presidio of Tubac, their first permanent military presence in Arizona.

The fifty soldiers stationed with their families at Tubac succeeded in quieting the Pimas, but the Apaches proved to be the presidio's doom. In 1774 Tubac's commander, Juan Bautista de Anza, made his famous expedition to open a route to California and established the settlement that would become San Francisco. Two years later the Tubac garrison was moved to Tucson where it could more effectively protect the route. Thus disarmed, Tubac was repeatedly raided, abandoned and resettled. Journalist J. Ross Browne, who passed through Tubac in 1864, described it in the most pathetic terms: ". . . harassed on both sides by Apaches and Mexicans and without hope of future protection, the inhabitants of Tubac for the last time have abandoned the town, and thus it has remained ever since, a melancholy spectacle of ruin and desolation."

Eventually Tubac did rise again, phoenix-like; the grasslands of the surrounding Santa Cruz Valley seemed ideal for ranching. Then in 1948, a nationally known artist named Dale Nichols established an art school in Tubac, and even though it lasted only a year, it placed Tubac on the map as an art center.

The unincorporated village is charming, slow-paced and unpretentious, with some 50 galleries and boutiques and a state historical park with exhibits on the settlement's long history. Prices for art are substantially lower than in Arizona's other major art centers, Scottsdale and Sedona. One gallery owner, however, sounded an alarm: while the number of galleries in Tubac is growing, the number of working artists is dwindling. "The cost of housing is climbing out of their reach," he said.

Visiting Tubac: Important events are the annual Cinco de Mayo (May 5) fiesta and the **Tubac Festival of the Arts** in February. Many shops close for the summer. Four miles south, the ruin of the 1822 mission of **San José de Tumacácori**, now a national monument, is open every day.

Jesus with the crown of thorns at San Xavier del Bac.

Lonely graves lie behind the mission of Tumácacori.

■ PRESCOTT

"Norman Rockwell America," the *Los Angeles Times* once called it. "For those of us who grew up in bland, instant slurbs, Prescott is a glimpse of a childhood we might have chosen instead, had anyone thought to ask," pined the *Tucson Citizen.* When *Arizona Highways* dedicated a full issue to Prescott (August 1985), its cover headline read "Prescott: Everybody's Hometown."

Prescott, a small city of 25,773, is indeed a gentle, civilized and picturesque place, and its collection of prim Victorian homes—more of them, by far, than anywhere else in Arizona—inevitably triggers these wistful lines from visiting writers. Add a near-perfect mile-high climate with four distinct seasons, none of them harsh, and Prescott seems like everyone's choice for an ideal place to live. Of course there is a catch: no industry. It's tough to earn a living in Prescott.

The town was founded, curiously, as a consequence of the Civil War. President Lincoln had designated Arizona a territory in 1863 and dispatched his appointed governor, John G. Goodwin, to set up a government. En route Goodwin heard that there was a nucleus of Confederate sympathizers at Tucson, the presupposed capital. The gubernatorial party went instead to Fort Whipple, an army post in northern Arizona, and in 1864 wisely founded the capital of Prescott on politically virgin ground.

Prescott lost the capital to Tucson just three years later (eventually it migrated yet again to Phoenix), but nearby gold mining and ranching delivered a boom to the town anyway. It became as legendary for drinking as Tombstone for gunfighting; by the early 1900s there were about 40 saloons lining Montezuma Street, still known today as "Whiskey Row." In *Roadside History of Arizona*, Arizona historian Marshall Trimble swears that, "The macho custom of thirsty cowboys in off the range was to start their binge, or 'whizzer' as they called it, at the Kentucky Bar and take a drink in every bar all the way to the Depot House, thirty-nine saloons away." Forty drinks!

There remain a few token historic bars on Whiskey Row, and on Saturday nights they sound boisterous enough to convince passersby that at least a sliver of the tradition endures.

Visiting Prescott: The excellent **Sharlot Hall Museum** sprawls through several historic buildings and details the history of Prescott and Arizona Territory. The surrounding **Prescott National Forest** is laced with delightful mountain hiking trails; ask for a map at the Forest Service office in town. No other Arizona town of its size seems to have as many festivals and annual events as Prescott. A sampling: Territorial Days (crafts, entertainment and historic home tours—June), Frontier Days and World's Oldest Rodeo (July), Bluegrass Festival (July). Horse racing season at Prescott Downs is from late May to late August.

To understand the enduring charm of Prescott, simply walk the Victorian neighborhoods that stretch about six blocks in each direction from downtown. In these neighborhoods, domestic life still spills from house out to street; people lounge on their cool porches, greeting strangers as well as neighbors. On a winter evening, as a light snow slowly blankets the town, families walk downtown under umbrellas to stroll and throw snowballs in the park surrounding the county courthouse. Norman Rockwell, indeed.

■ SEDONA

"There are only two places in the world I want to live," Max Ernst, the German-born surrealist painter who emigrated to Arizona in the 1940s, told his friends. "Paris and Sedona."

Ernst built a house in the lee of the red rocks of Sedona; he was one of many thousands who have been enchanted by the place. Another typical Sedona story was that of the New York stockbroker who flew in on a visit in 1973, fell instantly in love with the rocks, and bought a house the next day. Impulsive? "No," he said. "Impulsive would be the same day." The famed jazz drummer Louis Bellson, who appeared at the Jazz on the Rocks festival, looked up at the great red buttes towering 500 to 2,000 feet (152 to 609 m) over the town and spoke for his wife, the legendary Pearl Bailey, who was ill at home. "If Pearly was here," Bellson said, "She would say, 'God lives here.'"

Maybe God does: the landscape certainly is supernal.

Bell Rock, Courthouse Butte, Capitol Butte, Bear Mountain—these erosion-sculpted rocks seem almost to be alive. They change color and character almost hourly. In a gray, woolly fog they seem to float, eerily, like velvet ghosts. Under a midmorning sun they can be a pale and cool violet, then as the day burns on they shift into the red and orange regions of the spectrum. After sunset, when the fire colors have burned out, the rocks turn the color of rust (which is what they are, on the surface) against a violet sky, and all their crevasses and canyons blacken into impenetrable, ominous mystery. It is the perfect stage set for a production of Wagner's *Götterdämmerung*—"Twilight of the Gods"—in a production staged by the gods themselves.

The town of Sedona has a short but intriguing history. It was founded in 1902 by a young Missouri couple, Carl and Sedona Schnebly. Beginning in the 1960s it became an art colony, and in the 1970s it exploded with retirees. In the early 1980s Page Bryant, a psychic, claimed to have divined four metaphysical vortices in the red rocks around it, and Sedona also became a New Age mecca. In 1987 the Harmonic Convergence drew at least 5,000 people to town, a few of whom willingly paid $75 for tickets to go sit on Bell Rock at the moment that it was supposed to depart for the galaxy of Andromeda. For the most part, however, the New Age crowd in Sedona has proven to be quiet, unobtrusive and simply searching for ways to heal the earth and its inhabitants.

Art remains Sedona's prime industry. Out of a population of 7,657 there are an estimated 300 professional artists in town, some 30 galleries, and an annual out-

Sculptor and rancher Marguerite Brunswig Staude commissioned Sedona's Chapel of the Holy Cross in 1953; she called it "a spiritual fortress so charged with God that it spurs man's spirit godward!" (Kerrick James)

(opposite) Oak Creek and Cathedral Rock, two of Sedona's loveliest attractions. (Kerrick James)

door sculpture exhibition on the banks of Oak Creek. In some inexplicable way, the Red Rocks are involved in all this. Touring the galleries, the visitor will notice that although there is a plentiful variety of art, there is seldom anything combative, confrontational or unyieldingly baffling. Jim Ratliff, owner of one of Sedona's prime contemporary galleries, said it isn't simple conservatism. There is an energy in red rock country, he explained; he doesn't know what it is, but he believes it is real, and that somehow it fuels the creative process.

"But it can only be used in a positive way," he said. "If someone tries to use that energy to create something negative, they don't stay around. They have to go somewhere else. The red rocks spit them right out of here."

Visiting Sedona: An essential stop is **Tlaquepaque**, a fetching collection of art galleries and boutiques built in the fashion of an eighteenth-century Spanish village. The Red Rocks must be explored at close hand, of course, and the best way is on foot. An excellent trail map, entitled *Experience Sedona*, is available at local bookstores and boutiques. Sedona firms also offer llama treks (the llamas carry packs, not riders) and jeep tours. Jazz aficionados who think their music is naturally a creature of the night, properly played only in smoky nightclubs, invariably are converted by Sedona's **Jazz on the Rocks** festival. It's a day-long September lawn party featuring stars as bright as Diane Schuur and the Count Basie Orchestra, and in the years since its 1982 inauguration, it has become Arizona's premier music festival. Tickets always sell out; order early.

■ LAKE HAVASU CITY

On its face, this appeared a truly absurd scene: a gaggle of sun-baked British tourists aboard an imitation sternwheeler named the *Dixie Belle*, sailing past a fake British village under the London Bridge on a man-made lake in the Mojave Desert.

The one American aboard wondered aloud whether any of the Britons found this just a touch silly. Three replies:

Julia Smyth: "A lot of people felt upset when London Bridge left London. It'd be the same if someone took your Golden Gate, wouldn't it? But all of us who've seen it here have found it quite lovely."

George Griffith: "It's wonderful; it's as if you've taken us back in time. When we go into a shop in England now we're bombarded with such horrible music. Here it's very quiet and pleasant."

Peter Penrose: "It's fantastic what you Americans can do. Where you don't have any history, you just make it."

In Penrose's few words is the story of Lake Havasu and the small, young city of 23,506 on its eastern shore. Until 1938, the year Parker Dam was completed downstream, there was no lake here—just the ruddy Colorado slinking its way through the parched Mojave Desert. The town dribbled into existence a couple of decades later. Its famous attraction, the London Bridge, went up in 1971. When the bridge arrived as a kit of 33,000 tons of Dartmoor and Aberdeen granite stones, there was nothing for it to span, so a channel was dredged at the edge of the lake, thereby manufacturing an island.

The town and the bridge were the brainchildren of California chainsaw magnate Robert McCulloch, who moved his factory to Lake Havasu in 1964. According to local legend, McCulloch and his partner, C.V. Wood Jr., were watching television one evening when Johnny Carson noted that the obsolete London Bridge, built in 1824, was for sale. McCulloch turned to Wood and said, "Let's buy it." They did, for $2.4 million.

McCulloch's purchase drew international ridicule at the time—Britons in particular were incensed—but it turned out to be a remarkably canny purchase. It became the second biggest tourist draw in Arizona (after the Grand Canyon) and brought a constellation of supporting attractions, from an English heraldry shop to speedboat regattas. McCulloch died in 1977, and 10 years later his chainsaw factory, which at its peak had employed 1,800, moved to Tucson. Without tourism, Lake Havasu City would have vanished as quickly as a puddle in the Mojave Desert. McCulloch's flight of whimsy, the London Bridge, saved the town from the flight of McCulloch's factory.

Visiting Lake Havasu City: Fishing enthusiasts face a dilemma here. The best months for fishing the lake's bass, crappie, catfish and bluegill are May through September, but these are truly hot times in the Mojave Desert. Lake Havasu City's average May daily high is 95.3 F (35.1 C); July is 108.6 F (42.5 C); September is 102.5 F (39.1 C). Early mornings on the lake are reasonably cool, of course, but what does one do the rest of the day?

(following pages) Exotic Lake Havasu—a man-made lake, an imitation sternwheeler, a fake English village, and the real London Bridge.

The rest of the year at Lake Havasu is very pleasant (January's average high is 67.3 F/19.6 C) for anyone not frustrated by the uninterested fish. Winter boating is a popular pastime, and the major local festival is **London Bridge Days** (with a British theme, of course), held in October. The **London Bridge** itself is more than a curio (or Arizona's heaviest antique, as some wags have called it). Look closely for the many pock marks on its stones; these are the mementos of Nazi fighters strafing the bridge.

■ FLAGSTAFF

Except for the winter and spring winds, which can be ferocious, this town of 45,403 enjoys the best location in the state. It curls around the southern foot of 12,643-foot (3,851-m) Humphreys Peak, the highest point in Arizona. In winter, people flock to Flagstaff to ski; in summer the perspiring lemmings swarm up from Phoenix and Tucson to escape the heat. So many geologic and prehistoric attractions cluster around Flagstaff that one suspects the town was founded as a tourist magnet (it wasn't). The ruins of Walnut Canyon and Wupatki lie respectively 11 and 25 miles (18 and 40 km) away. Oak Creek Canyon creases into the plateau 10 miles (16 km) south; the Grand Canyon is 80 miles (128 km) north. Sunset Crater, looking like the mother volcano to a brood of baby cones, is 15 miles (24 km) out of town; Meteor Crater, the best preserved crater on the planet, is 45 (72 km).

Flagstaff will regret this spectacular setting only if a new or reactivated volcano someday appears on its horizon. It could happen; Sunset Crater last erupted in A.D. 1065—a few moments ago in geologic time.

Like so many other Arizona settlements, Flagstaff hasn't made the best of its lovely physical setting. The main commercial arteries through town, Milton and Santa Fe (the old Route 66), are jammed with signs and billboards clamoring for attention. Off these streets, however, Flag's green, forested neighborhoods and cool, pine-scented air make it seem like a wonderfully enticing place.

Flagstaff's first permanent resident was a rancher and prospector named Thomas F. McMillan, who homesteaded a ranch in 1876. When the railroad arrived in 1881, both cattle and timber industries boomed. Tourists and astronomers followed. In 1894 Percival Lowell and his wife founded and personally supervised construction of the hat-shaped Lowell Observatory on a mesa just west of town. Lowell planned to map Mars; he theorized that its recently discovered patchwork of lines was a canal system to carry water from its polar icecaps to the arid red deserts. Lowell died in 1916 unable to prove that the Martian lines were in fact canals, but he correctly predicted the existence of a ninth planet from observing the minute wobble of Uranus. In 1930, Clyde W. Tombaugh discovered that planet, Pluto, with the Lowell scope.

Flagstaff's most important institution today is the University of Northern Arizona, which has an enrollment of 16,000 students. Since 1965 the city also has staged the **Flagstaff Festival of the Arts**. Its prime attraction is an excellent festival orchestra whose players are drawn from symphony orchestras that are dormant during the summer—something that Flagstaff decidedly is not.

Visiting Flagstaff: A high priority should be to see the Sinagua ruins of **Walnut Canyon** and **Wupatki National Monument** (see "THE FIRST ARIZONANS"). **The Museum of Northern Arizona** also demands a visit. Guided tours of **Lowell Observatory** are conducted weekdays at 1:30 p.m. The **Flagstaff Festival of the Arts** consumes most of July and early August, offering classical music, art films, dance and professional theater. **Fairfield Snowbowl** on the San Francisco Peaks offers Arizona's highest-elevation skiing, with runs dropping from 11,200 feet (3,412 m).

■ YUMA

Poor Yuma. Possibly no small city on the continent has suffered such consistently bad press for so long a time.

J. Ross Browne wrote of Yuma in 1864: "Everything dries: wagons dry; men dry; chickens dry; there is no juice left in anything living or dead by the close of summer. . . . Chickens hatched at this season, old Fort Yumers say, come out of the shell ready cooked; bacon is eaten with a spoon; and butter must stand for an hour in the sun before the flies become dry enough for use. . . ."

In 1882, Charles H. Phelps wrote a travelogue in verse that must surely rank among the nastiest poems ever published about a town. An excerpt:

> Through all ages baleful moons
> Glared upon thy whited dunes;
> And malignant, wrathful suns
> Fiercely drank thy streamless runs. . . .

It continues today, with hapless Yuma still suffering from missiles of hostile wit lobbed from afar. In 1984, Phoenix's satirical cartoonist, Bob Boze Bell, drew a two-page spread in the *New Times* weekly, proposing some fresh civic slogans to the Chamber of Commerce: "Join the YUMAn race—out of town" Or: "You don't live in Yuma, YUMArinate." The Chamber has responded, gamely enough, with brochures that begin by asking: "Where's Your Sense of Yuma?"

Yuma came into existence because of the California gold rush. To reach California and its promise of wealth, prospectors somehow had to cross the Colorado River—a much more formidable barrier than it is today, with five states now sucking water out of it. A U.S. Army report in 1846 estimated it was 600 feet (183 m) wide at its narrowest. By 1850, both Indian and Anglo entrepreneurs were operating ferry services, and, as happened at so many other points of commingling, friction ensued. The Army established Fort Yuma on the California side of the river (although it was under the Arizona command) and subdued the eponymous Yuma tribe. The wagon traffic increased, and a civilian settlement, originally christened Colorado City, began to grow across the river from the fort.

Modern petroglyphs at Chloride by R. Purcell.

(opposite) Paloverde (green stick), the state tree of Arizona, is a graceful part of the Sonoran Desert landscape. (Kerrick James)

Culture in territorial Yuma: the Philharmonic Band, 1895. (Arizona Historical Society)

It is not difficult to understand why Yuma had public relations woes. In territorial days it was the hottest and driest place Anglos had yet attempted to settle in Arizona, and with San Diego 170 miles (272 km) off over one treeless horizon and Tucson 220 (352) in the opposite direction, it was easily the most remote as well. In 1876 it won its second industry, the Territorial Prison, which was essentially carved into a bluff overlooking the river. Eventually inmates from around the country were shipped here; they termed it, without humor or affection, the "Hell Hole." Think about it: nine-by-eight-foot cells, (three-by-two-m) with two tiers of three bunks each, one bucket for a latrine (emptied once a day), and 120-degree (49 C) summer temperatures. By the time it closed in 1909, 3,069 convicts had slowly simmered through their sentences there, and only 26 of them—fewer than one per year—ever successfully escaped.

Modern Yuma, a city of 56,473, has managed to make an asset of its improbable climate. About 40,000 snowbirds, most from the Northwest and Canada, descend on the Yuma area every winter. Questioned by *Arizona Highways* on why they chose Yuma over Phoenix or Tucson, most cited the small-city friendliness and relaxed pace. The San Diego Padres play their spring training schedule in Yuma's Desert Sun Stadium, and the extreme rarity of freezes in this very low

Pearl Hart (with guitar) was one of Yuma Territorial Prison's celebrated inmates; she did hard time from 1899 to 1902 for robbing a mail stage. (Arizona Historical Society)

desert basin (elev. 141 feet/43 m) makes it an ideal location for citrus farming. In fact, if Arizona had huddled all its agriculture along the Colorado instead of trying to force the central deserts to bloom, the state would not have a serious water problem today, and the federal government would not have spent $3.6 billion creating that uphill river known as the Central Arizona Project. That, and not this quiet and unpretentious town on the riverbank, qualifies as YUMAn folly.

Visiting Yuma: The **Territorial Prison**, now a state historical park, is a captivating attraction—an illustration of how the low Sonoran Desert environment could formally function as punishment. As one Arizona Historical Society employee said, this prison is "the bleakest place in Arizona."

SPRING TRAINING

For the most concentrated dose of Arizona Spring Training fever, take a hotel room in Scottsdale, a suburb of Phoenix. Preferably, find a hotel (like the Safari) that also houses the players of one of the eight or so major league teams that base their training operations in the Phoenix area. Then again, it isn't really necessary; after all, you're pretty close to most of the action just being in Scottsdale.

Within a few blocks of the major hotels on Scottsdale Boulevard is Scottsdale Stadium, where the San Francisco Giants play their games. A 20-minute drive will pass at least three other ball parks, one of which is sure to have a game. It's a good idea to order your tickets before you even go to Arizona; spring baseball has become awfully fashionable these past few years.

Several other baseball stadiums lie within 45 minutes of Scottsdale. The town of Chandler is the cool-weather home of the Milwaukee Brewers, and Mesa is home to the Chicago Cubs. The Oakland Athletics play in Phoenix at Phoenix Municipal Stadium and the California Angels are close by at Tempe Diablo Stadium.

Two hours down Interstate 10 is Tucson, where the Colorado Rockies hold forth in a very charming, old-fashioned ball park. If you follow the San Diego Padres, they train in Yuma, in the southwestern part of the state.

In addition to the regularly scheduled major league games, you should consider other, potentially more intimate baseball experiences. You can call the team offices to learn when the "B" games are scheduled. Usually they are played in the mornings at smaller facilities that allow real contact with the younger players. (As a rule, you won't find too many front line players at these games.) You can also search out training fields where teams teach technique and hold intra-squad minor league scrimmages (e.g., on Indian School road in Scottsdale, or near Tempe Diablo Stadium).

After the game, or for dinner, try the Pink Pony on Scottsdale Boulevard, traditional stomping ground of real baseball people but now more of a hot-spot for visitors and fans. The steaks are good and the bar is hopping. Not too far away is Don and Charley's, which is "home" to Cubs and Giants and their fans. The waitresses are often wives or girlfriends of players, and they can talk baseball knowledgeably.

Outside of Scottsdale, there is good food and lots of baseball life at Avanti's, in Phoenix. Be sure to make reservations at these places, as they're crowded all spring.

When you come, expect the weather to be good and hot. Bring your swimsuit, sun block, and extra-dark shades. Plan on renting a car (a pink Cadillac convertible is the automobile of choice), because Phoenix is laid out like Los Angeles and public transportation is inconvenient.

— Gene Seltzer, owner of the Riverside Pilots in Riverside, California.

Oakland A's pitcher Dennis Eckersley warms up during spring training. (Kerrick James)

VISITING MEXICO

"Sonora is where civilization ends and *carne asada* begins," wrote the Mexican philosopher José Vasconcelos. Sonora is the Mexican state adjoining Arizona. Carne asada (literally "roasted beef," although it is normally grilled) is one of its great attractions—along with sensational seafood, not-yet-spoiled beaches, folk-baroque Spanish missions and, once away from the border, warm and hospitable people.

Tourists in Southern Arizona invariably visit **Nogales**, the industrial Mexican border city 60 miles (96 km) south of Tucson. Generally they travel nowhere else in Sonora. This is a mistake.

Nogales ("Walnuts" in translation) is neither historic, charming, nor quaint. It is a teeming chemical reaction between an affluent nation and the edge of the Third World. The tragedy is that the *norteamericano* who becomes acquainted with Mexico through Nogales (or any other border city) not only will misunderstand the country, but also may leave with unwarranted prejudices. A few years ago, shopping in Nogales was trying to negotiate the best price on a painting of Jesus or Elvis on black velvet. In the last few years, many shops have gone upscale, offering impressive Mexican folk art, crafts, and imports. Their sheer variety is almost entertainment enough; in one small shop shoppers may find: leather duffel bags, fake Toltec icons, margarita glasses, statues of St. Francis of Assisi, and double basses. Bargain prices, for the most part, are history. Most of the tourist shops are along the first three blocks of Calle Obregón, up to its intersection with Calle Aguirre. Obregón continues south for about five miles, however, with shops mainly serving Mexican clientele. These are interesting, too.

A different experience awaits the visitor in Sonora's interior. There is little developed tourism in the state, so visitors see Mexican society as it really is—the unrestrained passion of the crowd at a semi-pro *beisbol* game; the old itinerant tool sharpener who plods through the residential streets of Hermosillo, the capital, playing melodies on his panpipes. Sonorans are outgoing and curious about foreigners, and it's easy to strike up conversations in the streets (providing you speak some Spanish—few Sonorans, other than those who work in the tourist shops and hotels, have studied English).

Rocky Point and **Guaymas**, two shrimping towns on the Gulf of California, offer superb seafood in unpretentious restaurants at prices that are at most half what one would pay on the coasts of California or Texas. **San Carlos**, adjacent to Guaymas, also has excellent restaurants and seaside resorts. San Carlos, however, is mostly a colony of U.S. expatriates and weekend condo dwellers, and exudes little of the character of a Mexican town.

Far off any beaten track is the quiet village of **Tubutama**, which is worth visiting just to see the folk-baroque mission church of **San Pedro y San Pablo de Tubutama**, built in 1788. Its facade is an architectural carnival of spirals, quatrefoils, sculpted seashells and flowers, and even a pair of angels with the bodies of children and the faces of old men, floating heavenward and carrying what appear to be chickens. It is naive and ambitious at once, and it radiates a sensation of perfect innocence and purity. There are no hotels or even restaurants in Tubutama.

Alamos is a seductively beautiful Spanish colonial town that grew out of the wealth generated by the nearby Sierra Madre silver mines in the 1700s. Scores of restored mansions line its narrow, tunnel-like streets, their rhythmic Romanesque colonnades forming a kind of visual music that serenades the stroller. The central plaza and courtyards of the mansions are awash in bougainvillea, jasmine and the poplar trees (*alamos*) that gave the town its name. Most of the mansions have been restored by Americans, a few as hotels and restaurants. Alamos is no more typical of Sonora today than is Nogales, its cultural opposite, but it is lovely.

U.S. citizens need no passport or visa for visits to Mexican border towns unless the stay exceeds 72 hours. For visits to the interior, take proof of U.S. citizenship (passport, birth certificate or voter registration) to Mexican customs at any border crossing and obtain a visa and *turista* permit for the car. Ideally, this process should take only a few minutes.

But should one drive? There are some difficulties. First, most U.S. auto insurance companies do not insure policyholders driving into the interior of Mexico; supplemental insurance must be bought from a company specializing in it (see the Yellow Pages in Tucson or Nogales). Major U.S. auto rental companies do not allow their cars to be taken into Mexico, although a handful of local firms do. Supplies of unleaded gasoline (*sin plomo*) are undependable, although the Mexican government is working to improve the situation: highway signs now advise where it will be available ahead. As for the issue of road safety, it depends on the individual's level of comfort in coping with unfamiliar situations. Mexican traffic may appear anarchic to *norteamericanos*, but at least everything happens in slow motion. In my experience, it is easier than driving in Europe.

For those not wanting to drive in Sonora, there is an inexpensive train linking Nogales, Hermosillo, Guaymas and Ciudad Obregon. Tickets may be purchased through Arizona travel agencies specializing in Mexican travel or at the Nogales, Sonora, train station. There also are some organized tours that travel by bus. The best-known are the delightful three-day Kino Mission Tours conducted every fall and spring by the non-profit *Southwest Mission Research Center* in Tucson (tel. 621-6278). This tour visits the historic mission churches at **San Ignacio, Tubutama, Oquitoa, Pitiquito and Caborca.** The missions are wonderful and these small towns, all but untouched by tourism, represent the real Mexico.

A glum-looking donkey awaits its next assignment in Nogales, Sonora.

A R T S

TELEVISION AND MARKETING, claims conventional wisdom, have almost finished transforming the United States into one homogenized, continental village. From Seattle to Miami our skylines cut similar profiles, our symphony orchestras play the same music and shudder through identical financial crises, and artists everywhere pursue the same bankable trends.

This guidebook dissents. The arts in Arizona are and always will be unique because they are driven by engines that are uniquely our own: our history, which still lies close to the surface. Our simmering stew of three distinct human cultures. Our landscapes. Our light. These are cultural and environmental imperatives that always will influence art—for the better, usually.

The sculpture of Prescott artists Rebecca Davis and Roger Asay is one example. They make intellectually challenging art out of the everyday stuff of the Arizona environment: pebbles, boulders, saplings, trees. It isn't just avant-garde kitsch. On the south shore of the little lake in Tucson's Reid Park, Davis and Asay have planted five pecan trees—trees stripped of all leaves, bark and small branches, sanded smooth, painted five different tones of red and, finally, turned upside down. They are as sensuous, in their own curious way, as Renoir's sun-dappled nudes. "We inverted them," Asay explained, "to take them out of context so people don't just dismiss them as bare trees. What we hope is that people will begin to see the trees differently, and more intently." People do.

In 1989, New Mexico architect Antoine Predock attempted an astoundingly deep and intellectually thorny abstraction of both Arizona's culture and landscape in his design for a single building: the Nelson Fine Arts Center at Arizona State University. Its complex profile, a ramble of colliding boxes, triangles, terraces and plazas, resembles at once a Hopi pueblo and a desert mountain range. Its color, a washed-out gray-purple stucco, was borrowed from a rock the architect found on a nearby hill. The building's story line, as Predock has explained it to baffled visitors, is a cultural cross-section of the site: the gurgling pools in its underground lobby recall the canals of the vanished Hohokam, while a flat panel jutting into the sky suggests an endangered artifact of the modern West, the drive-in movie screen. It is a mystical and magnificent building, and *The New York Times* architecture critic, Paul Goldberger, was exactly on target when he wrote that it illustrates "how it is possible for a piece of architecture to be deeply ingrained in the architectural traditions of a place, yet unlike anything we have seen before."

Traditions of a place. This is what is to be most cherished in the arts of Arizona.

■ ARCHITECTURE

Arizona is the only state in which the oldest functioning architecture is also the best. This is a prodigious tribute to the unknown designer of San Xavier del Bac, but also a raincloud over the résumés of all the architects since. This mission was built 200 years ago, probably by itinerant Spanish craftsmen and bewildered native laborers, in an Apache-beseiged outpost a thousand miles from any building of comparable ambition. And yet architects even today seem helpless to do much except sigh in envy, bow in humility, and muddle on making lesser buildings.

San Xavier was intended, wrote the captain of the Spanish presidio at Tucson in 1804, "to attract by its loveliness the unconverted [Indians] beyond the frontier." Ironically, this was both naivete and arrogance on the founding Jesuits' part; the Tohono O'odham people's concept of God was and still is rooted in nature, not at the altar of a transplanted Spanish baroque church.

But the builders spared no expense on their magic show. The church is built in the traditional cruciform plan, crowned with two belfries and a bravura dome, and decorated with a portal of such architectural sizzle that the eye hardly knows where to alight. This portal has everything—spires, scrolls, seashell motifs, eggs, arches, saints, even a cartoon: a cat and a rodent crouch on opposing scrolls just below the parapet, glaring at each other in eternal standoff. And after this the interior is no letdown, strutting a cavalcade of statuary, murals, and a stunning reredos that echoes the organization of the portal. In his three-volume survey of American buildings, architectural historian G.E. Kidder Smith called the interior "hair-raising." His late colleague Reyner Banham went even farther: San Xavier del Bac, he flatly proclaimed, "is the most beautiful man-made object in America Deserta."

From the coming of the railroad in 1880 to 1900, Arizonans were infatuated with Victorian architecture; it was a symbolic way of proclaiming the frontier civilized (and Americanized). In a quick 20 years it seemed to the residents that they were civilized enough, and the time arrived to declare cultural independence from those effete Eastern shores. The result was the Mission Revival of 1900-1915, and the still more romantic Spanish Colonial Revival of 1915-1930. These two movements left Arizona with some of its loveliest buildings. San Xavier, though, was not their inspiration; California was. These "Spanish" styles were encouraged by West Coast promoters eager to capitalize on the romantic mythology of the *conquistadores*. Like Californians, Arizona newcomers were not particularly interested in participating in Hispanic culture, but they loved wrapping themselves in its imagery.

In the 1930s came another reversal. Phoenix and Tucson, finally edging toward the country's economic mainstream, felt they had to begin looking like real cities instead of pink Iberian fantasylands. Color, ornament and romance became high crimes, and from then until the 1970s most architecture in Arizona echoed the modernist credo of "less is more" in vogue everywhere else. Modernism left Arizona with many of its least ingratiating buildings. Finally, then, yet another re-thinking—and yet another Hispanic revival. This one, still in progress, has no formal name, although one hostile critic has proposed "Taco Deco." It is simpler and cheaper than its predecessors, and repetitive to the point of cliché, but it also is an effort—if not quite a noble one—to perpetuate an architecture with a sense of place.

Since 1970, a growing minority of Arizona architects have tried to establish a different tradition: buildings that reside in harmony with the land. Their inspiration, if not their style, stems from the ideas of Frank Lloyd Wright (see sidebar). These buildings may take their colors, their forms, even their moods from the land. Along with Predock's Nelson Fine Arts Center, one of the best examples is The Boulders Resort in Scottsdale. A sculptural, free-form main building embraces a little "mountain"—a grumpy 200-foot-high (61-m) pile of feldspar and granite boulders. It has the grace of a coolly contemporary ballet on a Fred Flintstone stage set. Guest "casitas" are strewn around the jumbled, rocky landscape with no attempt to impose order where it would not naturally exist. As successful as the building is, the philosophy of designer Bob Bacon should, in the long run, be even more appreciated. When asked what he would have designed for this site had the assignment been a cathedral instead of a resort, Bacon replied, "Nothing."

The connoisseur of architecture should see numerous other Arizona buildings, most of them around the two metropolitan areas.

In Tucson: the 1927 Spanish Colonial Revival **Pima County Courthouse**, Church and Congress Streets; the historic west end of the **University of Arizona** campus, Park Avenue and University; and **Loews Ventana Canyon Resort**, 7000

FRANK LLOYD WRIGHT

On a warm October Sunday morning in 1987, some 250 disciples of organic architecture from around the world gathered on a Scottsdale hillside to celebrate, reminisce, and listen to words of inspiration. The occasion was the fiftieth anniversary of Frank Lloyd Wright's creation of Taliesin West, and the atmosphere was more like a religious service than a gathering of architects.

The prelude was a suite for violin and piano composed by Wright's third wife, Olgivanna—confident, big-boned music with a whiff of Rachmaninoff about it. The sermon was a recording of Frank Lloyd Wright speaking on the spiritual value of education. The missionary report previewed a touring exhibition on the architect's life and work, about to go on the road in search of new converts. "We feel this exhibition has the possibility of changing the architecture of America by the twenty-first century," said the managing trustee of the Taliesin Fellowship, "and possibly the world."

Wright died in Phoenix in 1959, a few miles away from his beloved Taliesin West. His had been the longest, most creative and most controversial career of any architect in modern history. What followed his death, however, had no precedent except in the ranks of religious prophets and political leaders. Wright, even today, lives on among his former associates and apprentices as the guiding spirit, the one fountain of Truth in architecture. The commune-like Taliesin fellowship continues as ever, spending its summers in Wisconsin and winters in Scottsdale. The Frank Lloyd Wright School of Architecture still instructs its students in a curriculum more like a medieval apprenticeship than a modern university education. Most oddly of all, the design vocabulary of the Taliesin architects has not changed since Wright's death. They talk of preserving only the *spirit* of Wright's philosophy of organic architecture, but in practice they also perpetuate his exuberant geometry, his contrapuntal massing, his repetitive ornamentation—all the elements that together make up the thing Wright claimed to despise so virulently: style.

Wright designed roughly 50 buildings for Arizona, about one-third of which were built (some, like Phoenix's First Christian Church, were finished posthumously by Taliesin Associated Architects). Among them are both masterpieces and flights of silly fantasy. They have not had widespread influence on architecture in Arizona (except that practiced at Taliesin), which is unfortunate. Wright early on developed a philosophy of desert architecture that took its inspiration from the spare, angular landscape, and at its best, it was and is beautifully harmonious.

"I suggest that the dotted line is the line for the desert; not the hard line nor the knife edge," he wrote in 1940. He had studied the desert's thorn forest—cholla, saguaro, ocotillo—and noticed how the needles of these plants broke up and filtered the harsh sunlight spraying through them. Obviously, a building couldn't literally wear a skin of needles, but an architect could articulate and shade and texture wall surfaces for the same effect. A high, straight, flat wall surface would reflect light and appear as a foreign presence imposed on the landscape, but a broken one—a "dotted line"—would settle gracefully into it. In this respect Taliesin West is the masterpiece; perhaps no other Wright building, architect Pietro Belluschi once said, so perfectly gathers in "the mood of the land."

Wright, however, blithely violated his own philosophy whenever he felt like it. There is little "mood of the land" in Gammage Center, his 1959 auditorium at Arizona State University. Originally designed as an opera house for Baghdad, it looks like a great pink wedding cake festooned with hoops and baubles that appear to have been inspired by the tales of Scheherezade, or that may simply have floated down from Mars. Its acoustics, however, are stunning. Wright's Arizona Capitol, which he designed in one morning in 1957, still generates debate—even though it was never built. It was a geometry student's nightmare, a gigantic, lacy gridlock of triangles and hexagons and heaven-storming spires. Reviewing a show of Wright drawings in 1990, *The Arizona Republic's* art critic Richard Nilsen declared flatly that Wright was a crackpot and that this project was a perfect "capitol for the planet Mongo." But it was perfectly in tune with the baroque sci-fi aesthetic of the 1950s, and had it been built, in two or three generations it would have gracefully aged into one of Arizona's architectural treasures, a rival to San Xavier del Bac.

Wright was both genius and hypocrite, visionary and gadfly. In deifying him, the disciples at Taliesin have done him no favor. His buildings speak better for him.

Taliesin West, four miles east of Scottsdale Road on Shea Boulevard, offers student-led tours daily. **Gammage Center** at Mill Avenue and Apache Boulevard in Tempe can be viewed from outside, but normally is locked except for scheduled concerts. **First Christian Church,** 6500 N. 7th Avenue in Phoenix, welcomes visitors from 8:30 to 5 on weekdays. Check in the church office. The **Arizona Biltmore,** 24th Street and Missouri in Phoenix, actually was designed by Albert Chase McArthur; Wright's contribution as "consultant" was smaller than is popularly believed. The rest of Wright's Arizona buildings are private homes, and are not open to the public.

Taliesin West: Frank Lloyd Wright's timeless essay in desert architecture. (Top photo by Kerrick James

N. Resort Drive. The latter, designed in 1984, drew considerable inspiration from Wright's unbuilt San Marcos-in-the-Desert hotel of 1928.

In Phoenix: the **Luhrs Tower** (1929), 45 W. Jefferson, a successful marriage of Art Deco and Spanish Colonial Revival—and to this day, the best of Phoenix's several dozen high-rises. **Brophy Prep** (1928), 4701 N. Central Avenue, is the most lyrical Spanish Colonial Revival building in the state. **Tempe City Hall** (1971), 31 E. 5th Street, Tempe, is a personal favorite, although many still condemn it as architectural conceit: an inverted pyramid of glass and steel bursts up from street level, shading a lovely subterranean courtyard. The one work of Paolo Soleri worth visiting is **Cosanti**, 6433 Doubletree Road, Paradise Valley, an intimate village of earth-cast organic forms. Soleri's much better-known **Arcosanti**, 70 miles (112 km) north of Phoenix, is uninteresting as architecture; as a social experiment it has more to do with totalitarianism than harmonious living with the Earth. Essentially, Soleri would have us all live in concrete beehives.

Near Tubac, see the mission of **San José de Tumacácori.** In Sedona, the 1956 **Chapel of the Holy Cross**, wedged between a pair of ruddy buttes, is the provocative retort to Wrightian organic architecture, an impassive, defiant creation that appears more powerful than the mountains around it. Finally, the 1905 **El Tovar Hotel** at the Grand Canyon's South Rim is a truly amazing accomplishment: a sprawling wooden pile of styles from the Victorian Gothic to Richardsonian Romanesque that still manages, somehow, to seem elegant, and that does no dishonor to the great spectacle at its back.

■ THE VISUAL ARTS

Virtually all artists who come to Arizona from somewhere else are changed by the environment here. It is not only that new subjects materialize on their canvases; that would be expected. But a fresh temperament, a different attitude, perhaps even a new spirit may also pervade their work. Sometimes it is subtle; more often it is a dramatic change.

Howard Conant, a painter who for 10 years also headed the University of Arizona Department of Art, moved to Arizona from New York City in 1976. He was a geometric abstractionist, and his New York paintings often seemed to express tension and energy and violence, even when the subject had nothing at all to do with the city. They were jagged and searing. After five years of work in a quiet desert studio, his paintings were still as crisp as ever, but the fury had all evaporated. Gentle, rolling lines had replaced processions of severe, knifelike triangles. He even gave in and painted a sunset, albeit an abstract one.

"A sunset is just about the lowest thing a professional artist can do," he said. "Postcard artists do sunsets. Cowboy artists do sunsets. But I'd fallen so in love with the desert that I finally just decided, what the hell—I've got to do it. I succumbed."

Artists have been interpreting the Arizona environment since some anonymous Hohokam first scratched the likeness of a scorpion onto a boulder. Possibly he was expressing a vivid encounter with that environment—a nasty sting. In 1873, the famous painter Thomas Moran accompanied John Wesley Powell on the latter's third expedition into the Grand Canyon, and the following year completed what is still one of the grandest and most evocative paintings ever made of Arizona, *The Chasm of the Colorado*. On a single gigantic canvas (7 by 12 feet/2 by 4 m), Moran portrayed the canyon splashed with golden sunlight, splattered by a furious thunderstorm, and haunted by clouds of mist lurking in shadowy abysses—all at once. Moran wrote that the canyon was "by far the most awfully grand and impressive scene I have yet ever seen," and it may be that his imagination outpaced even the canyon's real-life grandness. The painting was hung in the U.S. Senate lobby, and viewers were electrified. From there it played a role in the transformation of Arizona. Inspired by the tremendous public reaction, the promotion-minded Santa Fe Railway a few years later began commissioning artists to come out and paint Southwestern subjects, particularly Arizona and New Mexico. Their work helped create the tourism boom and promote the settlement of these scenic and exotic lands.

Arizona's visual art separates into several basic categories. Landscapes are the most obvious, and among the most abundant, as a day's gallery browsing will show. Western art, less respectfully called "cowboy art," is another.

Western art is controversial in Arizona. The intelligentsia scorns it. Collectors are enchanted by it. The average person cannot afford it—not the capably executed works, at least. Paintings by Howard Terpning, among the most highly regarded of Arizona's living Western artists, have sold for as much as $312,500.

Yet art critics turn apoplectic virtually in unison when the subject of Western art arises. In Tucson's *City Magazine*, writer Karin Demorest concluded:

[The Western Artist] is on a treadmill, telling the same story over and over again, stubbornly refusing to stray from the stock images of the genre —the cowboy, the Indian, the horse, the desert landscape, the mountains, the sunset. Furthermore, his preoccupation with authenticity and technique deprives him of real expressiveness and individuality. . . . Subject matter, authenticity and technical skill are the standards by which Western art is both made and judged, with little if any attention paid to composition, spatial quality or drawing. A piece is considered good, even great, if the subject looks utterly real: the number of feathers in the Indian's headdress correct, the spots on the Appaloosa just the right color, the stirrups flawlessly rendered. . . .

So why the popularity? The answer is as obvious a cliché as the classic cowboy-in-the-sunset painting: the themes in these scenes from a romanticized past are those cherished by the collectors themselves (who, according to Demorest, are almost exclusively white males, over 45): independence, heroism, nature in its raw form (and so awaiting a man's challenge), and nostalgia for a bygone era free of cynicism and ambiguity. Interestingly, women seldom appear on Western artists' canvases, except as idealized and therefore untouchable Indian squaws.

Native American art, and art portraying Native Americans, are two other prominent categories. Among the former are some well-known tribal specialties: Tohono O'odham wire baskets, Apache ga'an masks and Navajo sand paintings and rugs. Most prized in Arizona, however, are Hopi kachina dolls.

Like so many other Native American art forms, kachina (pronounced "kat-SEE-na") dolls now serve both ceremonial and commercial roles in Hopi life. Some Hopis benefit: a top-drawer doll can sell for several thousand dollars. Others grieve: the most beautiful and intricate dolls no longer go to young Hopi girls, but to tourists and collectors. The positive note, however, is that because of their commercial success, the art of Hopi kachina carving has grown much more intricate and elegant over the last two or three generations.

Kachina dolls traditionally are carved from cottonwood roots by men as gifts for their female children. The dolls represent the living kachinas, masked intercessors to the Hopi spirit world who help to guarantee such critical matters as rain. Many published sources say that the gifts are to educate the children in the Hopi way, but the more important reason is to insure their eventual fertility.

Nineteenth-century kachina dolls were rudimentary and statically posed, and the arms, legs and fingers were simply implied by bulges extruded from the torso. Modern kachinas explode with energy and detail; they frequently are frozen in a dance pose, and their very distinct limbs ripple with musculature. On the most intricate dolls, even individual strands of hair and barbs of feathers are carved. At the risk of taking sides in a Hopi controversy, the view here is that this is one treasured Native American art that has benefitted from its commercialization.

Art portraying Native Americans, however, deserves the most respect when it is least commercial. Mass-marketed images of Indians, which have made more than a few Arizona artists wealthy, invariably reduce their subject to cliché: the noble savage, the stoic squaw, the innocent, saucer-faced infant. Some artists have been more honest. Among them is Barry Goldwater, later elected to the U.S. Senate, who took a celebrated series of photos of the Navajo people in the 1930s. Even today, the best art portraying Native Americans remains photographic: it is easier to tell the truth through a lens.

Viewing art: The principal art museums in Arizona are all noted in "PHOENIX," "TUCSON," AND "ARIZONA TOWNS." One generalization: the various university museums stay closer to the cutting edge and take more risks than the municipal museums. One special museum is the University of Arizona's **Center for Creative Photography,** one of the best photographic museums in the country. Its shows change periodically, and its archives house works of more than

Pots on display at Hubbell Trading Post, Ganado.

(opposite) A Hopi kachina doll. (photo by Paul Chesley)

1,400 photographers—including the complete *ouevre* of Ansel Adams, Edward Weston, W. Eugene Smith and Richard Avedon. Their prints are normally stored away from public view, but visitors may make requests (well in advance, the center recommends) for private print-viewing sessions.

Buying art: Scottsdale's **Fifth Avenue** galleries are the best-known in the state, and they serve the well-heeled traditionalist best. Tucson's **Congress Street** galleries mostly feature price tags a fraction of Scottsdale's and offer more adventure—though the quality varies wildly. **Sedona** has many excellent galleries but little provocative art; **Tubac's** shops also tend toward conservatism but are lower-priced. **Bisbee** is a good place to catch emerging artists' work on the cheap. **Jerome** defies categorization; it is the least predictable art center of all—a welcome characteristic for adventurous buyers. There are galleries specializing in Native Americana in every city, but the **Hubbell Trading Post**, a National Historic Site founded in 1876 at Ganado on the Navajo Reservation, is one worth a special trip: its selection of quality Navajo rugs is staggering. For Western art collectors, October brings the Phoenix Art Museum's annual **Cowboy Artists of America** sale, a social event that always grosses more than $1 million in sales.

■ PERFORMING ARTS

Another cliché: Because Arizona is a young state, and because it has relatively little in the way of old wealth, its performing arts organizations are still struggling through their adolescence. Like many clichés, this one has a nucleus of truth in it. But it isn't the full story.

The oldest arts organization still performing is the Tucson Symphony Orchestra, which was founded in 1928—an accomplishment for what was then a town of about 30,000 souls. The Phoenix Symphony followed later, but it was the first arts organization in the state to take the plunge into "major" status, meaning full-time employment for its musicians. That decision was made in 1981, and the years since have, in truth, been difficult: chasmic deficits have plagued the orchestra, and emergency fund drives and staff layoffs have been necessary to keep it afloat. One of its peculiar curses is, strangely, Phoenix's attractive winter climate. Wealthy and cultured people are drawn by it to retire in Phoenix (or commute to winter homes here), and while they *attend* the Phoenix Symphony, some of their *dona-*

tions still go back to the great old orchestras in their snowbound home towns—Minneapolis, Cleveland, Boston.

The highly acclaimed Arizona Theatre Company is even younger—it was founded in Tucson in 1967—and it also has faced tough financial times and emerged intact. It now functions as a statewide organization, still headquartered in Tucson, but staging six plays each season in both Tucson and Phoenix. The Arizona Opera Company, likewise based in Tucson but serving both cities, produces four operas per season. It lives scrupulously within its budget, a considerable achievement for any opera company, and one reason is its conservative "Top 40" repertoire of operas—Mozart, Rossini, Puccini & Co. In fairness, the Arizona Opera probably can't afford many artistic risks at this awkward point in its life. It is too mature and established to take a wild, youthful plunge into the avant-garde, and yet not secure enough to produce, say, John Adams's *Nixon in China*, lose money on it, and not be hurt. Call it, if you must, adolescence.

Risks are being taken in abundance, however, by smaller groups and determined individuals. In Phoenix, the *Teatro del Valle* puts on thought-provoking plays by Hispanic playwrights, including world premieres. In Tucson, the tiny but popular a.k.a. Theatre has carved out a miniature specialty staging the confrontational plays of Sam Shepard. In this end of the spectrum of the performing arts, such unrestrained vitality equals the confidence of maturity.

■ FOLK ART

Thanks to its profusion of cultures (once again), Arizona also is spectacularly rich in folk art—from cowboy poetry to Mexican murals to Tohono O'odham "chicken scratch," a musical style apparently transmitted to the tribe by the Jesuit and Franciscan missionaries long before Anglo settlement. (Certainly no other tribe plays a repertoire of polkas and two-steps on accordion, saxophone, drums and electric guitar.)

No broad survey of folk art is possible in this short treatment, but one curiosity unique to Arizona seems especially worth describing: the century-old tradition of Arizonans wryly poking fun at their own habitat in verse, gag and cartoon image.

Most of this folk art, predictably, plays on the heat or the desert's general inhospitality. One reliable place to find it is in *Phoenix Gazette* columnist Sam Lowe's

(following pages) The historic Hubbell Trading Post now stocks everything from Doritos to exquisite Navajo rugs costing several thousand dollars.

annual Hot Weather Poetry contest. This semi-Elizabethan quatrain was among 1988's published entries:

> Helios, thou are gross,
> Filled with strange desire.
> Thou rendereth Phoenix comatose
> Then rape us all with fire.

This poetic tradition dates back at least to 1879, when a ballad attributed to a pioneer Tucson bartender first circulated. A remarkably clever and well-paced tale, it begins with the Devil being given permission (presumably by God, though this detail is left unstated) to select a land as a special annex for Hell. It is, of course, Arizona—and Satan undertakes to improve on it:

> . . . He filled the river with sand till it was almost dry,
> And poisoned the land with alkali
> And promised himself on its slimy brink
> The control of all who from it should drink.
> He saw there was one more improvement to make,
> He imported the scorpion, tarantula and rattlesnake,
> That all who might come to its country to dwell
> Would be sure to think it was almost hell.
> He fixed the heat at one hundred and seven
> And banished forever the moisture from heaven . . .

The punchline, of course, is inevitable: when the Devil at last completes his "improvements":

> . . . For his own realm compares so well
> He feels sure it surpasses Hell.

None of this is serious put-down: anyone who actually disliked this environment would not be moved to write wry and ironic verses about it. In truth, it is a form of braggadocio. Wrote James S. Griffith, Arizona's preeminent cultural anthropologist of folk art, "One of the points of the genre is that it takes a real tough character to put up with whatever country is being described." This seems to be no less true today, even given the palliative of air conditioning, than it was in 1879. Wimps dwell not in this land.

■ KITSCH

Arizona may well lead the nation in the production of kitsch, a distinction that need not cause us embarrassment. Kitsch is the natural consequence of having rich landscapes and cultures that invite reduction into sentimental or cartoonish images, along with a vibrant tourist industry that supplies customers with cash in hand. *Objets de kitsch* generate jobs and revenue today, and over two or three generations they undergo a quiet metamorphosis into important cultural artifacts—i.e., antiques. The only immediate problem is telling folk art and kitsch apart. The line is blurry.

Architectural kitsch abounds in Arizona. A fine example is the giant stucco teepee in the old mining town of Globe; it currently houses a pizza parlor. A better-known institution is Bedrock City, a Fred Flintstone theme park of free-form boulder-like buildings strategically placed at the intersection of US 180 and Arizona State Highway 64, the two main routes to the Grand Canyon's South Rim. More extravagant is the downtown Phoenix Mercado, a boutique fantasyland that marries Taco Deco to the recklessly festive pink, purple, yellow and turquoise colors of postmodernism.

Arizona's animals and plants lead to endless production of kitsch. The scorpion and the saguaro seem especially inspirational. In 1971 the legislature proclaimed the bola the state tie of Arizona, and the quintessential bola (for tourists, that is) must have an authentic Arizona scorpion encased in a transparent plastic clasp. (Few Arizonans under retirement age would be caught dead in a bola of any sort today; as Arizona novelist Ray Ring explained, "The official necktie, the string bola, is so goofy most wives won't let their husbands appear in one.")

The saguaro, perhaps because of its anthropomorphic friendliness, pops up in boutiques everywhere. There are saguaros made of green-painted stovepipe, stuffed felt, soldered copper, blown glass and glowing neon. The Arizona State Museum even has a miniature saguaro made by a Tohono O'odham artist out of scrap telephone wire. None of Arizona's cultures seem able to resist the siren of kitsch.

Other examples: there is a peculiar building in Amado whose very entrance is a gigantic cow skull and horns. Numerous Arizona towns and cities have "Old West" shopping villages with a steak house and assorted curio shops. (Pinnacle Peak steak house in Tucson's Trail Dust Town even has an especially kitschy ritual:

(top) Where's the beef? Amado's longhorn architecture is on the auction block. (above) Pueblo Kitsch: a ceramic miniature recalling historic pueblo architecture. (opposite) Romanticizing the nineteenth century in Chloride, an old Mojave Desert mining town.

any unsuspecting customer who wears a tie to dinner will be attacked by waitresses ringing cowbells and wielding scissors; they snip off the tie and staple it to the ceiling.) A recent development is chile kitsch: red peppers are turning up in stained glass windows, dangling from people's ears, and glowing on Christmas trees.

Any image, if replicated over and over, eventually ceases to be usable in fine art or even folk art. It parks in the province of kitsch and from there it will not budge. This is the one thing to regret about kitsch. It is all but impossible today for anyone to paint a saguaro in a sunset, a noble and honest Arizona image, and have it be taken seriously. Literal paintings of Indians have long been snubbed by everyone outside the Western art establishment; recently even highly stylized renderings have become suspect—those images of Navajo women in immense, flowing robes have badly overpopulated the galleries.

Arizona, however, seems inexhaustably rich in subject matter. If the saguaro is for now too hazardous for the serious artist to approach, there are a few dozen neglected species of cacti still out there, waiting.

ARIZONA DREAMS

IT IS A WARM WINTER DAY IN 1987, and I am walking in a park in downtown Mesa listening to a developer talk penguins.

"You know how hot it is here in the summer," he says, unnecessarily. "So imagine the effect of watching 19 penguins frolicking in a fountain around an igloo. It would be absolute dynamite!"

He's serious, he swears; his plan is just on the back burner at the moment because the projected cost of the desert penguin habitat has bloated to about 10 times the original projection. I soberly record all this in my notebook, and a few weeks later report it as part of a special newspaper project commemorating the 75th anniversary of Arizona statehood.

The reason I didn't simply laugh and dismiss him as a crackpot is that his scheme nestled seamlessly into the continuum of Arizona's story.

From the Gadsden Purchase of 1853 to today, Arizona has always been a land for dreamers, "a blank slate on which they could etch their visions of the future," in the words of Arizona State Museum ethnohistorian Thomas E. Sheridan. If penguins and igloos in downtown Mesa seem preposterous, they are hardly more so than the necklace of lakes that now drapes through the heart of the Mojave Desert (complete with London Bridge), or the Victorian hotels in the mining towns, clasped desperately to the sides of mountains and gulches. We have remodeled the land to meet our needs and dreams, rather than accepting it on its own terms. Often we have done no good. Wrote Charles Bowden in *Blue Desert*, "Here the land always makes promises of aching beauty and the people always fail the land." A harsh judgment, but not one without the resonance of much truth in it.

The first miracle of technology that reconstructed the face of Arizona was the railroad. Until this, virtually all the architecture had been native—that is, built with the materials at hand. In the desert towns, that meant dirt, primarily—dirt mixed with water, poured into a form, and dried in the abundant sun to make adobe. The word descends from the Arabic *al-tub*, "the brick," which suggests its fundamental importance in arid lands everywhere. Adobe made perfect sense in the Arizona deserts. Its great thermal mass helped keep interiors cool through the torrid summer. Houses were built close together, which helped shade the spaces between them. Instead of front and back yards patterned after the rural English

model, they incorporated shady, enclosed Mediterranean courtyards. But once the railroads came, bringing building materials from back East, pioneer Arizonans couldn't wait to discard adobe in favor of Victorian architecture. Mud was symbolic of the Mexican past; gables and balustrades represented an affluent, expanding America—even though this architecture made little sense, environmentally or aesthetically, in the desert.

The hunger of the pioneers to make Arizona look like someplace else meant that it would never again have a unique and environmentally sensible built environment. When mirrored glass towers burst into vogue nationally in the 1970s, architects dutifully reproduced them in Phoenix. No one asked the obvious question: why bounce more sunlight around in a place that already has quite enough of it?

Water projects were the next phase in the makeover of Arizona. Mining and farming both require generous and reliable water supplies, which never existed naturally here. Arizona's rivers are trickles one season, torrents the next. It took a network of dams to control them: Roosevelt in 1911, Coolidge in 1929, Hoover in 1935. All were federal projects, as their names imply. Arizona didn't have the money to tame its own rivers, and at that time it didn't have the political influence to wrestle Washington into paying, either. These dams exist because there was money to be made in Arizona, and the people flocking here to make it needed the water.

Thus tricked into unnatural behavior, these rivers made Phoenix green and created the spectacle of vast recreational lakes—Powell, Mead, Havasu, Roosevelt—in treeless landscapes that enjoy 3 to 10 inches (8 to 25 cm) of rain in a year. Other water projects have changed the landscape in ways less obvious to the casual visitor. Driving south toward Tucson along I-10, one views tens of thousands of acres of farmland now lying fallow, choked with tumbleweeds. Thirsty Tucson has bought this farmland for the rights to slurp the aquifer underneath.

But the most important effect of all the water projects has been that they have made big cities possible. This has been both boon and curse. Without the cities, Arizona would have had little to contribute to the arts and sciences, it would hardly seem cosmopolitan, and it wouldn't offer either its residents or visitors the diversity it now does. At the same time, these cities are draining the water, fouling the air and gnawing away the desert and mountains around them. This cannot go on forever.

(previous pages) Construction of Hoover Dam, in 1935 the world's largest, claimed the lives of 96 workers.

A perceptive visitor to Arizona may discern a messy contradiction in what we say about the land and what we do to it. For example, we rhapsodize endlessly over the sunsets and mountain views, but we don't prohibit billboards. Several other scenic states do, notably Vermont, Maine, Alaska, and Hawaii. In Sedona, arguably the town with the loveliest natural assets in all of Arizona, there is no public access to its sparkling little river—it's all private property barred by a phalanx of "No Trespassing" signs. No one thought of a riparian park until it was too late.

The contradiction can be explained, even if not easily forgiven. Arizona has grown up too fast for its own good. Our population was 749,587 in 1950, 3,619,064 in 1990. Most Arizonans are newcomers; too few of us have the deeply bedded roots that would give us a better understanding of and stewardship for the land. Too many of us moved here pursuing private dreams, and with the notable exception of the pioneer Mormons, we have always been busier developing personal resources than communal ones. City councils find themselves under constant pressure to allow new housing developments and shopping centers (and widen the streets on the way), but there is not enough competing clamor for more parks and greenbelts. Development is enormously controversial in Arizona today, but for 40 years it has been happening so fast that proponents and opponents only lurch from one battle to the next, never finding the time to take a long, careful look at what we really want to do with the land.

There are some positive signs. In 1980 the legislature finally enacted a statewide groundwater code, which mandates that by the year 2025, Arizona wells may draw no more water out of their aquifers than is being replenished by nature. There is a growing positive environmental activism. The Nature Conservancy's Arizona chapter, for example, is buying up endangered land at an astounding rate. The Conservancy fielded a three-year, $3.98 million fund drive to protect 14 threatened riparian corridors along rivers and arroyos. It comes almost too late, however. According to the Conservancy, 90 percent of Arizona's prime riparian woodlands already are gone.

In his bicentennial history of Arizona, author Lawrence Clark Powell articulated our difficulties in a few perfectly chosen words. The state's most serious problem, he wrote, is "peculiarly Arizonan, that of a rising flood of people into a land naturally unsuited to large numbers of people." Yet this land's promises of aching beauty have always drawn people with their dreams, and in successive laminations of civilizations they always will. Ours will not be the last.

BACK ROADS OF ARIZONA

I EASE MY CAR OFF THE DESERTED FOREST ROAD by the Mogollon Rim and onto a carpet of straw-colored pine needles. This is very close to the place, as best as I can tell, where the Tonto Apaches introduced themselves to Gen. George Crook, the U.S. Army's top Indian fighter, one autumn afternoon in 1871. Crook and his men were blazing a trail and gaping at the scenery, just as tourists do today, when suddenly the crisp alpine air was clotted with arrows. The troops scrambled for cover. Most of the Apaches melted back into the woods, but two found themselves trapped right on the rim, a sheer escarpment overlooking another forest 2,000 feet (610 m) below.

The soldiers closed in. The Apaches leaped over the edge, apparently choosing suicide over capture. Crook's men stared in horrified amazement. But when they peered over the rim to look for the corpses, what they saw were two very live Apaches spidering down the near-vertical wall. Crook fired, and an arm of one of the fugitives went limp, blood spurting from an artery. His pace never slowed.

I peer over the rim myself and try to imagine doing that with one arm—and suddenly I feel very much like Crook did. Because of encounters like this, he eventually developed a profound respect for the people he had been sent to Arizona to subdue. They understood this beautiful but treacherous land in ways that the incoming wave of white settlers never would. If I had not made the effort to get to the Mogollon Rim—and it took three attempts, because the gravel road is often blocked by snow—I never would have fully understood this chasmic difference between our culture and theirs. This is one of the compelling reasons for leaving Arizona's cities and freeways behind, and taking the back roads. There is no better way to get to know the state except to walk it.

This chapter outlines eight drives, all rich in scenery, history, and surprises—such as the world-class bookstore on a desert ranch 40 miles from the nearest city. All start from one of Arizona's three main urban areas: Phoenix, Tucson, or Flagstaff. Some are easy day trips; some will take two, three, or four days. Most of the roads on the suggested routes are paved, and all are accessible to two-wheel-drive passenger cars except in heavy rain or snow.

One's sense of adventure may occasionally be called upon. The last time I drove US 666 from Alpine to Clifton, I encountered exactly three other cars in 95 miles

Snowfall on the red rocks near Sedona as seen from Schnebly Hill Road. (Kerrick James)

(152 km). It's a great scenic highway, but not a great place for your fuel injection to take early retirement. Summer or winter, *always* carry emergency drinking water while driving in Arizona.

■ ANCIENT ARIZONA TRAIL

This trip begins and ends in Flagstaff. As outlined here, it would cover about 575 miles (920 km) and take four full days. Along the way is a wealth of prehistoric ruins, petroglyphs, and the most improbable land forms in North America. Most of the drive is on the Navajo Reservation, offering opportunities to engage a distinct contemporary culture, as well. *Best times: April through October.*

DAY 1: From Flagstaff, drive seven miles (11 km) east on I-40 to **Walnut Canyon National Monument,** a V-shaped furrow 385 feet (117 m) deep, lined with Sinagua ruins halfway down the canyon walls. This is a perfect place to contemplate the question of whether Arizona's prehistoric cultures, in the throes of a population boom after A.D. 1100, faced the threat of war over limited resources. Walnut Canyon's settlements certainly *look* defensive; why else would they have been built in such preposterous locations? Tantalizingly, an archaeologist has found one "foreign" arrowhead in the rib cage of a Sinagua woman buried here—but just one.

Next stop is **Petrified Forest National Park,** 105 miles (168 km) east on I-40. Petrified Forest's ruins aren't worth a long visit, but near the Puerco Ruin is one of the most prolific and astounding collections of Anasazi petroglyphs in existence. The Park Service doesn't point it out, so most visitors miss it. Walk south from the ruin to the edge of the mesa it's on and look among the rocks just below.

After Petrified Forest, turn north into the Navajo Reservation and visit the **Hubbell Trading Post,** in business since 1876, and now a National Historic Site. The days when you could buy an inexpensive Navajo rug are now as remote as the era of nickel Cokes, but the weaving is more lovely and imaginative than ever. The prehistoric and geologic wonders of **Canyon de Chelly,** another 36 miles (58 km) north on US 191, have been described in some detail in the "FIRST ARIZONANS" and "CANYONS" chapters. Stay overnight, preferably in the historic Thunderbird Lodge.

DAY 2: Take the 18-mile (29 km) South Rim Drive to Canyon de Chelly's Spider Rock Overlook early in the morning, then take either a half-day or full-day tour of the canyon floor and its Anasazi ruins with a (required) Navajo guide. Anyone who hasn't done this hasn't experienced even a fraction of the wonders of this canyon. Guides may be hired at the visitors center, or at Thunderbird Lodge (which arranges trips in six-wheel military surplus vehicles).

In late afternoon, hike the 2.5-mile (4 km) round-trip trail to White House Ruin, the one trail on which visitors are allowed without guides. In the evening, drive 81 miles (130 km) to Kayenta, where you will need reservations (there are only two motels). Next morning, you'll visit the largest and most astonishing Anasazi ruins in Arizona.

DAY 3: The two ruins of **Navajo National Monument** are **Betatakin** and **Keet Seel**, both built in deep sheltering alcoves in the walls of Tsegi Canyon. Betatakin is a three-hour hike in and out, led by a park ranger, and limited to 60 people a day (first come, first served). Keet Seel is a 16-mile (26 km) round trip best taken on horseback; the hike is a death march through soft, wet sand. Because of a budget squeeze, the Park Service opens Betatakin only from the beginning of May to the end of September, and Keet Seel from Memorial Day through Labor Day.

Reservations for Keet Seel are essential and must be made one to two months in advance (Navajo National Monument: [602] 672-2366). If you take only the half-day Betatakin tour, return to Kayenta in the afternoon, then take US 163 19 miles (30 km) north to **Monument Valley.** The 17-mile (27-km) dirt road through the Navajo Tribal Park is rough but manageable. Plan to be on the mesa at the park entrance for sunset.

DAY 4: West on US 160, then south on US 89 to **Wupatki National Monument** and **Sunset Crater.** Skip the northernmost ruins, Lomaki and the Citadel, and go to the Wupatki ruin (behind the visitors center) and Wukoki. These ruins are labeled as Sinaguan, but their architecture has Anasazi written all over it. At the end of the Ancient Arizona Trail, you now know enough archaeology to be suspicious.

■ SCENIC SEDONA TRAIL

Everyone staying in Flagstaff visits Sedona, 28 miles (45 km) to the south. There are two scenic ways to go, however, and a day trip offers an opportunity to experience both. *Best times: March through November.*

From the beginning of I-17 in Flagstaff, drive south 19 miles (30 km) to

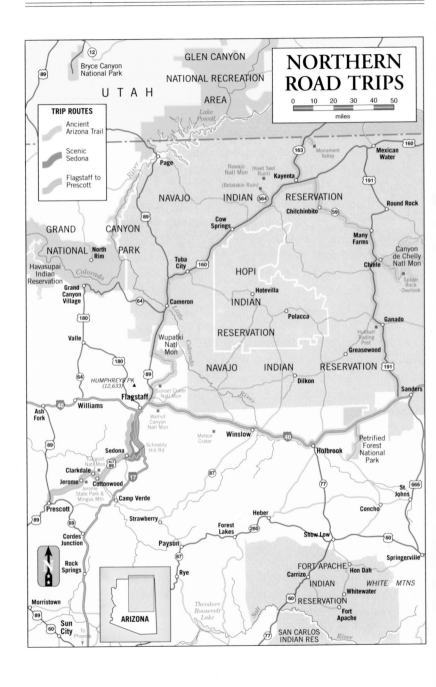

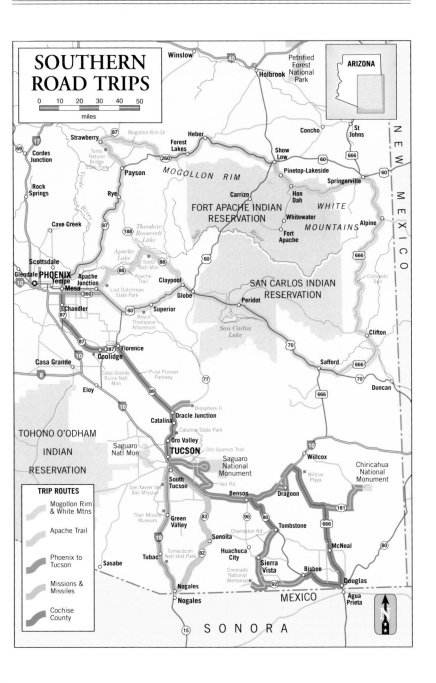

SOUTHERN ROAD TRIPS

0   10   20   30   40   50
miles

ARIZONA

TRIP ROUTES

Mogollon Rim & White Mtns

Apache Trail

Phoenix to Tucson

Missions & Missiles

Cochise County

Schnebly Hill Road, then take this 15-mile (24-km) graded dirt road into Sedona. Few people do, but their reward is a spectacular view into the gaping mouth of Oak Creek Canyon from 1,800 feet overhead. The mountain road "demands a driver's attention," as *Arizona Highways* author James E. Cook has written, but it normally isn't dangerous. A good friend advises, however: don't do it at night. After a day among Sedona's galleries and red rocks, take US 89a back to Flagstaff. For about 15 glorious miles (24 km), the road winds alongside the creek on Oak Creek Canyon's floor. En route, gape at the polychromatic sandstone and limestone strata on the canyon walls, and the erosion-sculpted gargoyles on the ridges. Special recommendation: it's almost impossible to get an overnight reservation at Garland's Oak Creek Lodge, eight miles of Sedona on US 89a. The regulars book it a year in advance. Dinner reservations, however, are obtainable. The menu is fixed nightly, you'll be seated with strangers (who generally prove engaging), and you'll enjoy the best dinner between Phoenix and Denver (602) 282-3343. *Open April 1 through November 15.*

■ FLAGSTAFF TO PRESCOTT, SCENIC ROUTE

This drive begins in Flagstaff and ends in Prescott, a distance of just 90 miles (144 km) over the prescribed highways. With all the attractions and mountain switchbacks en route, this is a long one-day trip, although the actual driving time is just three hours. *Best times: March through November.*

Take US 89a 28 miles (45 km) through Oak Creek Canyon to Sedona. Continue on 89a to **Tuzigoot National Monument,** a fascinating Sinagua pueblo ruin on a hill cresting 100 feet (30 m) over the Verde River Valley. Like Walnut Canyon, this defensive citadel implies a distinct fear of invasion. Continue south on 89a to Jerome and Mingus Mountain. **Jerome** is a retired Victorian mining town now blossoming with boutiques and art galleries, funkier and cheaper than Sedona's. Continuing on over 7,743-foot (2,360-m) Mingus Mountain, 89a offers rim-of-the-world views. Around the junction of US 89a and 89 five miles (8 km) north of Prescott are the Granite Dells, a garden of Precambrian boulders weathered into improbable shapes. There's no state or national park at the Dells, but they're worth an exploratory stop.

■ MOGOLLON RIM/WHITE MOUNTAIN SCENIC DRIVE

Most visitors to Arizona, if they encounter the Mogollon Rim at all, see it from below: as a vast, green wall, planed flat on the top, butting against the sky 90 miles (144 km) northeast of Phoenix. Looking up, it's an odd sight. Looking down, it is considerably more dramatic. Seeing it for the first time, a wide-eyed U.S. Army Capt. John C. Bourke wrote in 1891, "it is a strange upheaval, a strange freak of nature, a mountain canted up on one side."

The Coronado Trail, a.k.a. US 666, which various chambers of commerce would like to have us believe traces the route taken by Francisco Vásquez de Coronado in 1540, is the loneliest and loveliest mountain highway in Arizona. Elk, deer, raccoon, wild turkey, and even black bear can often be sighted from the car, and brief side excursions on gravel logging roads will take you to pristine streams and canyons that aren't seen by more than a few dozen people a year. This 582-mile (931-km) round trip from Phoenix will take two full days to cover both lonely wonders. *Best times: April through October.*

<u>DAY 1</u>: Leaving Phoenix, head north on Arizona Highway 87 to Tonto Natural Bridge State Park. The 90-mile (144 km) drive, which climbs gradually from the low Sonoran Desert to the 5,500-foot (1,675-m) elevations of Tonto National Forest, skirts lovely mountain scenery. After a wet winter, the roadside parade of wildflowers in March and April is spectacular. **Tonto Natural Bridge,** a 400-foot (122-m) limestone arch spanning a 150-foot-deep (46 m) canyon, deserves a visit. From the natural bridge, continue up Highway 87 to the top of the rim. Just beyond milepost 281 is the Mogollon Rim Road (Forest Road 300), to the right. It's 42 miles (67 km) of well-graded, lightly traveled, gravel road with vertiginous views over the rim, just to your right. Stop often to stare. Beware of logging trucks rumbling around blind curves, and the wind gusts which may whip you while you are peering over the rim. At day's end, stay either in Pinetop-Lakeside or Springerville. The former has more interesting choices in accommodations; the latter is 56 miles (90 km) on down the road, which will slice an hour's driving time off the next day's rather long route.

<u>DAY 2</u>: From Springerville, head south on US 666 to Clifton. This 123-mile drive will demand four to five hours even without stops, and you should stop frequently to enjoy the astounding mountain scenery and wildlife. Check weather forecasts before departing; a sign just south of Alpine warns: RT 666 NOT

MAINTAINED NIGHTS, WEEKENDS, OR DURING STORMS. Another adds: NEXT SERVICES 90 MILES [144 KM].

The highest paved road in Arizona, US 666 crests at 9,092 feet (2,771 m) at Hannagan Meadow. Between Hannagan Meadow and Clifton, US 666 resembles a 60-mile-long (90-km) corkscrew mashed into the Ponderosa pine forest and lathered with asphalt. Its hairpin turns are as tight as Scrooge's Christmas budget; the 15- and 20-mph (24- and 32-kph) warnings are, for once, realistic. Several automotive magazines have cited it as one of the best serious-driving roads in America. Decide early on whether you intend to enjoy serious (i.e., quick) driving or the scenery; you cannot do both. Either way, watch out for wildlife crossing the highway. A few miles from the highway, excursions off US 666 to the **Blue River** or **Black River** are particularly rewarding, but the state highway map offers little help in navigating these dirt and gravel roads. Stop at the **Apache-Sitgreaves National Forest** office in Springerville or Alpine and buy a detailed forest map ($3). Rangers are happy to direct visitors to the prettiest scenery and offer advice on road conditions.

Twelve miles (19 km) north of Clifton the highway exits the national forest and begins weaving down toward the desert. Six miles (10 km) later is the **Morenci Mine,** the second largest open-pit copper mine in the world. Reactions of passers-by range from awe at the astounding scale of the operation to revulsion at the indelible scarring of the now lifeless land. One mile (1.6 km) farther, off the east side of the road, is an oddly poignant sight: a hillside cemetery, not moist and green and shady, but choked with prickly pear and cholla cacti. The graves, dating from 1900 to the 1930s, are marked with handmade wrought-iron memorials and lead-pipe crosses, works of folk art. They form a silent monument to the harshness and bleakness of these early miners' lives. Until 1937, Clifton's copper all was extracted in underground mines.

From Clifton, take US 70 west to Globe, then US 60 to the **Boyce Thompson Arboretum** three miles (5 km) west of Superior. The arboretum offers a fine nature trail through a virtual desert forest, and has a good variety of desert plants for sale. From the arboretum, continue on toward Phoenix, and at Apache Junction take Arizona Highway 360 (the Superstition Freeway) into the city—*not* the traffic-light-clotted US 60/89.

The alpine beauty of the Mogollon Rim offers a welcome respite from the desert.
(Kerrick James)

■ APACHE TRAIL

This one-day, 164-mile (262-km) loop through the Sonoran Desert east of Phoenix today has nothing to do with Apaches—it doesn't even quite reach the San Carlos Indian Reservation. During the Apache wars, however, U.S. Army troops and Indian scouts combed the desert and mountains around here, trying to track down bands of Apache guerrillas. The loop passes the dramatic **Superstition Mountains,** three of the lakes devised by damming the Salt River in the early 1900s, a lovely **Salado Indian ruin,** and the **Boyce Thompson Arboretum.** Despite the short distance, it could be a long day. *Best times: October through April.*

From Phoenix, take Arizona Highway 360 (the Superstition Freeway) east and then Arizona Highway 88 to **Lost Dutchman State Park** at the base of the Superstitions. The park itself offers little except camper spaces, but its loop drive provides a gateway for day hikes into the Superstitions. Walk the **Siphon Draw trail** at least a couple of miles into the mountains; the awesome brute thrust of the craggy walls at your side will make you feel altogether insignificant.

Past Tortilla Flat, the highway deteriorates into a gravel road on its way toward Roosevelt Dam. President Teddy Roosevelt, who came to dedicate the dam in 1911, called this road "one of the most spectacular, best-worth-seeing sights of the world." Roosevelt's eponymous structure, claimed to be the world's largest masonry arch dam, isn't a disappointing sight either, and the road provides a striking view of it. Roosevelt Lake, an improbable sprawl of water 17 miles (27 km) long, is well stocked with fish, and, on weekends, party animals from Phoenix. Five miles (8 km) southeast of the dam, still on Highway 88, stop at **Tonto National Monument,** the lone ruin of the prehistoric Salado people open to the public. The Salado furrow archaeologists' brows; they can't agree on who these people were or where they came from. The main cliffside pueblo of 16 (remaining) rooms was inhabited from about A.D. 1250 to 1450. See the Boyce Thompson Arboretum (described in the preceding drive) en route back to Phoenix.

■ PHOENIX TO TUCSON, SCENERY AND SCIENCE

The 110-mile (176-km) commute between Arizona's two large cities normally takes just under two hours on Interstate 10, but nobody enjoys the desolate drive. A slightly longer route of 132 miles (211 km) offers less traffic, more scenery,

A Navajo horseman herds his sheep in Monument Valley.

several bits of history, and a convenient opportunity to visit the controversial **Biosphere II**. *Best times: October through April.*

From Phoenix, take Arizona Highway 360 (the Superstition Freeway) east to Apache Junction, then US 89 south to Florence. This little desert town doesn't draw many tourists; it is best known for its several state and federal prisons (about 4,700 of Florence's population of 7,510 view the world through bars). However, there are a couple of reasons for non-felons to do time in the town. One is its architecture. Florence has several interesting Territorial adobe buildings, including one, the **Clark House**, that features Italianate Victorian detailing. (Unfortunately, it's nearly in ruins.) More extravagant is the second **Pinal County Courthouse,** a sprawling Victorian pile with a French Second Empire cupola. Built in 1891, it still serves as a three-dimensional billboard advertising a grand future for Florence that never materialized. The other is the **Pinal County Historical Society Museum,** the only museum in Arizona to maintain a room devoted to execution paraphernalia. In here are the actual nooses used in 25 hangings at the Arizona State Prison between 1920 and 1930, complete with mug shots of the men (and one woman) whose necks they embraced. There's also a chair from the gas chamber and other grisly tools of the executioner's trade. The museum is at 715 South Main Street.

A short nine-mile (14-km) side trip from Florence is **Casa Grande Ruins National Monument,** the one remaining high-rise left from the prehistoric Hohokam civilization. This four-story mud building in the flatlands of the desert also has an attitude that is unmistakably defensive. Archaeologists theorize that it was used as a solar observatory to mark summer and winter solstices, and perhaps as housing for a Hohokam priesthood or managerial elite. Visitors theorize: yes, but they also must have needed to keep watch on, and keep out, some external threat.

Forty-two miles (67 km) south from Florence on US 89, turn left on Arizona Highway 77 for a visit to **Biosphere II**. The sealed, three-acre terrarium, which at this writing is sustaining eight human bionauts in their second year of experimental captivity, is five miles (eight km) east of the highway junction. Serious science, monumental performance art, or tourist trap? Visitors will find evidence of all three at Biosphere II.

For this privately funded $150 million project, bionauts were locked into the near-airtight terrarium with 3,800 species of plants and animals. The immediate objective was to see if the eight humans could sustain themselves for two years with only the food and oxygen generated inside the container. In the long term, it seems to be a feasibility study for colonizing Mars. Since its inauguration, Biosphere II has come under fire from an increasingly skeptical press. Visitors still seem to enjoy the tours, however.

A guide will walk you through experimental greenhouses and around the outside of the enormous Biosphere, where you might catch a glimpse of one of the crimson-suited Bionauts tending the gardens. You won't get to meet them, but a stop on the tour called *Meet The Biospherians* provides videotaped answers to the most predictable questions. Yes, the *most* predictable: are the four men and four women, all unmarried, Doing It in there? The reply is more coy than conclusive, and it helps confirm the suspicion that this is more entertainment than science.

Return to US 89 and drive 27 miles (43 km) south to Tucson. If enough daylight is left, stop at Catalina State Park, which offers a wonderful hiking trail—Romero Canyon—probing the north face of the Santa Catalina Mountains.

■ MISSIONS AND MISSILES

Visitors staying in Tucson routinely make the swift 60-mile (96-km) drive down I-17 to the Mexican border city of Nogales. Here's how to make a very full day of it, and see much more than the tourist shops of Nogales' Calle Obregón. *Best times: any.*

The not-quite-twin bell towers of **San Xavier Del Bac** pop into view to the west off I-17 soon after you leave Tucson. (The east tower was never crowned with a dome; the least exotic but most likely explanation is that the remote parish simply ran out of money.) The church is the most elaborate and lovely Spanish mission in what is now the United States, and no one should miss it.

Twelve miles (19 km) south on I-17 is the **Titan Missile Museum,** an actual (though now disarmed) ICBM resting in its underground silo. Once it was programmed to target a Soviet city; the museum will not say which one. In a fascinating reversal of Cold War tensions, Russian visitors now tour it alongside Americans.

Another few minutes' drive south on I-17 finds the historic Spanish presidio of **Tubac,** now jammed with art galleries and boutiques. Practically next door is Arizona's other Spanish mission, **San José de Tumacácori,** now a national monument. Just south along the access road from Tumacácori is a local monument to the olfactory sense: the retail store of the Santa Cruz Chili & Spice Co., the most seductively aromatic room in Arizona.

Nogales, Sonora, is the obvious stop for lunch. Tourists generally gravitate toward one of three restaurants, all under the same ownership: La Roca on Calle Elias and El Cid and El Greco, both on Calle Obregón. All three offer seafood, steaks, and Mexican food; El Greco is at once the least expensive and the most pleasant. All three are only a few blocks across the border; park in one of the pay lots on the U.S. side and walk—you'll be happy you did.

The best route back to Tucson is not the same quick zip up I-17, but a leisurely 80- to 100-mile (128- to 160-km) meander through what is becoming known as Arizona's wine country. From Nogales, drive north on Arizona Highway 82. These beautiful rolling grasslands, punctuated by groves of billowing oak trees wherever a depression collects extra rain, used to be prime rangeland. The recent discovery that the soil underneath is of the helpfully acidic *terra rossa* variety is now encouraging a boomlet in grape cultivation and winemaking. In 1992,

Arizona had 360 acres (146 hectares) of commercial vineyards and six wineries, up from zero of either in 1980. **Sonoita Vineyards,** in the nearby village of **Elgin;** and **R.W. Webb Winery,** on the I-10 frontage road west of the Sonoita exit, offer tasting and tours; others certainly will follow. Arizona wine is not yet a match for California's, either in consistency or value. But it has come a long way in a very few years. Return to Tucson via Arizona Highway 83 and I-10—after no more than modest indulgence in some Arizona wines.

Wine grapes flourish in the acidic terra rossa *soil of southern Arizona. Above, a vintner shows off his wines.*

■ COCHISE COUNTY

Cochise County is 6,400 square miles (16,576 sq. km) bristling with history and breaking hearts with its scenery. Birders worldwide know about Cochise County; the San Pedro riparian forest alone supports more than 350 species of migratory or breeding birds. The original county seat was Tombstone, the old West's most notorious town; the present county seat is Bisbee, modern Arizona's most entertaining town. On a lonely ranch out here is the Southwest's most engaging bookstore. Although the Cochise County line lies only 30 miles (48 km) east of Tucson, a basic introduction to its scenery and civilization will cover some 425 miles (680 km) in three days. *Best times: any.*

DAY 1: Don't take any of the obvious connections from Tucson to I-10. Drive east on Broadway to Old Spanish Trail and meander southeast: this is the scenic route, and it's worth the few extra minutes. **Old Spanish Trail** winds past **Saguaro National Monument** and **Colossal Cave,** a Pima County park; and a private castle crowning a ridge half a mile southeast of the cave. At I-10, drive 23 miles (37 km) east and take the US 80 exit to **Tombstone** (see p. 164). From Tombstone, veer southwest to **Coronado National Memorial,** a Huachuca Mountain preserve that probably was never even approached by Sr. Coronado, but perhaps appreciated in the distance as his band slogged along the San Pedro River 10 miles to the east. Take the snaking drive up the paved Memorial road to 6,575-foot (2,004-m) **Montezuma Pass,** and you can see the obvious route the Spanish explorers would have taken through the valley below. In summer, you also will see squadrons of hummingbirds assaulting the plentiful flowers of the mountain yucca here, and possibly even the elusive coati—a raccoon relative that moves with the grace of a cat. Spend the night in Sierra Vista if you prefer predictable chain-motel comfort, or in **Bisbee** (see page 162) if you're open to steep, crumbling streets, bed-and-breakfasts in old rooming houses, and unsolicited entertainment. Last time I was just about to drift off to sleep in Bisbee, someone in Brewery Gulch began serenading the moon on a tenor sax. Bisbee is built on the sides of two intersecting gulches, so the wail echoed all over town. No matter, this was Bisbee, and nobody had anything important to do tomorrow anyway.

DAY 2: Rise early and drive to the **Chiricahua National Monument** on Arizona's eastern edge, the most dramatically sculpted mountain range in the state. Plan to spend half the day on one or more of the monument's many hiking trails.

En route to or from the Chiricahuas, stop in the border town of **Douglas** to see a drop-dead architectural masterpiece: the lobby of the 1907 **Gadsden Hotel**, an opulent, two-story marble neo-Renaissance wonderland. The architect was Henry Trost, who had fallen under the spell of Louis Sullivan in Chicago a dozen years earlier. Don't be discouraged by the rather plain exterior of the building; go inside. If you want to spend the night, rooms are inexpensive ($30 and up in 1992) but hardly as stunning as the lobby. Otherwise, return to Bisbee.

DAY 3: Take US 666 north for a sneak visit to the **Willcox Playa**, that strange Pleistocene dry lake bed—which may become a vast, few-inch-deep wet lake with the rains of late summer. The playa is no state or national park; there are no posted instructions for going there. Look for the railroad tracks 3.5 miles (5.6 km) south of I-10, turn left and follow the dirt road paralleling the tracks to the edge of the playa. En route back to Tucson, stop first at the **Amerind Foundation** in Dragoon. Dragoon is just an unincorporated clump of ranches, but Amerind is one of the Southwest's best museums of archaeology, founded in 1937 by a Connecticut businessman who became mesmerized by the remnants of prehistoric Arizona.

Fifteen miles (24 km) west off I-10, even more improbably, is the **Singing Wind Bookstore**, which has enjoyed acclaim in the *Los Angeles Times*, the *Wall Street Journal*, and even the *Congressional Record*. It's the dream of ranchwoman Winn Bundy, who has more than 100,000 titles for sale, along with a wealth of free literary wisdom, in two rooms of her ranch house. The shop's emphasis is on books of the Southwest, but anything else that happens to interest Bundy or her fanatically loyal customers is here also. Take the Ocotillo exit at Benson, drive 2.3 miles (3.7 km) north, look for the "Singing Wind Ranch" mailbox ventilated with bullet holes, turn right, and let yourself through the gate. For any pilgrimage through Arizona and the Southwest, this place is both the beginning and end.

PRACTICAL INFORMATION

■ AREA CODE

The Area Code for Arizona is **602**.

■ WHEN TO COME

Ideally, a prolonged visit to Arizona will be in the fall or spring; these seasons offer temperate weather in the deserts and high country at the same time. Cost-conscious travelers may want to schedule their visits in these seasonal windows that include both (usually) tolerable weather and off-season hotel/motel rates:

> Flagstaff and the high country: April-May and November
> Phoenix: April and October-December
> Tucson: April and October-December

If economy is not the most important consideration, simply see the high country May through October and the deserts November through March.

(following pages) The best photographs of Monument Valley usually are made around sunrise and sunset.

Here are the monthly temperature and precipitation statistics for Phoenix, Tucson, and Flagstaff:

AVERAGE MAXIMUM DAILY TEMPERATURES (F)

CITY	JANUARY	MARCH	JULY	SEPTEMBER	NOVEMBER
PHOENIX	65°	75°	105°	98°	75°
TUCSON	64°	72°	98°	94°	73°
FLAGSTAFF	42°	49°	82°	74°	51°

AVERAGE MONTHLY PRECIPITATION (IN INCHES)

CITY	JANUARY	MARCH	JULY	SEPTEMBER	ANNUAL AVG.
PHOENIX	.75	.80	.74	.60	7.01
TUCSON	.86	.71	2.54	1.34	11.09
FLAGSTAFF	2.21	2.30	2.45	1.54	21.07

■ GETTING AROUND

Arizona's four largest airports with commercial service are: Tucson International, Phoenix Sky Harbor, Flagstaff Pulliam Airport, and Grand Canyon Airport. Fares to and from Phoenix are much cheaper than to the other cities; many Tucsonans drive the 110 miles to Sky Harbor to take advantage of round-trip fares to the East Coast that are at least $100 less. Sky Harbor has a convenient close-in location—it's 10 minutes to downtown—but the airport's layout, with no fewer than three separate terminals connected by shuttle buses, is a paradigm of inconvenience. Allow a few minutes extra when departing or making connections.

Both Phoenix and Tucson have extensive municipal bus services, but in these sprawling, low-density cities, mass transit simply is not practical for most users. Taxis are expensive because there are long distances to cover. For the visitor arriving by air, frankly, a rental car is the only realistic choice.

Speed limits on the interstates are 65 mph rural and 55 (104 and 88 kph) in the cities. Radar enforcement is ubiquitous, but detectors are legal and in common use. With long distances to cover between settlements, Arizonans tend to drive fast. State law requires the use of seat belts.

TEN INDISPENSABLE ATTRACTIONS

If you have limited time to tour Arizona, what should you see? In this state, conventional wisdom is hard to challenge; the best-known attractions clearly deserve their popularity. Still, there is room for some personal idiosyncracy. My indispensible 10, traveling (roughly) north to south:

Grand Canyon. Remember, in summer the South Rim is a teeming amusement park. North Rim is preferable.

Canyon de Chelly. As spectacular as the Grand Canyon, in a more quiet and intimate way. Navajo residents limit access to the canyon floor unless you hire a guide.

Hubbell Trading Post, Ganado. Not only a National Historic Site and museum, but the most complete and most fascinating Native American art and crafts gallery (Navajo) in Arizona.

Flagstaff. The city is not remarkable, but the profusion of attractions—ruins, mountains, craters, festivals, winter sports—within an hour's drive makes it a very attractive place to spend several days.

Sedona. The surrounding red rocks form the most spellbinding scenery in the state, Grand Canyon notwithstanding.

Heard Museum, Phoenix. The best museum dedicated to Native Americana in the nation.

Arizona-Sonora Desert Museum, Tucson. One of the world's ten best zoos, and a place to fall in love with the Sonoran Desert.

San Xavier del Bac, Tucson. The most lovely and extravagant Spanish mission on what is now United States soil.

Bisbee. Still on the comeback, a bohemian ragamuffin of a town clinging to the sides of a gulch, fascinating in its very unpredictability.

Aravaipa Canyon. A primitive, rugged and enchanting wilderness. You need a permit to hike it.

The state highway map, published by *Arizona Highways,* is available at tourist information centers in every town, as well as at many bookstores. For extensive travel on the Navajo and Hopi reservations, a very detailed map called "Indian Country" is published by the Automobile Club of Southern California; it shows minor roads not found on the official state map. *Arizona Highways* publishes a variety of lavishly illustrated and authoritative books to help guide the traveler around the state. They include *Travel Arizona, The Back Roads,* and three volumes titled *Outdoors in Arizona,* covering hiking, camping and fishing and hunting. The address is *Arizona Highways,* 2039 W. Lewis Ave., Phoenix, AZ 85009; or call (800) 543-5432.

■ ACCOMMODATIONS

This is by no means a comprehensive list, but rather a few hotels, motels and B&Bs in different price ranges that I have particularly liked. In a few outlying areas I am simply listing what is available. All phone numbers are area code 602 unless otherwise noted.

B = under $60   M = $60-120   L = over $120

ALPINE

Judd's Ranch • 339-4326 • 0.5 miles (1 km) north of Alpine • Open April-October • B

BISBEE

Bisbee Grande Hotel • 432-5900 or (800) 421-1909 • 57 Main St. • Elegantly furnished Victorian hotel, breakfast included • B-M

Bisbee Inn • 432-5131 • 450 K St. • Nice renovation of historic miners' rooming house. No individual baths, but breakfast is included • B

DOUGLAS

Gadsden Hotel • 364-4481 • 1046 G Ave. • Stunning lobby in 1907 hotel; headless ghost inhabits basement • B-M

FLAGSTAFF

Little America • 779-2741 or (800) 352-4386 • I-40 at Butler Ave. • Flagstaff's premier motel • M

Quality Suites • 774-4333 or (800) 228-5151 • 706 S. Milton Rd. • Includes breakfasts in sunny dining room, adjacent to Northern Arizona University • B-M
(Note: Flagstaff has many inexpensive motels along E. Santa Fe St., the famous old US

Route 66. However, the Southern Pacific railroad tracks parallel this street, and patrons of those motels near crossings will be serenaded by train whistles all night.)

GRAND CANYON (NORTH RIM)

Grand Canyon Lodge • (801) 586-7686 • Reservations through TWR Services, Cedar City, UT. Inside park, close to rim • B

GRAND CANYON (SOUTH RIM)

Grand Canyon National Park Lodges • 638-2401 • Box 699, Grand Canyon, AZ 86023 • Use the above address to reserve space at all South Rim lodges, plus **Phantom Ranch** on the canyon floor.

Descending in cost are **El Tovar** (M-L), designated a National Historic Landmark, dramatic and luxurious; **Thunderbird** and **Kachina** lodges (M); **Yavapai** lodges (M); **Bright Angel Lodge** and cabins (B-M); and **Maswik Lodge** (B). All except Yavapai and Maswik lodges are very close to the rim. Best value: Bright Angel.

JEROME

Nancy Russell's Bed and Breakfast • 634-3270 • In town • M

KAYENTA

Wetherill Inn • 697-3231 • P.O. Box 175, Kayenta • Pleasant motel with Navajo gift shop on US 163 in town • M

LAKE HAVASU CITY

Ramada London Bridge Resort • 855-0888 or (800) 624-7939 • 1477 Queen's Bay Rd. • Luxurious Olde English theme resort. Overlooks lake and London Bridge • M

Best Western Lake Place Inn • 855-2146 or (800) 258-8558 • 31 Wings Loop • Five blocks from lake and bridge • B-M

PATAGONIA

Stage Stop Inn • 394-2211 • Center of town • B-M

PHOENIX AND ENVIRONS

Arizona Biltmore • 955-6600 or (800) 528-3696 • 24th St. and Missouri, Phoenix • Built in 1929, this remains the Valley's most beautiful resort • L

Los Olivos Executive Hotel • 258-6911 or (800) 776-5560 • 202 E. McDowell Rd., Phoenix • A quiet motel a mile north of downtown • M

Westcourt in the Buttes • 225-9000 or (800) 843-1986 • 2000 W. Westcourt Way, Tempe • Luxury hotel dramatically built into the top of a small mountain. Near Arizona State University and airport • M-L

PINETOP (WHITE MOUNTAINS)

Whispering Pines Resort • 367-4386 • Individual log cabins with kitchens and fireplaces • B-M

PRESCOTT

Hassayampa Inn • 778-9434 • 122 E. Gurley St. • Historic downtown hotel (1927), nicely renovated • M

Marks House Inn • 778-4632 • 203 E. Union • Victorian mansion B&B with 5 rooms • M

Prescott Pines Inn • 445-7270 or (800) 541-3574 • 901 White Spar Road • A pleasant B&B with stunning breakfasts • B

SEDONA

Forest Houses Resort • 282- 2999 • Oak Creek Canyon. • Eleven rustic cabins 10 miles (16 km) north of Sedona in Oak Creek Canyon; request the Lower Sycamore with its bedroom fireplace and dramatic cantilevering over the creek • M

Canyon Villa B&B • 284-1226 or (800) 453-1166 1 • 25 Canyon Circle Drive • Six miles south of town, a B&B rivaling Sedona's big resorts in luxury • M-L

Quality Inn King's Ransom • 282-7151 • M

Junipine • 282-3375 or (800) 542-2121 • 8351 N. Hwy. 89A. • Condo-like resort 9 miles (14 km) north of Sedona in Oak Creek Canyon; units have full kitchens • L

L'Auberge de Sedona • 282-1661 or (800) 272-6777 • 301 L'Auberge Lane–Uptown • Lovely resort beside Oak Creek in a sycamore forest; rates include six-course dinner at L'Auberge's excellent French restaurant • L

TUCSON

Doubletree Hotel • 881-4200 or (800) 528-0444 • 445 S. Alvernon Way • A high-rise hotel in a residential midtown location • M-L

El Presidio Bed & Breakfast • 623-6151 • 297 N. Main Ave. • Lovely B&B in an 1879 Victorian adobe • M

La Posada Del Valle • 795-3840 • 1640 N. Campbell Ave. • Southwest adobe with 5 rooms, circa 1920, patio • M

Loews Ventana Canyon Resort • 299-2020 or (800) 223-0888 • 7000 N. Resort Dr. • Tucson's most beautiful destination resort, nested in a saguaro forest at the foot of the Santa Catalina Mountains • L

WICKENBURG

Rancho de los Caballeros • 684-5484 • 3.5 miles (6 km) west on US 60, south 2 miles (3 km) on Vulture Mine Rd. Resort with golf course. Open Oct-May • L

WINDOW ROCK

Navajo Nation Inn • 871-4108 • Located on AZ 264, east of shopping center • B

YUMA

Best Western Chilton Inn • 344-1050 or (800) 528-1234 • 300 E. 32nd St. • B-M

Best Western Yuma Inn-Suites • 783-8341 or (800) 528-1234 • 1460 S. Castle Dome Rd., off I-8, 16th St. exit • B-M

■ GUEST RANCHES

(Area code is 602.)

AMADO

Reventone Ranch • 398-2883 • P.O. Box 504, AZ 85645

DOUGLAS

Price Canyon Ranch • 558-2383 • P.O. Box 1065, AZ 85607

DRAGOON

Triangle T Guest Ranch • 586-3738 • P.O. Box 218, AZ 85609

EAGER

Sprucedale Ranch • 333-4984 • P.O. Box 880, AZ 85925

MESA

Saguaro Lake Guest Ranch • 984-2194 • 13020 Bush Highway, AZ 85205

PATAGONIA

Circle Z Ranch • 287-2091 • P.O. Box 194, AZ 85624

PAYSON

Kohls Ranch • 826-4211 • Highway 260, AZ 85541

PEARCE

Grapevine Canyon Ranch • 826-3185 • P.O. Box 302, AZ 85625

SASABE

Rancho de la Osa • 823-4257 • P.O. Box 1, AZ 85633

TUCSON

Elkhorn Guest Ranch • 822-1040 • Sasabe Star Route, Box 97, AZ 85736

Hacienda Del Sol Ranch Resort • 299-1501 • 5601 N. Hacienda Del Sol Rd., AZ 85718

Lazy K Bar Ranch • 744-3050 • 8401 N. Scenic Dr., AZ 85743

Tanque Verde Ranch • 296-6275 • Route 8, Box 66, AZ 85748

White Stallion Ranch • 297-0252 • 9251 W. Twin Peaks Rd., AZ 85743

WICKENBURG

Flying E Ranch • 684-2690 • P.O. Box EEE, AZ 85358

Kay El Bar Ranch • 684-7593 • P.O. Box 2480, AZ 85358 • 3 miles (5 km) north of town on US 89. Rates include meals. On National Register of Historic Places. Open Oct-April.

Rancho Casitas • 684-2628 • P.O. Box A-3, AZ 85358

Wickenburg Inn Tennis & Guest Ranch • 684-7811 • P.O. Box P, AZ 85358

■ RESTAURANTS

What follows is an abbreviated and thoroughly subjective blitz through some of the more interesting restaurants in Arizona, based largely on foraging for my magazine food column, which is headlined *EAT*. Visitors will want to consult longer lists. Most reliable (i.e., not in bed with advertisers) are the weekly guides in Phoenix's *New Times* and the *Tucson Weekly*. Both are free alternative newspapers published on Wednesdays.

It clearly is reckless to proclaim any one Mexican restaurant the best in Arizona, but I will not flinch (nor accept debate): it is **El Bravo**, a small, family-run Sonoran-style cafe in north-central Phoenix (8338 N. 7th St., 943-9753.) Proprietor Carmen Tafoya labored for years at a Motorola plant in Phoenix, and every time her department would have a potluck, her co-workers would shower her with choruses of "Carmen! You should open a restaurant!" In 1980 she did, and years later her walls are groaning with awards—all deserved. The succulent *chile colorado* tastes as if it has been simmered for a week. Green corn and chicken tamales braid the prickly flavor of green chiles with sweet corn *masa*. The prices are barely higher than fast food. Unlike many larger Mexican restaurants, success has shown no sign of spoiling El Bravo.

Other Mexican recommendations: A Mexico City-based chain called **La Parrilla Suiza** (Phoenix and Tucson, several locations) offers delectable food from the Mexican heartland. Seafood prepared in Mexican styles—for example, *camaron al mojo de ajo*, shrimp sauteed with garlic—is a specialty at a growing number of restaurants. In Phoenix, check out **San Carlos Bay Seafood Restaurant** (1901 E. McDowell, 340-0892) and **Rocky Point Restaurant** (6021 S. Central, 243-3371). The state's best Mexican buffet, a lavish and eclectic affair, is featured every Wednesday night at **Los Abrigados** resort in Sedona (in Arizona 800-822-2525; out of state 800- 521-3131).

Spanish cuisine resembles Mexican in no respect other than a common ardor for garlic, but it seems altogether appropriate in the continuum of Arizona's history. One Arizona resort, **The Scottsdale Princess** (7575 E. Princess Drive, 585-4848) has boldly chosen a Spanish theme (or, more specifically, Catalan) for its signature restaurant, **Marquesa**. Specialties such as *zarzuela,* a garlicky stew of sea creatures, are expensive but lavish. **Havana Cafe of Phoenix** (4225 E. Camelback, 952-1991) serves moderately priced "pre-Castro" Cuban cuisine, in which nearly every region of Spain is represented with Caribbean influences. In Tucson, **Encore Med** (5931 N. Oracle Road, 881-1130) offers excellent Spanish cuisine, or diners

Tucson's citizens love to dine out. El Charro, the city's oldest Mexican restaurant, is popular with tourists. (Kerrick James)

can make a full meal out of three or four *tapas* (appetizers) at **La Paloma's Desert Garden** (3800 E. Sunrise Dr., 742-6000).

Every other ethnic cuisine imaginable is available in Arizona's metropolitan areas, from Russian to Cajun and Creole. One special favorite is the mini-chain of Punjabi Indian restaurants run by the London-born Khangura brothers (**New Delhi Palace**, Tucson, 6751 E. Broadway, 296-8585; in Tempe 933 E. University, 921-2200; in Flagstaff, 2700 S. Woodland Village, 556-0019). In Tucson, **Seri Melaka** (6133 E. Broadway, 747-7811) serves both Malaysian and Chinese cuisine. The Malaysian owners, who often wait tables themselves, are enthusiastic ambassadors for their country; if you arrive knowing nothing about Malaysian culture, you won't leave that way. In Phoenix, **Greekfest** (1940 E. Camelback Rd., 265-2990) serves the best Greek cuisine in the state.

Fine (and expensive) dining in Arizona 20 years ago was basically limited to ponderous "continental" restaurants. Happily, this is no longer true; nouvelle ideas and techniques, more often than not drawn through Mexico, have invaded all but the crustiest of establishments. In Sedona, **L'Auberge**, (282-1661), a lovely and intimate creekside resort, offers six-course French dinners with both classic and nouvelle strains. In Phoenix, **Vincent's on Camelback** (3930 E. Camelback, 224-0225) appears to be the hottest thing going, experimenting with everything from classically inspired rack of lamb to duck tacos. *New Times* has said owner-chef Guerithault is "certainly one of the finest chefs in the West." Arguably the most innovative chef in Arizona, however, is Janos Wilder, owner-chef of Tucson's **Janos** (150 N. Main, 884-9426). Wilder began cooking in a Menlo Park, California pizza parlor at the age of 16, apprenticed at La Réserve in Bordeaux, and in 1983 he started his own restaurant in one of Tucson's oldest buildings, the Hiram Stevens House of 1865. Between appetizers of chiles stuffed with lobster and brie and a main course of black pepper-encrusted tenderloin with apple brandy sauce, diners can ponder the house's territorial ghosts. In 1893 a despondent Stevens, a distinguished man who had been a delegate to Congress, went into his wife's room and fired a shot at her head. It glanced off a silver comb in her hair, which spared her life. Stevens then aimed the revolver at his own head and successfully dispatched himself.

A couple of restaurants in very small Arizona towns deserve mention; Arizonans happily drive 100 miles (160 km) or more for the experience. One is the iconoclastic **House of Joy** in Jerome, once a miners' bordello, now a small, eclectic gourmet restaurant that only opens Saturday and Sunday afternoons and evenings. Call at least a month in advance for reservations (634-5339), and place the call *only* on a Saturday or Sunday—these are the only days they answer. Rather more accessible is **Sonoita's Er Pestaro** (455-5821), a tiny and urbane trattoria in a cow-country crossroads. Rome-born owner-chef Giovanni Schifano serves the finest plates of pasta in Arizona, and the marvelously inexpensive wine list includes an '83 Barolo with enough body to bench-press Switzerland. It is not, in the end, so strange to find such a restaurant in rustic Sonoita; Schifano says he was tired of serving spoiled celebrities in New York City. "Here," he smiles broadly, "you see millionaires driving pickups."

Among my favorites in Phoenix is **Tomaso's** (3225 E. Camelback, 956-0836), serving high-end Italian cuisine. **The Fish Market** and **Top of the Market** (both in the same building at 1720 E. Camelback, 277-3474) offer excellent fresh seafood; the upstairs **Top of the Market** is fancier and pricier. **La Chaumiere** (6910 Main, Scottsdale, 946-5115) is one of the Valley's finest French restaurants and arguably its most charming. There must be three dozen Thai restaurants around the Valley; the best of the several I've tried is **The Siamese Cat** (5034 South Price, Tempe, 820-0406). The most dramatic overlook of the city is at **Top of the Rock** (2000 Westcourt Way, Tempe, 225-9000)— this hotel restaurant literally buds from the top of a butte. Finally, in downtown Phoenix, try the cioppino at **Lombardi's** (Arizona Center, 257-8323), a noisy but very competent Italian bistro that also provides good value for the money.

In Tucson, **Jack's** (5250 E. 22nd, 750-1280) has been dishing out no-nonsense barbecue since the dawn of civilization. **Boccata** (5605 E. River Road, 577-9309) is my choice among the city's several upscale Northern Italian bistros; an added attraction is the daily Mussel Madness happy hour offering a drink and a great bowl of steamed mussels for $6. **Big A** (2033 E. Speedway, 326-1818) is your classic college hangout, but this one has the added attraction of world-class burgers. **Samurai** (3912 N. Oracle, 293-1963) is the best fast-food-style Japanese restaurant I've sampled in any city anywhere; order the dumpling-like *gyozi*. **The Tack Room** (2800 N. Sabino Canyon Road, 722-2800) has scored five stars from the Mobil Travel Guide every year since 1977, the only Arizona restaurant to be so honored. Lastly, **Ventana** at Loews Ventana Canyon Resort (7000 N. Resort Dr., 299-2020) is my choice among Tucson's destination resort restaurants; the excellent classic and nouvelle dishes are complemented by stunning views of the city lights.

Those restaurants marked in **bold** have been written about in the text and are recommended by the author. Those restaurants in *italic* have been included in this list by the publisher for the purposes of geographic diversity. Area code is 602.

Prices for one, excluding liquor and tip are as follows:

B = Budget, under $10; M = Moderate, $10-20; E = Expensive, over $20

DOUGLAS

La Fiesta Cafe • Mexican • 364-5854 • 524 Eighth St. • B

FLAGSTAFF

Cafe Express • Homemade natural foods • 774-0541 • 16 N. San Francisco St. • B

Macy's European Coffee House and Bakery • Gourmet café food • 774-2243 • 14 S. Beaver St. • B

New Delhi Palace • Indian • 556-0019 • 2700 S. Woodland Village • B-M

GRAND CANYON (NORTH RIM)

Grand Canyon Lodge • 638-2611 • open May-October • M

GRAND CANYON (SOUTH RIM)

El Tovar Hotel • Elegant dining • 638-2631 • Grand Canyon Village • E

Moqui Lodge • Mexican/American • 638-2424 • Tusayan • B

JEROME

House of Joy • Eclectic gourmet • 634-5339 • Saturday and Sunday only • B

KAYENTA

Amigo Cafe • Mexican, Arizona's hottest *salsa* • 697-8448 • US 163 • B

KINGMAN

Nick's Coffee Mill • Local atmosphere • 753-3888 • 2011 E. Andy Devine • B

LAKE HAVASU CITY

London Arms Pub & Restaurant • American/British • 855-8782 • English Village • M

PHOENIX

Chirstopher's • French nouvelle • 957-3214 • Biltmore Financial Center, 2398 E. Camelback Rd. • E

El Bravo • Sonoran-style café • 943-9753 • 8338 N. 7th St. • B

The Fish Market • Seafood • 277-3474 • 1720 E. Camelback • M

Greekfest • Greek cuisine • 265-2990 • 1940 E. Camelback • M

La Parrilla Suiza • Mexican • Various locations • B-M

Lombardi's • Italian bistro • 257-8323 • Arizona Center • M

Rocky Point Restaurant • Mexican seafood • 243-3371 • 6021 S. Central • M

San Carlos Bay Seafood Restaurant • Mexican seafood • 340-0892 •
1901 E. McDowell • M

Tomaso's • Italian • 956-0836 • 3225 E. Camelback • E

Top of the Market • Seafood • 277-3474 • 1720 E. Camelback • M

Vincent's on Camelback • Nouvelle American excellence • 224-0225 •
3930 E. Camelback • E

SONOITA

Er Pastaro • Trattoria • 394-2676 • B-M

SCOTTSDALE

La Chaumiere • French • 946-5115 • 6910 Main • E

Marquesa • Spanish/Catalan • 585-4848 • at the Scottsdale Princess,
7575 E. Princess Dr. • E

SEDONA

Fournos Restaurant • Greek, Continental • 282-3331 • 3000 W. Hwy. 89a • M

L'Auberge de Sedona • French cuisine • 282-1667 • 301 Little Lane (off N. Hwy. 89A
one block north of Hwy. 179) • E

TEMPE

Delhi Palace • Indian/Punjabi • 921-2200 • 933 E. University • B-M

The Siamese Cat • Thai • 820-0406 • 5034 South Price • B-M

Top of the Rock • 225-9000 • 2000 Westcourt Way • M-E

TOMBSTONE

Nellie Cashman Restaurant and Pie Salon • Western • 457-2212 •
Fifth and Toughnut • B

Lucky Cuss Restaurant • Western • 457-3561 • Allen St. between Fourth and
Fifth • B

TUBAC

Joanna's Café International • German cuisine • 398-9336 • Mercado de Baca • B-M

TUCSON

Big A • Hamburgers, college hangout • 326-1818 • 2033 E. Speedway • B

Boccata • Italian bistro • 577-9309 • 5605 E. River Rd. • M

Cafe Terra Cotta • Nouvelle southwestern • 577-8100 • St. Philip's Plaza, 4310 N. Campbell Ave. • E

El Charro • Oldest Mexican restaurant in Tucson • 622-5465 • 311 N. Court Ave. • B-M

Encore Med • Spanish • 888-1130 • 5931 N. Oracle Rd. • E

Jack's • Barbecue • 750-1280 • 5250 E. 22nd • B

Janos • Nouvelle cuisine • 884-9426 • 150 N. Main • E

La Parrilla Suiza • Mexican • 747-4838 • 5602 E. Speedway Blvd. • B-M

New Delhi Palace • Indian • 296-8585 • 6751 E. Broadway • B-M

Samurai • Japanese • 293-1963 • 3912 N. Oracle • B

The Tack Room • Classic cuisine • 722-2800 • 2800 N. Sabino Canyon Rd. • E

Ventana • Classic/nouvelle cuisine • 299-2020 • Loews Ventana Canyon Resort, 7000 N. Resort Dr. • E

WICKENBURG

Frontier Inn • Barbecue, steaks • 684-9501 • 466 E. Wickenburg Way • B-M

La Casa Alegre • Mexican • 684-2152 • 540 E. Wickenburg Way • B

YUMA

Beto's Mexican Food • 782-6551 • 812 E. 21st St. • B

Golden Corral Family Steakhouse • American • 726-4428 • 2401 S. Fourth Ave. • B-M

EATING IN ARIZONA

Oh! If we could only live as the Mexicans live, how easy it would be!" pined Martha Summerhayes, a young Army bride who came to Arizona in 1874. "For they had their fire built between some stones piled up in their yard, a piece of sheet iron laid over the top: this was the cooking-stove . . . a kettle of *frijoles* (beans) was put over to boil. These were boiled slowly for some hours, then lard and salt were added, and they simmered down until they were deliciously fit to eat, and had a thick red gravy. . . ."

Ms. Summerhayes went on to rhapsodize about several other staples of the Mexican table in Arizona Territory, including *chile colorado* and *chile verde* (red and green chile beef stew, respectively), *tortillas*, and *carne seca* (sun-dried beef simmered with onions and peppers). Recipes for these dishes have endured virtually unchanged for more than a century, and Arizonans, both newcomers and natives, rhapsodize still. Mexican food is Arizona's culinary religion.

This is only proper. In fact, it should be in the state constitution. It perpetuates our historic roots. For gringos, it cracks open a door, at least, into Mexican culture. And of course it tastes wonderful. Forgive me if I turn moist-eyed and mystical, but there is something about Mexican cuisine that seems akin to the essence of life. Its forms are those of nature's geometry: the circle (*tortilla*), the cylinder (*flauta*), the arch (*taco*). Its flavors are likewise elemental: *chile habanera* evokes pure fire; a very fresh *guacamole* laced with lime and cilantro captures both the color and mood of springtime. Mexican food also can reflect the complexity of nature; it isn't merely hot. *Huachinango a la Veracruzana* is a perfect example. This is red snapper filet sautéed with onion, garlic, tomatoes, green olives, capers, and—if the chef is really cookin'—nutmeg. All these flavors form rival factions of piquancy that circle each other warily, struggle briefly for power on the taste buds, and finally embrace and trip down the tube dancing and singing in tight-woven harmonies. Snapper can be a dull fish, but not when prepared in a Veracruz pan.

Huachinango a la Veracruzana remains relatively rare on Mexican restaurant menus in Arizona. Most kitchens still cling to the frontier; this is a conservative religion.

The traditional Mexican restaurant meal here invariably begins with a basket of deep-fried tortilla chips (usually complimentary) and an accompanying *salsa* of chopped or puréed tomato, *jalapeño* chile, onion, and cilantro. Depending on how the restaurant perceives its clientele, this *salsa* may range from annoyingly mild to incendiary. The entrées typically consist of a wide choice of "combination plates" mixing *tacos, enchiladas, tamales, flautas, burros,* and *chiles rellenos,* accompanied by rice, beans and warm flour tortillas. Dessert is likely to be either *sopapaillas,* fried bread puffs with honey; or *flan,* a creamy cinnamon-flavored custard. Nobody pretends that this is a heart-smart diet, but some restaurants at least have begun to substitute lower-fat vegetable oils for the traditional lard. This has a slightly deleterious effect on the flavors of some dishes, but it seems like a sensible tradeoff.

There are some other pleasing trends developing in Mexican dining around the state. One is the gradual appearance of regional cuisines other than the beefy ranch-style Sonoran that has prevailed since—well, since Arizona was part of Sonora. Mexican food is a far larger universe than most *norteamericanos* ever imagine, and this should come as no surprise: Mexico comprises tropics, deserts and more than 5,000 miles (8047 km) of seacoasts; and Aztecs, Mayas, Pimas, Spaniards, French, and Americans have all exerted their influence in different regions. Thus a *pan de cazon,* which is kind of a shark-and-bean sandwich from the Yucatán peninsula, has no family ties to *birria,* a savory goat pot roast from Guadalajara. Both, along with other regional specialties, gradually are becoming more widely available in Arizona. So is Sonoran coastal cooking, in which spicy shrimp replace shredded beef in *tacos* and *enchiladas.* Finally, there are several new shoots and permutations of Mexican cuisine that fall under no single culinary label, although "nouvelle Southwestern" covers some of it. This cooking weds Mexican ingredients to the latest French techniques, often to smashing effect but occasionally to bizarre ends. I have tried Anaheim chiles stuffed with lobster and brie and fried with beer batter, which were stunning, and Mexican sea bass swimming in blueberry sauce, a very unstable marriage of ingredients. Generally, the new cuisine is much more expensive than the old.

Innovation and a wide variety of ethnic dining have come fairly late to Arizona. There are at least a couple of reasons. Our two principal cities were not large until recently, and except for Mexican-Americans, they had no concentrated ethnic enclaves. The influence of the frontier may have had a lingering effect, too: a mean land demands a mean cuisine. Emblematic of territorial Arizona was cowboy stew, or, as more colorfully labeled in Louise DeWald's *Arizona Highways Heritage Cookbook,* "Son-of-a-Bitch Stew." Ingredients: all the meat and most of the internal organs of a freshly butchered calf, slowly boiled for five hours. Warns the classic recipe, "Never add spices or vegetables to a Son-of-a-Bitch; spoils the true flavor of the ingredients."

By the late 1970s the last remnants of the S.O.B. culinary philosophy finally were swept aside by new waves of immigrants and an increasingly alert tourist industry. The growing-up process has been astoundingly rapid: today you can eat as well in Arizona as in California. A Tucson bistro serves wine-steamed mussels year-around for happy hour; a Phoenix cafe introduces cuisine from El Salvador to Valley residents. A trattoria in Patagonia, pop. 874, serves pasta that draws customers from all over Arizona. There is not yet a distinctive "Arizona cuisine" except for traditional Sonoran, but this simply reflects the character of our land: a young, volatile, attractive haven for a great stew of immigrants. A London-born Indian who along with his three brothers has built a successful trio of Punjabi restaurants in Flagstaff, Tempe, and Tucson explained it simply: "Arizona looked like an interesting change for us."

(Kerrick James)

CHILE SCORCH SCALE

Chiles enhance taste, are intriguing to look at, and can scorch the unsuspecting. How is chile heat measured? In 1911 a Mr. Scoville gave us a guide to chile heat by testing a range of chiles on some non-chile eaters (how they later fared is unrecorded). Some common chiles and their heat levels are recorded below.

CHILE	SCOVILLE HEAT UNITS	RATING
Mild Bell	0	0
R-Naky, Mexi-Bell	100-500	1
NuMex Big Jim	500-1000	2
Pasilla, Española	1000-1500	3
Sandia, Cascabel	1500-2500	4
Jalapeño, Mirasol	2500-5000	5
Serrano	5000-15,000	6
Cayenne, Tabasco de Arbol	15,000-30,000	7
Aji, Piquin	30,000-50,000	8
Santaka, Chiltepin	50,000-100,000	9
Habanero, Bahamian	100,000-300,000	10

■ NATIONAL PARKS, MONUMENTS, AND RECREATION AREAS

(All telephone numbers are in area code 602 unless otherwise noted.)

Apache-Sitgreaves National Forest • P.O. Box 640, Springerville, AZ 85938 • 333-4301

Aravaipa Canyon • BLM Safford District Office • 425 E. 4th St., Safford, AZ 85546 • 428-4040

Canyon de Chelly National Monument • P.O. Box 588, Chinle, AZ 86503 • 674-5213 • Navajo Rt. 64 through Chinle • Admission fee

Casa Grande Ruins National Monument • P.O. Box 518, Coolidge, AZ 85228 723-3172 • Take AZ 87, 2 mi. (3 km) north of Coolidge • Admission fee

Chiricahua National Monument • Dos Cabezas Rt. Box 6500, Willcox, AZ 85643 • 824-3560 • AZ 186, 27 mi. (43 km) southwest of Willcox • Admission fee

Coronado National Forest (Santa Catalinas-Mt. Lemmon) • 5700 N. Sabino Canyon Rd., Tucson, AZ 85715 • Sabino Canyon information, 749-3223; Mt. Lemmon information 749- 3349

Glen Canyon National Recreation Area • P.O. Box 1507, Page, AZ 86040 • 645-2511

Grand Canyon National Park • Grand Canyon, AZ 86023 • 638-7888 • South Rim: AZ 64 58 mi. (93 km) north of Williams • North Rim: AZ 67, 45 mi. (72 km) south of Jacob Lake • Admission fee • For all South Rim lodging reservations, Phantom Ranch and mule trips inside the canyon, call 638-2401. North Rim lodging: TWR Services, Cedar City, UT, (801) 586-7686

Grand Canyon Railway • from Williams to South Rim: 518 E. Bill Williams Ave., Williams, AZ 86046 • 800-843-8724

Kitt Peak National Observatory • P.O. Box 26732, Tucson, AZ 85726 • tour information 623-5796 • ext. 250, AZ Hwy. 86, 37 mi. (60 km) west from Tucson; turn south on AZ Hwy. 386

Monument Valley • P.O. Box 93, Monument Valley, UT 84536 • (801) 727-3287 • Take US 163, 22 mi. (35 km) north from Kayenta • Admission fee

Montezuma Castle National Monument • P.O. Box 219, Camp Verde, AZ 86332 • 567-3322 • Take I-17 to Exit 289, 87 mi. (140 km) north of Phoenix • Admission fee

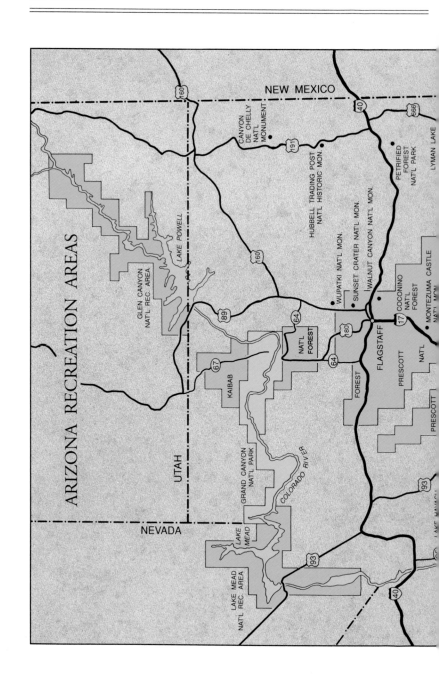

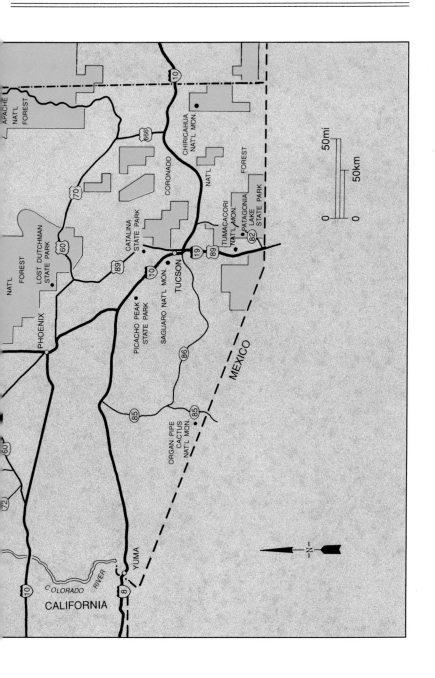

Navajo National Monument • HC-71 Box 3, Tonalea, AZ 86044 • 672-2367 • Take U.S. 160 18 mi. (29 km) south of Kayenta, then AZ Hwy 564 north to monument • Admission fee, ranger-guided tours. Call in advance; only limited numbers of visitors allowed

Oak Creek Canyon • Coconino National Forest, 2323 Greenlaw Lane, Flagstaff, AZ 86004 • 527-7400 • US 89A between Flagstaff and Sedona

Organ Pipe Cactus National Monument • Rt. 1, P.O. Box 100, Ajo, AZ 85321 • 387-6849 • Hwy. 85 22 mi. (35 km) south of Why • Admission fee

Paria Canyon • Bureau of Land Management, P.O. Box 459, Kanab, UT 84741 • (801) 644-2672

Petrified Forest National Park • Petrified National Forest, AZ 86028 • 524-6228 • Take I-40 to Exit 311 30 mi. (48 km) east of Holbrook • Admission fee

Prescott National Forest • 344 S. Cortez St., Prescott AZ 86301 • 445-1762

Saguaro National Monument • 296-8576 • East unit: 3693 S. Old Spanish Trail, Tucson, AZ 85730 • West unit: 2700 N. Kinney Rd., Tucson, AZ 85743 • Admission fee

Sunset Crater National Monument • Rt. 3, Box 149, Flagstaff, AZ 86004 • 527-7042 • US 89 10 mi. (16 km) north of Flagstaff • Admission fee

Tonto National Forest • Superstition Mountain Wilderness, P.O. Box 5348, Phoenix, AZ 85010 • 225-5200

Tonto National Monument • P.O. Box 707, Roosevelt, AZ 85545 • 467-2241 • AZ 88 5 mi. (8 km) south of Roosevelt Lake • Admission fee

Tumacácori National Monument • P.O. Box 67, Tumacácori, AZ 85640 • 398-2341 • I-19, 45 mi. (72 km) south of Tucson • Admission fee

Tuzigoot National Monument • P.O. Box 219, Camp Verde, AZ 86322 • 634-5564 • Follow signs 3 mi. (5 km) east of Clarkdale • Admission fee, ranger-guided tours

Walnut Canyon National Monument • Walnut Canyon Rd., Flagstaff, AZ 86004 • 526-3367 • Take I-40 to Exit 204 7 mi. (11 km) east of Flagstaff • Admission fee

White Mountains • Pinetop-Lakeside Chamber of Commerce, P.O. Box 266, Pinetop, AZ 85935 • 367-4290

Wupatki National Monument • P.O. Box 444A, Flagstaff, AZ 86001 • 527-7040 • US 89 24 mi. (39 km) north of Flagstaff • Admission fee

Unusual rock formations fire the imagination.

■ MUSEUMS AND CULTURAL ATTRACTIONS

Amerind Foundation • Exhibits of prehistoric and contemporary Native American life and culture • Dragoon. Take I-10 to Exit 318, 58 miles (93 km) east of Tucson • 586-3666 • Admission fee

Arizona Historical Society • 949 E. 2nd St., Tucson • 628-5774

Arizona Museum of Science and Technology • 80 N. 2nd St., Phoenix • 256-9388 • Admission fee

Arizona-Sonora Desert Museum • 2021 N. Kinney Road, Tucson • 883-2702 • Admission fee

Arizona State Museum • University of Arizona, Tucson • 621-6302 • Exhibits are divided between two buildings flanking the main west campus entrance at Park and University

Boyce Thompson Southwestern Arboretum • P.O. Box AB, Superior • 689-2811 • US 60 4 mi. (6 km) west of Superior

Center for Creative Photography • University of Arizona, Tucson • 621-7968

Copper Queen Mine • Bisbee • 432-2071 • Admission fee

Desert Botanical Garden • 1201 N. Galvin Parkway, Phoenix • 941-1225 • Admission fee

Flandrau Planetarium • University of Arizona, Tucson • 621-7827 • Admission fee

Fleischer Museum • Art museum of American impressionism • 17207 N. Perimeter Dr., Scottsdale • 585- 3108

Hall of Flame • Museum of antique fire trucks and firefighting equipment • 6101 E. Van Buren St., Phoenix • 275-3473 • Admission fee

Heard Museum • 22 E. Monte Vista Road, Phoenix • 252-8848 • Admission fee

International Wildlife Museum • 4800 W. Gates Pass Road, Tucson • 624-4024 • Admission fee

Lowell Observatory • 1400 W. Mars Hill Road, Flagstaff • 774-2096

MARS Gallery *(Movimiento Artistico del Rio Salado)* • 130 N. Central Ave., Phoenix • 253-3541

Museum of Anthropology • Eastern Arizona College, Thatcher • 428-1133

Museum of Northern Arizona • Rt. 4, Box 720, Flagstaff • 774-5211 • Admission fee

Nelson Fine Arts Center • Arizona State University, Tempe • 965-ARTS

Old Tucson Studios • 201 S. Kinney Road, Tucson • 883-6457 • Admission fee

Phoenix Art Museum • 1625 N. Central Ave., Phoenix • 257-1222 • Free on Wednesdays, admission fee other days

Phoenix Zoo • 5810 E. Van Buren St., Phoenix • 273-1341 • Admission fee

Pima Air Museum • 6000 E. Valencia Road, Tucson • 574-9658 • The Air Museum also operates the **Titan Missile Museum**, I-19 to Duval Mine Road exit 20 mi. (32 km) south of Tucson • 625-7736 • Admission fees, guided tours at the Titan Missile Museum

Pueblo Grande Museum • 4619 E. Washington St., Phoenix • 275-3452

Sharlot Hall Museum • 415 W. Gurley St., Prescott • 445-3121

Reid Park Zoo • 900 S. Randolph Way, Tucson • 791-4022 • Admission fee

San Xavier del Bac • Rt. 11, Box 645, Tucson. Nine mi. (15 km) south of Tucson on I-19 • 294-2624

Taliesin West • From Scottsdale Road take Shea Blvd. 4 miles (6 km) east to Via Linda, turn left, then left again on 108th St. and follow signs • 860-8810 • Admission fee

Tucson Museum of Art • 166 W. Alameda, Tucson • 628-1754 • Free on Tuesdays, admission fee other days

University Art Museum • Nelson Fine Arts Center, Arizona State University, Tempe • 965-2787

University of Arizona Museum of Art • University of Arizona, Tucson • 621-7567

Wildlife World Zoo • 16501 W. Northern Ave., Litchfield Park • 935-WILD • Many exotic species in a privately owned suburban Phoenix zoo • Admission fee

Yuma Territorial Prison • **State Historic Park** • Yuma. Take Giss Parkway to Prison Hill Road • 783-4771 • Admission fee

■ FESTIVALS

The following are some of the better-known annual festivals in Arizona, but there are hundreds of smaller or more esoteric ones around the state. The best way to obtain information is to write or call a town's chamber of commerce; they all maintain informational sheets on cultural events up to a year in advance. For the Phoenix metro area, contact the Phoenix & Valley of the Sun Convention & Visitors Bureau, 505 N. 2nd St., Suite 300, Phoenix, AZ 85004, 254-6500. For Tucson, contact the Metropolitan Tucson Convention & Visitors Bureau, 130 S. Scott Ave., Tucson, AZ 85701, 624-1817. Area code is 602.

FEBRUARY

Tubac Festival of the Arts • Tubac Chamber of Commerce, P.O. Box 1866, Tubac, AZ 85646 • 398-9201 • Oldest arts and crafts fair in Arizona, mostly visual arts

FEBRUARY-MARCH

Festival in the Sun • 800 E. University Blvd., Suite 110, Tucson, AZ 85719 • 621-3364 • Very ambitious music and theater festival sponsored by the University of Arizona

APRIL

International Mariachi Conference • P.O. Box 3035, Tucson, AZ 85702 • 884-9920 ext. 245 • North America's largest festival of mariachi performances and workshops. Always a sellout; obtain tickets in advance

JULY

Prescott Bluegrass Festival • Chamber of Commerce, P.O. Box 1147, Prescott, AZ 86302 • 445-2000

JULY-AUGUST

Flagstaff Festival of the Arts • 403 N. Agassiz, Flagstaff, AZ 86002 • 774-7750 or 800-332-9444 (in Arizona only) • Classical music, dance, theater, film, and art exhibits

SEPTEMBER

Grand Canyon Chamber Music Festival • P.O. Box 1332, Grand Canyon, AZ 86023 • 638-9215

Jazz on the Rocks • P.O. Box 889, Sedona, AZ 86336 • 282-1985 • The state's top jazz festival, with a full day of outdoor performances. Always a sellout; request tickets several *months* in advance

Navajo Nation Fair
P.O. Box 1687, Window Rock, AZ 86515 • 871-4108 • Powwow, singing, weaving, arts and crafts

Old-Time Fiddlers' Contest
Payson State Championship, Chamber of Commerce, P.O. Box 1380, Payson, AZ 85547 • 474-4515

A mariachi band entertains festival goers. (Kerrick James)

OCTOBER

Arizona State Fair • Arizona Veterans Memorial Coliseum, 19th Avenue and McDowell Road, Phoenix • 252-6771 • Rides, concerts, Native American and cowboy dancing, 4-H Club events—a classic American state fair

Helldorado Days • *Tombstone Epitaph,* P.O. Box 917, Tombstone, AZ 85638 • 457-2211 • Shootouts, 1880s fashion show, parade, street entertainment

Tucson Meet Yourself • Southwest Folklore Center, University of Arizona, Tucson, AZ 85721 • 621-3392 • A downtown festival celebrating Tucson's ethnic diversity

■ GOLF COURSES

Jack Rickard, a tireless golfing enthusiast and a full-time golf writer, has provided this selective guide to the best courses open to the general public. In this section, we've listed towns that courses are near, then the name of the golf course. An additional source of information for golfers is the *Arizona Golf Course Directory,* 7124 E. First Street, Scottsdale, AZ 85251, 949-7201. Use area code 602.

CASA GRANDE
Francisco Grande • resort • 426-9205

FLAGSTAFF
Fairfield Elden Hills • public • 527-7999

GREEN VALLEY
Canoa Hills • public • 648-1880

KINGMAN
Kingman Golf Course • public • 753-6593

LAKE HAVASU CITY
London Bridge Golf Club • public • 855-2719
Stone Bridge Golf Course • public • 855-2719

LITCHFIELD PARK
Wigwam Golf & Country Club • resort • 935-9414

NOGALES
Rio Rico Resort • resort • 281-8567

PAGE
Glen Canyon Golf Club • public • 645-2715

PARADISE VALLEY
Stonecreek, the Golf Club • public • 953-9100

PINETOP
Silver Creek Golf Club • public • 537-2744

PHOENIX
Arizona Biltmore Country Club • resort • 955-9655

SCOTTSDALE
The Boulders Club • resort • 488-9028

Camelback Golf Club • resort • 948-6770

McCormick Ranch Golf Club • public • 948-0260

Scottsdale Country Club • public • 948-6911

Tournament Players Club • public • 585-3939

Troon North • resort • 585-5300

SEDONA
Verde Valley Country Club • public • 634-5491

SIERRA VISTA
Pueblo del Sol • public • 378-6444

TUBAC
Tubac Resort • resort • 575-7540

TUCSON
Ventana Canyon • resort • 577-2115

Randolph Park North • public • 325-2811

La Paloma Country Club • resort • 742-6100

Tournament Players Club at Star Pass • public • 622-6060

WICKENBURG
Los Caballeros Golf Club • resort • 684-2704

Wickenburg Country Club • public • 684-2011

YUMA
Cocopah Bend Resort • resort • 343-1663

Mesa de Sol Golf Course • public • 342-1283

(following pages) Indian children light bonfires during the Spring Festival at Mission San Xavier in Tucson. (Kerrick James)

■ SPORTS

Phoenix is embroiled in a seemingly endless debate over whether to build a domed stadium that will, it is hoped, attract a major-league baseball team—it's currently the largest city in the U.S. without one of its own. It does, however, have a successful and popular NBA team, the Phoenix Suns, and the NFL Phoenix Cardinals, which cannot be described as popular. The Cards moved from St. Louis in 1988, which infuriated that city; then owner Bill Bidwill promptly set Phoenix afume by charging the highest ticket prices in the NFL. Bidwill lowered prices the next year, but the Cards have yet to come up with a winning season in their new home.

The Cards play in Arizona State University's 72,000-seat Sun Devil Stadium in Tempe and rarely sell out; the Suns occupy America West Arena and almost always do.

Seven major-league baseball teams hold their spring training in Arizona; they're collectively known as the Cactus League. Their exhibition games attract more than 600,000 fans every year. The Oakland A's play in Phoenix, Milwaukee Brewers in Chandler, Chicago Cubs in Mesa, San Francisco Giants in Scottsdale, California Angels in Tempe, Colorado Rockies in Tucson, and San Diego Padres in Yuma. Local newspapers carry game schedules. (Also see p. 184.)

For the last several years, the hottest Arizona team of any sort has been the University of Arizona's Wildcat basketball team. The Cats went to the NCAA Final Four in 1988 and won the PAC-10 championship in 1986, 1988, 1990, and 1991.

Coach Lute Olson's program is so clean it squeaks like a gym shoe: virtually all the players graduate, and there's never been even a hint of recruiting violations. A Tucson reporter once described the team as "St. Lute and his leaping apostles." The only discouraging word is that you cannot get a ticket. McKale Center's 13,800 seats sell out long in advance to season ticket holders every year. Most games, fortunately, are broadcast live on KMSB-TV (Channel 11) in Tucson.

■ RODEOS

Professional "Turquoise Circuit" rodeos are held in Arizona. They are listed by the month in which they occur. As specific dates and times are apt to change, it's best to call the chamber of commerce in the towns where the rodeos are held. For Indian reservation rodeos, contact All-Indian Rodeo Cowboy Association, Box 305, Window Rock, AZ 86515, 657-3240.

JANUARY
Turquoise Circuit Finals, Tucson
Jaycees Parada del Sol, Scottsdale

FEBRUARY
Jaycees Silver Spur, Yuma
La Fiesta de los Vaqueros, Tucson

MARCH
Jaycees Rodeo of Rodeos, Phoenix

APRIL
Desert Foothills Fiesta, Cave Creek
Copper Dust Stampede, Globe

JUNE
Pine Country Rodeo, Flagstaff

JULY
Frontier Days, Prescott
Navajo Nation Celebration, Window Rock

AUGUST
Payson Annual Rodeo, Payson
Gila Valley Pro Rodeo, Safford

OCTOBER
Rex Allen Days, Willcox
Andy Devine Days, Kingman

■ RIVER RAFTING

Arizona offers river trips on several different rivers. A short list of companies follows. Unless otherwise noted, area code is 602.

Arizona Raft Adventures • 526-8200

Canyoneers, Inc. • (800) 525-0924 (out of state) • 526-0924 (in state)

Expeditions, Inc. • 779-3769

Moki Mac, River Expeditions • (800) 284-7280 or (801) 943-6707

Rivers & Oceans—A Travel Company • 526-4575

Wild & Scenic Expeditions, Inc. • 774-7343 or (800) 231-1963

Wilderness River Adventures • 278-8888 or (800) 528-6154

Worldwide Explorations • 774-6462 or (800) 272-3353

■ GENERAL INFORMATION

Arizona Office of Tourism Phoenix, • 542-8687

Phoenix Chamber of Commerce • 254-5521

Phoenix Convention and Visitors Bureau • 254-6500

Tucson Chamber of Commerce • 792-1212

Tucson Convention and Visitors Bureau • 642-1817

■ EXPOSING ARIZONA

Arizona's landscapes and various human cultures form a photographer's dream, but there also are a few difficulties.

The light is one. Except on overcast days, the Arizona sky is brighter than in most places in North America. A modern camera's metering program doesn't realize that it's *supposed* to be bright, and often will choose a smaller aperture or higher shutter speed than it should. Then the rest of the picture will be underexposed. The solution is to point the camera a bit downward, at what appears to be an average brightness level in the scene, and use that meter reading. Also, remember that in the deserts, broad daylight is flat light. It bleaches color and nuance out of your pictures. The best landscape photos are shot in the early morning, late evening, or when a storm is threatening.

Another problem is overexposure—not of your film, but of the state itself. Arizona has been photographed so extensively (and so expertly) that it is quite a challenge to come up with a fresh image of a familiar attraction such as Monument Valley. Keep alert for unusual details—say, a rattlesnake on a boulder that could be used for a foreground—and pray for unsettled weather.

Finally, Arizona's natural environment is not particularly gentle with camera equipment. Camera repair shops warn customers not to leave cameras in a car parked in the sun on a hot day; the heat can melt lubricants and allow them to ooze onto components where they don't belong. The heat will not affect unexposed film, but do have it processed promptly after shooting.

■ ARIZONA PUBLICATIONS

Arizona's most famous publication is, interestingly, owned by the state of Arizona itself: *Arizona Highways* magazine has a circulation of 410,000, about 80 percent of it out of state, and a nonpareil reputation for spectacular photography.

It was founded in 1925 as a newsletter published by the Arizona Highway Department and sold for 10 cents per copy. It chronicled highway construction and administrative humdrum within the department, and its purpose was to promote roadbuilding in the young state.

Tumacácori Mission decorated for a December festival. (Kerrick James)

The modern concept of *Arizona Highways* began in 1938 with the editorship of Raymond Carlson, which lasted three decades. Carlson introduced four-color photography, which was rare at the time, and rhapsodic prose. Today the photography is better than ever, the writing more journalistic than promotional. But its mission remains the same: to promote tourism in Arizona. It does so with great success.

For a one-year subscription write *Arizona Highways*, 2039 W. Lewis Avenue, Phoenix, AZ 85009.

The state's largest newspaper, the *Arizona Republic*, is available in every town and hamlet. Its daily columnist, E. J. Montini, is worth the price of the paper; he's one of the few columnists anywhere who still bases his commentary on solid reporting. The *Arizona Daily Star*, published in Tucson, is available all around southern Arizona. Once a fine newspaper, it has been in a deep slumber since the mid-1980s. Its evening competitor, the *Tucson Citizen*, will give a visitor a better feel for the city.

Other publications of use to the visitor include *Tucson Guide* and *Valley Guide*, both quarterly magazines with features and entertainment suggestions; *Phoenix* magazine, which has some excellent writing and provocative features; *Tucson Lifestyle*, which is relentlessly upscale; and Phoenix's *New Times* and the *Tucson Weekly*. Both the latter are available free in street boxes and in stores on Wednesdays; they offer the best guides to dining and entertainment.

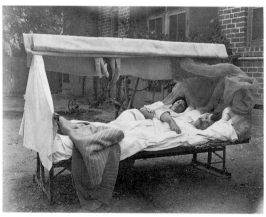

Summer sleeping in central Arizona before air conditioning. (Arizona Historical society)

■ HOW TO
LOOK LIKE A
NATIVE

Arizona is largely an informal state, although Phoenix, sad to say, is growing steadily less so (See the "PHOENIX" chapter for a discussion). In the smaller towns and cities, only the lawyers ever wear suits. For the casual visitor, casual, comfortable clothing is recommended—especially including shorts in summer. Only a handful of restaurants in Phoenix require jackets for men at dinner; in Tucson, at this writing, none do.

One important accessory, summer and winter alike, is sunblock with a protection factor no lower than 15. This is not only to prevent sunburn: southern Arizona has the world's second highest rate of melanoma, a deadly skin cancer, and cumulative exposure to sun is the prime cause. As enticing as sporting a well-bronzed body may seem, Arizona doctors speak as one in this recommendation: forget sunbathing.

RECOMMENDED READING

ARIZONA'S PHYSICAL CHARMS AND CULTURAL INTRIGUE have been luring painters and photographers to the state for more than a century, and the result is an uncommonly rich documentation of this land through the visual arts. Less obviously, this is equally true of its literature. Writers are smitten with Arizona for precisely the same reasons as artists.

The literature of the Sonoran Desert begins in the sixteenth century with the meticulous chronicles of Spanish explorers such as Diego Pérez de Luxán, and continues with the accounts of soldiers and evangelists over the next two centuries. These journals are invaluable to historians, but some also offer entertaining insight to the casual reader. One in particular crackles with immediacy and lucid detail: Father Ignaz Pfefferkorn's *Sonora* (see below), which has been translated into English and is currently in print.

This tradition of perceptive journalism continues into the period of early Anglo occupation. Some remarkably good writers, curious about the remote frontier, came to Arizona between 1860 and 1900. While their prose may seem excessively florid by today's standards, the meticulousness with which many described their encounters is (or ought to be) a model for journalism in any age. John G. Bourke's *On the Border With Crook* is an indispensable account of 1870s Arizona, written by an aide to Gen. George Crook, most successful commander of the Apache campaigns. Bourke's high respect for the Apaches is revealing, and he insightfully observes that "The moment (the Indian) concludes to live at peace with the whites, that moment all his troubles begin. Never was there a truer remark than that made by Crook: 'The American Indian commands respect for his rights only so long as he inspires terror for his rifle.'"

In modern times Arizona has been tamed—some believe—but its endangered beauty, continuing cultural conflict and very rapid pace of change generate more words than ever. Some come from unexpected sources. Former Gov. Bruce Babbitt, originally educated as a geologist, edited and annotated a superb anthology on the Grand Canyon. William K. Hartmann, an astronomer, recently authored the definitive work on the Sierra Pinacates, the remote black volcanic mountains in the heart of the Sonoran Desert. Eva Antonia Wilbur-Cruce, a woman who grew up on a ranch near the Mexican border in the first two decades of this century, finally has

Havasu Falls in the Grand Canyon at the Havasupai Indian Reservation is a Shangri-la still unreachable, fortunately, by car. (Kerrick James)

transformed that experience into a personal history graced with lovely and softly lyrical prose. (All these are listed below.) And there are books that are anything but lovely and soft, that instead glow red with outrage over the depredations that humankind has visited on this fragile land. Of these, the works of Edward Abbey and Charles Bowden lodge at the top of any list.

This bibliography of 32 books on Arizona and its neighboring lands is colored without apology by this author's own tastes and convictions. All books listed below are in print and easily available at this writing.

■ MODERN DESCRIPTION AND TRAVEL

Miller, Tom (ed.): *Arizona, the Land and the People*. University of Arizona Press, Tucson 1986. Not the pretty but superficial coffee-table volume it appears to be, but an authoritative and literate anthology of articles covering the state's natural history and human cultures.

Weir, Bill: *Arizona Traveler's Handbook*. Moon Publications Inc., Chico, California 1989. An exhaustively detailed general guide for the traveler.

■ ESSAYS

Abbey, Edward: *Desert Solitaire: A Season in the Wilderness*. University of Arizona Press, Tucson 1988 (reprint). Originally published in 1971, this is the earliest and most treasured of Abbey's collections: passionate, combative, keenly focused, and achingly beautiful in its use of the English language. Much of this book describes Arches National Monument in Utah.

Abbey, Edward: *The Journey Home: Some Words in Defense of the American West*. E.P. Dutton, New York 1977. A more quixotic, irritatingly self-indulgent Abbey lurks in this collection, but it remains a flinty and entertaining read.

Banham, Reyner: *Scenes in America Deserta*. Peregrine Smith Books, Salt Lake City 1982. The late Reyner Banham, an architectural historian, shaped these essays around human beings' impact on the Mojave and Sonoran deserts. They are not academic, but sharp-eyed, passionate, and occasionally eccentric.

Bowden, Charles: *Blue Desert.* University of Arizona Press, Tucson 1986. As is true of his friend Abbey, the earliest of Bowden's collections is also the best. These prickly essays cover an astonishing range, but the constant thread is decline and death—of animals, humans, and ways of life.

Bowden, Charles: *Frog Mountain Blues,* University of Arizona Press, Tucson 1986.

Shelton, Richard: *Going Back to Bisbee.* University of Arizona Press, Tucson 1992. Shelton has lived in Southern Arizona since 1958, and this gracefully written and entertaining book is a memoir of his encounters with the region's natural history, critters, and people.

Wilbur-Cruce, Eva Antonia: *A Beautiful, Cruel Country.* University of Arizona Press, Tucson 1987. (See comments above.)

◾ NATURAL HISTORY

Alcock, John: *Sonoran Desert Spring.* University of Chicago Press, Chicago 1985. A biologist writes both authoritatively and lyrically about the life of the Sonoran Desert. A highly readable and informative personal journal.

Alcock, John: *Sonoran Desert Summer.* University of Arizona Press, Tucson 1990. A wonderful second volume in what evidently will be a tetralogy.

Babbitt, Bruce (ed.): *Grand Canyon: An Anthology.* Northland Press, Flagstaff, Arizona. 1978. A perfect dip into the immense body of literature on the Grand Canyon, including trenchant commentary by former Arizona Governor Babbitt himself.

Hartmann, William K.: *Desert Heart: Chronicles of the Sonoran Desert.* Fisher Books, Tucson 1989. This superb book centers on the volcanic Sierra Pinacate that sprawls, black and malevolent, across the Arizona-Sonora border. But it manages to elucidate much of the natural and cultural history of the entire Sonoran Desert—from Hohokam to modern *narcotraficantes.*

Van Dyke, John C.: *The Desert.* Peregrine Smith Books, Salt Lake City 1987 (reprint). The classic 1901 work on the Southwest deserts, written by a New Jersey art historian and librarian who for three years explored this land, in his words, "as a lover."

Whitney, Stephen: *A Field Guide to the Grand Canyon*. Quill, New York 1982. The perfect companion for the amateur canyon naturalist, with exhaustive information and illustrations covering its geology and biology.

■ PREHISTORY

Lister, Robert H. and Florence C.: *Those Who Came Before*. University of Arizona Press, Tucson 1983. The best single volume encompassing all the prehistoric cultures of the Southwest.

Matlock, Gary: *Enemy Ancestors*. Northland Press, Flagstaff, Arizona 1988. A short but comprehensive non-academic book on the Anasazi.

Bronze bells in the patina curing room at the foundry in Arcosanti. (Kerrick James)

Modern Navajo rugs and blankets wear searing colors and aggressive geometry.

■ HISTORY

Bourke, John G: *On the Border With Crook.* University of Nebraska Press, Lincoln 1971 (reprint). The most essential book on the Apache wars and life in Arizona Territory.

Byrkit, James: *Forging the Copper Collar: Arizona's Labor-Management War of 1901-1921.* University of Arizona Press, Tucson 1982. The title does this superb book no favor. It is no dry and arcane navigation of an obscure historical narrows, but a dramatic story of Arizona's painful political puberty. Byrkit is both a careful historian and a fine, bold writer.

Luckingham, Bradford: *Phoenix: The History of a Southwestern Metropolis.* University of Arizona Press, Tucson 1989. The only available comprehensive history of the Southwest's largest city.

Officer, James E.: *Hispanic Arizona, 1536-1856.* University of Arizona Press, Tucson 1987. Definitive and fascinating.

Pfefferkorn, Ignaz: *Sonora: A Description of the Province.* University of Arizona Press, Tucson 1989 (reprint). A book about Sonora, not Arizona, but the two were culturally and politically one during Fr. Pfefferkorn's ramblings between 1756 and 1767. His curious and observant eye records details as fine as the Piman bowstrings: ". . . made by twisting the intestines of various animals, and about as thick as the quill of a raven's feather."

Sonnichsen, Leland: *Tucson: The Life and Times of an American City.* University of Oklahoma Press, Norman, Oklahoma 1982. Informal, but written by a man who takes a lover's care of the English language. Prime among the several available Tucson histories.

Summerhayes, Martha: *Vanished Arizona.* University of Nebraska Press, Lincoln 1979 (reprint). The fascinating memoir of a cultivated Massachusetts woman who came to Arizona as an Army bride in 1874.

Trimble, Marshall: *Arizona: A Cavalcade of History.* Treasure Chest Publications, Tucson 1989. Bursting with anecdotes, this history is written in a tone that occasionally crosses the line from informal to cloyingly folksy.

Tucson: A Short History (Anthology). Southwestern Mission Research Center, Tucson 1986. Engaging writing by six experts; more depth than one would expect in 150 pages.

■ NATIVE AMERICANS

Fontana, Bernard: *Of Earth and Little Rain.* University of Arizona Press, Tucson 1989. An intimate and affectionate portrait of the Tohono O'odham of southern Arizona, written by a field historian who has lived at the reservation's edge for 25 years.

Iverson, Peter: *The Navajo Nation.* University of New Mexico Press, Albuquerque 1983. A history of the Navajo people, with emphasis on the last 50 years.

Waters, Frank: *Book of the Hopi.* Penguin Books, New York 1977. Waters lived among the Hopis; he writes about their religion and ceremonies with insight.

Yetman, David: *Where the Desert Meets the Sea.* Pepper Publishing, Tucson 1987. A jewel-like book, sparkling with warmth, insight, and gentle humor, about the scarcely known Seri Indians of the Sonoran coast.

■ MISCELLANY

Griffith, James S.: *Southern Arizona Folk Arts.* University of Arizona Press, Tucson 1988. Griffith is the walking encyclopedia on the folk arts of Native American, Hispanic, and Anglo Arizonans; this book offers a well-researched introduction to many different traditions.

Watkins, Ronald J.: *High Crimes and Misdemeanors.* William Morrow & Company, New York 1990. For political junkies, this is the only thorough and relatively objective chronicle of Gov. Evan Mecham's chaotic 1987-88 administration and impeachment—a story with more drama and strange characters than most works of fiction.

(following pages) Rainbow over the Mittens and Merrick Butte in Monument Valley. (Kerrick James)

I N D E X

COMPASS AMERICAN GUIDES

WRITTEN FOR THE "LITERATE TRAVELER," this series of guides conjures up the images, explores the myths and legends, and reveals the spirit of America, its cities and states, and Canada.

Compass American Guides are available in general and travel bookstores, or may be ordered directly by calling 1-800-733-3000; or by sending a check or money order, including the cost of shipping and handling, payable to: Random House, Inc. 400 Hahn Road, Westminster Maryland 21157. Books are shipped by USPS Book Rate (allow 30 days for delivery): $2.00 for the 1st book, $0.50 for each additional book. Applicable sales tax will be charged. All prices are subject to change. Or ask your bookseller to order for you.

> *"Books can make thoughtful (and sometimes even thought-provoking) gifts for incentive travel winners or convention attendees. A new series of guidebooks published by Compass American Guides is right on the mark."*—SUCCESSFUL MEETINGS *magazine*
>
> Consider Compass American Guides as gifts or incentives for VIP's, employees, clients, customers, convention and meeting attendees, friends and others. Quantity discounts and customized editions are available.

Chicago   Veteran newsman and inveterate Chicagoan, Jack Schnedler, who writes regularly for the *Chicago Sun-Times,* captures the essence of this brawny, exuberant city, covering its history from swamp to skyscrapers, its architecture and urban essences.
Author: Jack Schnedler—Photographer: Zbigniew Bzdak
ISBN 1-878867-28-8; 320 pp; Price $16.95 (paper). ISBN 1-878867-29-6; Price: $24.95

Las Vegas   Deke Castleman's rollicking introduction to the capital of glitz, with a tale of fifty hotels, a celebration of tacky museums, a guide to quick weddings and sign language, and, of course, a system for playing slots, craps, blackjack, poker, and other games of chance.
Author: Deke Castleman—Photographer: Michael Yamashita
ISBN 1-878867-18-0; 304 pp; Price $14.95. Second edition.

Los Angeles   A hip and fast-moving tour of Los Angeles with special attention to those places where movies were filmed, movie stars lived and loved, and legends were born.
Author: Gil Reavill—Photographer: Mark S. Wexler
ISBN 1-878867-17-2; 324 pp; Price $14.95.

San Francisco and the Bay Area   San Francisco has something for everyone, whether your taste runs to cappuccino or dim sum, to downtown honky tonk or Davies Symphony Hall. Special emphasis on the surrounding Bay Area, from the Napa Valley to the markets of the East Bay.
Author: Barry Parr—Photographer: Michael Yamashita
ISBN 1-878867-16-4; 400 pp; Price $14.95. Second edition.

Arizona   From hidden canyons to museums of archaeology, from the civilized pleasures of Phoenix to jagged wildlands, author Larry Cheek reveals Arizona's scenic, cultural, and historical attractions and colorful eccentricities.
Author: Larry Cheek—Photographer: Michael Freeman
ISBN 1-878867-32-6; 288 pp; Price $16.95. Second edition.

Colorado   Champagne powder and cattle ranches, deserts and mountains, clean civilized cities, and classic American small towns—author Klusmire describes them all with wit, folksy humor, and a native's insight.
Author: Jon Klusmire—Photographer: Paul Chesley
ISBN 1-878867-07-5; 318 pp; Price $14.95 (paper). ISBN 1-878867-20-2; Price $22.95 (cloth)

Hawai'i   Some credit Hawai'i's magic to climate and scenery, others to its handsome people and spirit of *aloha*—but all are stirred by its royal history and its connection to the cultures of Polynesia. This guide helps you discover Hawai'i's magic for yourself.
Author: Moana Tregaskis—Photographers: Wayne Levin and Paul Chesley
ISBN 1-878867-23-7; 364 pp; Price $15.95 (paper). ISBN 1-878867-24-5; Price $22.95 (cloth)

Montana   Love of land and sky runs deep in Montana. Mountain ranges with names like the Crazies and the Sapphires. Legendary rivers—the Madison, Big Hole, and Yellowstone. Curiouser creeks—Froze-to-Death, Stinking Water, and Hellroaring. High plains, once home to buffalo, still offer wide vistas to the eye and soul. This land of the Big Sky may well be the last best place.
Author: Norma Tirrell—Photographer: John Reddy
ISBN 1-878867-10-5; 320 pp; Price $14.95 (paper). ISBN 1-878867-13-X; Price $22.95 (cloth)

New Mexico   Space, light, purity—New Mexico has cast a magical spell of mystery over its inhabitants for centuries. Rich in history, New Mexico has seen the sophisticated Anasazi culture, Spanish conquistadors searching for gold, 16th century colonists, and Pancho Villa. This truly is a Land of Enchantment.
Author: Nancy Harbert—Photographer: Michael Freeman
ISBN 1-878867-06-7; 336 pp; Price $15.95 (paper). ISBN 1-878867-22-9; Price $22.95 (cloth)

Utah   Unspoiled as the day Brigham Young proclaimed "this is the right place," this land of red-rock canyons and snow-capped mountains offers glorious scenery and a glimpse of the magnificent cliff-dwellings of the ancient Anasazi Indians. Special emphasis on outdoor recreation.
Author: Tom & Gayen Wharton—Photographer: Tom Till
ISBN 1-878867-31-8; 352 pp; Price $16.95. Second edition.

Wyoming   High, wide, and handsome, a land where tales of Indians, pioneers, gun slingers, cattle barons, cowboys and other characters of the Old West still cling to life. Nat Burt, son of pioneering dude ranchers, roams the state where the myth of the cowboy was born.
Author: Nathaniel Burt—Photographer: Don Pitcher
ISBN 1-878867-04-0; 392 pp; Price $14.95 (paper). ISBN 1-878867-03-2; Price $22.95 (cloth)

Canada   Veteran journalist Garry Marchant approaches the second largest country in the world as not one, but six different nations. Special sections on the Inuits, Canadian sports, rail hotels, 'Newfies,' Quebecois culture and the Calgary Stampede.
Author: Garry Marchant—Photographer: Ken Straiton
ISBN 1-878867-12-1; 308 pp; Price $14.95

■ About the Author

Lawrence W. Cheek worked for the *Tucson Citizen* for 14 years as a reporter, music and architecture critic, essayist, and Saturday editor. He then edited Tucson's *City Magazine,* a free-ranging monthly that comprised investigative reporting, politics, popular culture, and the arts. His work frequently appears in *Arizona Highways* magazine, which also has published two of his books: *Scenic Sedona* and *Photographing Arizona.* He lives with his wife, Patty, next door to the Santa Catalina Mountains, where he puts off writing by exploring their canyons.

■ About the Photographer

Michael Freeman is a noted photographer and writer who has traveled all over the globe for book and magazine publishers, both British and American. His work has appeared in the *Sunday Times of London* and *Smithsonian* magazine. Most recently, for the large-picture format book *Angkor,* he has undertaken the first study of this ancient Cambodian city in two decades.